Decoding

the

Energy Enigma

Improved Decision-Making on

This Generation's Most Pressing Issue

Michael J. Molnar

JIVA LLC
New York, NY

Editor: Linda Molnar

Cover Design: Jim DeLouise

ISBN (Electronic): 978-0-9972479-0-9

ISBN (Print): 978-0-9972479-1-6

Library of Congress Control Number: 2016901335

Dedicated to Tazia

Mom, Dad, Linda and Lisa

Jeffrey, Jessica, Alyssa and Brianna

I would like to thank Linda Molnar for her help editing this book

CONTENTS

Preface: Why Are Outcomes So Bad for Something So Important?

"Human behavior flows from three main sources:
desire, emotions and knowledge."
- Plato
Greek Philosopher (428 to 347 B.C.)

Energy is critical to national security, economic growth, the environment and individuals' health. It is a key area of focus for governments as well as business leaders and investors. Yet, for something so important, why are the decisions made and outcomes achieved often so poor?

For example: How has every U.S. President since the early 1970s adamantly declared energy independence as a crucial goal, yet none has achieved it? Why do some parts of the energy world repeatedly undergo phenomenal booms only to be followed by massive busts? How did some of the most sophisticated investors in the world lose billions on their solar investments? How did European carbon regulations lead to incentives to burn more coal – the exact opposite of their intention? How does a hedge fund lose $6 billion of its $9 billion under management in just a few weeks of trading natural gas? Why is the world so slow to react to global warming even though the scientific community has issued clear warnings since 1988?

This book is the culmination of two distinct passions of mine: the energy sector and decision-making. My time studying at The University of Chicago – an academic arena that is the center of the debate on rational versus behavioral thinking in economics – piqued my interest in how people form judgments and make decisions. My curiosity drove me to subsequently attend The London School of Economics to study Decision Sciences exclusively. This led to a Visiting Research Fellow role at a think tank. There, my work centered on providing insight into the stock market's valuation of companies, which is nothing more than the collective judgment of many individual participants in the market.

My focus on energy began after making a career move to Wall Street, as I wanted to focus on the part of the world economy that I believed mattered the most. Since then, I have held a variety of positions all with a focus on the energy sector: Founding Partner of a long/short equity hedge fund, Founding Partner of a boutique investment bank, and lead equity analyst for the coal and alternative energy sectors at Goldman Sachs. These roles have allowed me the opportunity to observe, advise and invest in countless situations in the energy sector.

Enigmas are typically defined as "something puzzling or difficult to understand." Decisions and the subsequent outcomes for governments, business leaders and investors in energy certainly qualify as enigmas. My goal is not to tell the reader *what* to think but rather to explain *why* poor thinking occurs and *how* it can be improved in the future. My hope is that the tools provided in this book decode the energy enigma, even if just a bit, to help governments, business leaders and investors make better decisions about what is arguably the most vital part of the world economy.

February 2016
New York, NY

Section I

Understanding Energy

and

Poor Decision-Making

Why The Energy Sector is So Important

"All truths are easy to understand once they are discovered;
the point is to discover them."
- Galileo Galilei
Italian Astronomer, Physicist, Philosopher (1564 to 1642)

Quick Primer on Energy

This book is not a detailed textbook on energy markets, technologies, or investment approaches; there are hundreds of these books available already. This is a book about understanding how energy systems – and the people within those systems – behave in order to improve decision-making. Given the energy focus, however, it does require a certain amount of industry-specific knowledge. While most of this is addressed within each section, there are certain core aspects of the energy world that are helpful to understand upfront.

The most fundamental question is: What is energy? While there are numerous definitions, below is a practical one based on Figure 1:

> *Energy is used to power and heat residential and commercial buildings, as key inputs into industry such as chemical plants or manufacturing facilities, and as fuel for transportation of people and goods. Key sources of energy include oil, natural gas, coal, nuclear and renewables.*

Figure 1 shows how energy in the U.S. is broken down by supply and demand. From the supply side, the U.S. is dominated by fossil fuels with petroleum, natural gas and coal making up 35%, 28% and 18% of supply, respectively. Renewable energy is 10% of the energy mix, which is composed of biomass (53%), hydroelectric power (28%), wind (19%) geothermal (<1%), and solar/photovoltaic (<1%). Solar is very small but growing rapidly, as we will discuss later. Nuclear is at the bottom, providing 8% of supply.

There are four large areas of energy demand: transportation, industrial, residential and commercial buildings, and electric power. On an energy-equivalent basis, electric power is by far the largest energy user, absorbing 39% of supply, followed by transportation at 27%, industrial usage at 22%, and residential and commercial usage at 12%. Each demand area is supplied by a certain mix of supply sources. Transportation is dominated by petroleum. Industrial usage is more balanced among all energy sources, except nuclear which is only used to produce electricity. Natural gas is used to heat the majority of residential and commercial buildings in the United States. Finally, electric power uses nearly all sources except for petroleum.

Figure 1: Sources and Uses of Energy in the U.S. (2014)

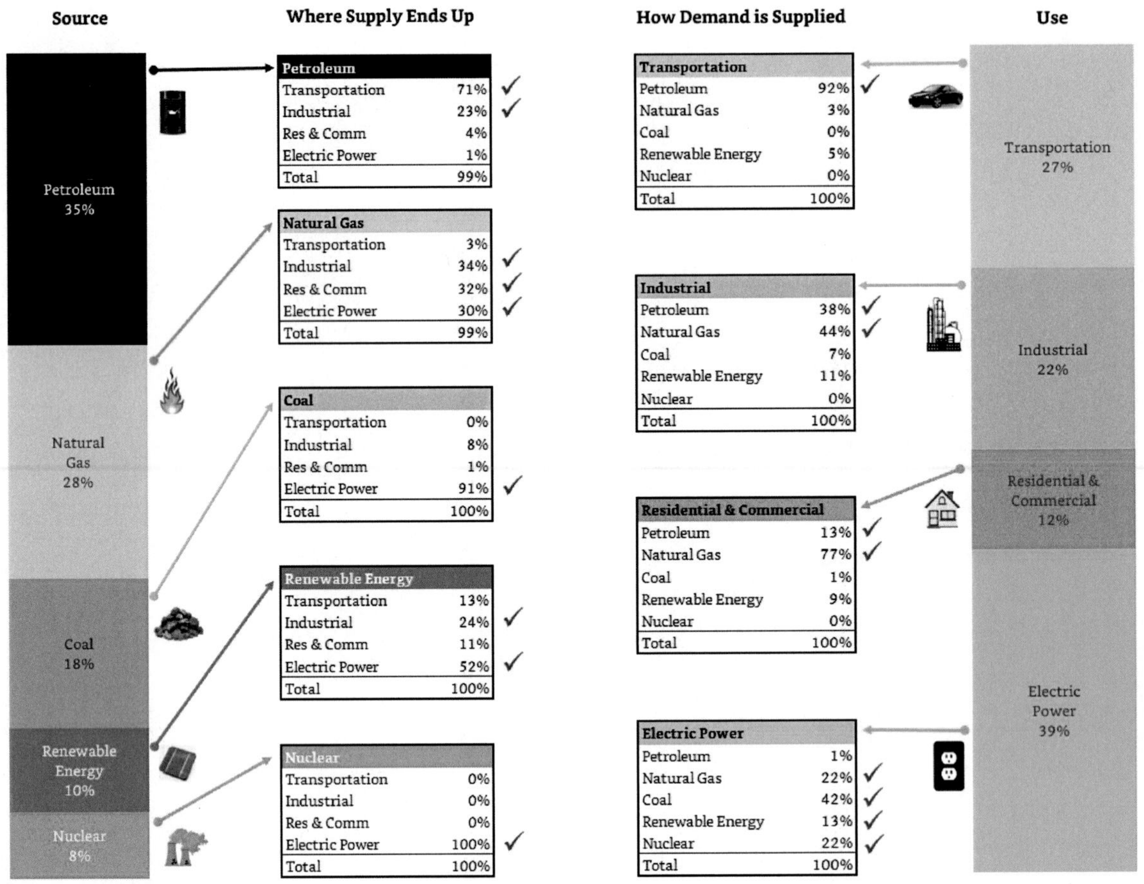

Source

Petroleum 35%
Natural Gas 28%
Coal 18%
Renewable Energy 10%
Nuclear 8%

Where Supply Ends Up

Petroleum
Transportation	71% ✓
Industrial	23% ✓
Res & Comm	4%
Electric Power	1%
Total	99%

Natural Gas
Transportation	3%
Industrial	34% ✓
Res & Comm	32% ✓
Electric Power	30% ✓
Total	99%

Coal
Transportation	0%
Industrial	8%
Res & Comm	1%
Electric Power	91% ✓
Total	100%

Renewable Energy
Transportation	13%
Industrial	24% ✓
Res & Comm	11%
Electric Power	52% ✓
Total	100%

Nuclear
Transportation	0%
Industrial	0%
Res & Comm	0%
Electric Power	100% ✓
Total	100%

How Demand is Supplied

Transportation
Petroleum	92% ✓
Natural Gas	3%
Coal	0%
Renewable Energy	5%
Nuclear	0%
Total	100%

Industrial
Petroleum	38% ✓
Natural Gas	44% ✓
Coal	7%
Renewable Energy	11%
Nuclear	0%
Total	100%

Residential & Commercial
Petroleum	13% ✓
Natural Gas	77% ✓
Coal	1%
Renewable Energy	9%
Nuclear	0%
Total	100%

Electric Power
Petroleum	1%
Natural Gas	22% ✓
Coal	42% ✓
Renewable Energy	13% ✓
Nuclear	22% ✓
Total	100%

Use

Transportation 27%
Industrial 22%
Residential & Commercial 12%
Electric Power 39%

Source: Energy Information Administration. Totals that do not equal 100% are due to rounding.

Worldwide energy demand has been growing at 2.6% per year since 1965 which has been driven by an increasing population, economic growth, and an expanding middle class around the world. In recent years, most of the growth has been driven by Asia, specifically China. For example, demand from Asia has been growing at 4.6% per year over the past 10 years whereas North America has been flat and Europe has declined. Overall growth in energy demand appears insatiable. Even the decline felt due to the calamitous Global Financial Crisis in 2008 only put a temporary dent in demand that was recovered in short time (See Figure 2).

Figure 2: World Energy Demand Has Been Driven by Asia in Recent Years

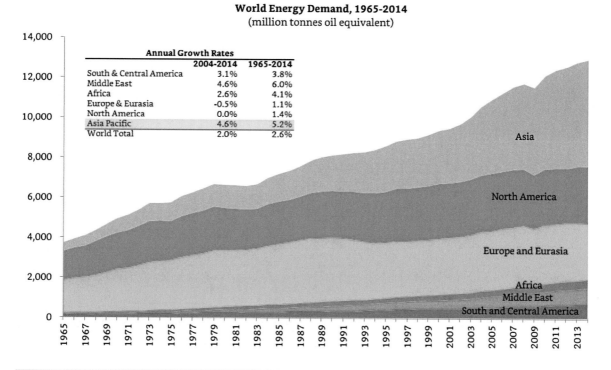

World Energy Demand, 1965-2014
(million tonnes oil equivalent)

Annual Growth Rates		
	2004-2014	1965-2014
South & Central America	3.1%	3.8%
Middle East	4.6%	6.0%
Africa	2.6%	4.1%
Europe & Eurasia	-0.5%	1.1%
North America	0.0%	1.4%
Asia Pacific	4.6%	5.2%
World Total	2.0%	2.6%

Source: BP World Energy Statistics

Another way to analyze the data is to look at worldwide energy demand by energy source (see Figure 3). The units used are millions of tonnes of oil equivalent (MTOE), which simply normalizes the different sources of energy to be comparable with one another. There are several takeaways:

- First, nuclear power is the only source that has declined over the past 10 years, a result of the Japan nuclear disaster at Fukushima in 2011.

- Second, all fossil fuels are continuing to grow, which might be surprising considering the large media attention on renewables.

- Third, renewables are the fastest-growing energy source in percentage terms, growing 15% per year over the past three- and 10-year time horizons.

While the growth in renewables might make some environmentalists feel good, it is important to remember that they are growing fast in percentage terms, but off of a very small base. Fossil fuels growth, while much lower in percentage terms, is significant in unit terms given its large base. The result is that, over the 2011 to 2014 time period, energy demand worldwide grew by 520 MTOE in total with oil, natural gas and coal making up 67% of that number.

Figure 3: Fossil Fuels Continue to Dominate but Renewables Are Growing at a Fast Rate

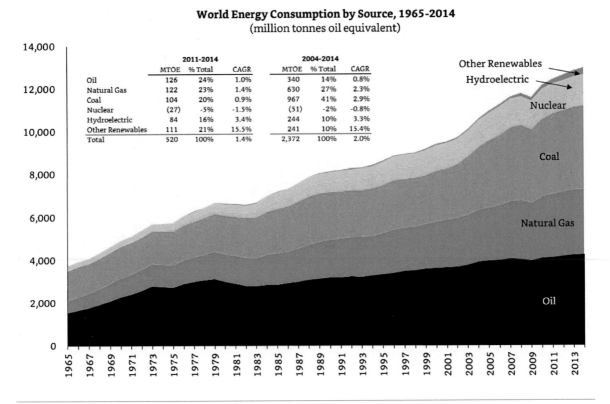

World Energy Consumption by Source, 1965-2014
(million tonnes oil equivalent)

	2011-2014			2004-2014		
	MTOE	% Total	CAGR	MTOE	% Total	CAGR
Oil	126	24%	1.0%	340	14%	0.8%
Natural Gas	122	23%	1.4%	630	27%	2.3%
Coal	104	20%	0.9%	967	41%	2.9%
Nuclear	(27)	-5%	-1.5%	(51)	-2%	-0.8%
Hydroelectric	84	16%	3.4%	244	10%	3.3%
Other Renewables	111	21%	15.5%	241	10%	15.4%
Total	520	100%	1.4%	2,372	100%	2.0%

Source: BP World Energy Statistics

Transitions in energy, where supply shifts from being dominated by one source to another, tend to happen over long timescales. Taking data from the 1700s to the present show the following Ages of Energy, where supply was dominated by one particular source:

- **Age of Wood:** From early times into the late 1800s, energy was mainly produced by burning wood.

- **Age of Coal:** With the discovery of coal in the mid-1800s, coal rapidly grew to about 80% of the energy supply by 1900.

- **Age of Petroleum and Natural Gas:** Discovery of oil and natural gas in the early 1900s has led to their dominance starting in the 1930s through the present day.

Renewables are growing fast but are very small in the context of the total energy mix. As advanced as society has become over the past several hundred years, power is still mainly generated by burning fossilized remains of dead organisms from millions of years ago.

Figure 4: Energy Transitions, 1776 to 2014

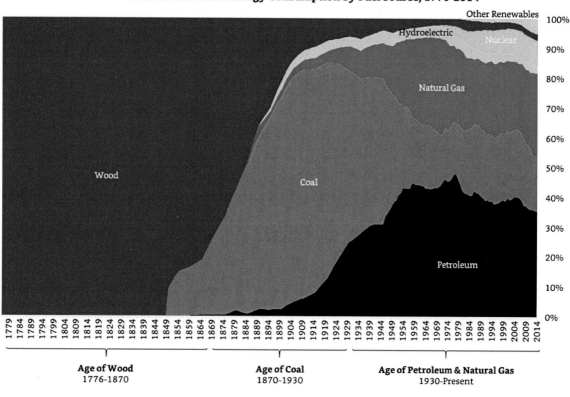

Source: *Energy Information Administration; Michael Molnar*

For a market as large as energy to transition to a new, dominant supply source, it takes many decades of substantial supply growth to make an impact. So, while the small percentage of total energy generated by renewables might be disheartening to some, the high growth rates are typical at the early stages of a transition.

Understanding Energy's Impact

Global Industry Classification Standards, commonly known by the shorthand "GICS," are a good way to frame the different areas of the economy. The classification has 10 sectors, which are then further subdivided into industry groups. Each of the 10 sectors is shown below with just two modifications. Consumer is considered one category, including both consumer discretionary and staples, and energy is grouped with utilities, industrials and materials.

To assess the impact of each sector, four criteria are evaluated:

1. **Economy**
2. **National security**
3. **Environment**
4. **Individuals' health**

Economically, all sectors have an impact. The companies in each sector, as well as employees and other stakeholders, are direct economic contributors. Indirectly, the products and services generated in one sector are often used in other sectors. Beyond the economy, sector impacts vary. By definition, healthcare obviously has a clear impact on individuals' health. The consumer sector, one can argue, impacts healthcare and the environment to a degree. The communications, financials and technology sectors have an impact on security.

By comparison, there is no sector of the economy that impacts the economy, national security, the environment and individuals' health as significantly as the energy sector. Foreign policy is massively influenced, and at times dictated, by energy issues. The air we breathe, the water we drink, and the land on which we live is often in conflict with the production of energy. Finally, energy production and usage is a major contributor to the economic output of nearly all countries.

Figure 5: Energy Impacts the Economy, Security, Environment and Health

Sector of Economy	Economy	Security	Environment	Health
		Issues Impacted		
Energy (plus utilities, industrials, materials)	✓	✓	✓	✓
Financials	✓	✓	✗	✗
Healthcare	✓	✗	✗	✓
Communications	✓	✓	✗	✗
Consumer (discretionary plus staples)	✓	✗	✓	✓
Technology	✓	✓	✗	✗

Source: Michael Molnar

The four criteria above highlight *what* is impacted, but exactly *who* are we talking about? Broadly speaking, we break down society into four constituents throughout this book: individual citizens, business leaders, investors and governments. Each of these groups have an impact on – and are impacted by – the energy sector in different ways.

Figure 6: Energy Issues that Different Constituents Face

	Economic	Security	Environment & Health
Individual Citizens	Cost of gasoline has climbed 20%, which has hurt the household budget. How long will this last?	A family member in the military is sent to the Middle East. What is driving our foreign policy?	What are the long-term effects on your health from the coal plant emissions in your area?
Business Owners & Investors	What will the impact to margins and profits be as my input energy costs have changed?	If political instability occurs due to energy price movements in areas we have assets, what will be the effect on value?	We have to dispose of waste but it is expensive. What are the costs involved?
Government Officials	Lower near-term energy costs are a stimulus to the economy – but at what long-term cost?	How does our energy policy drive strength or weakness in world affairs with allies and enemies?	How do we best regulate pollution of the air and water by energy producers?

Source: Michael Molnar

A more detailed discussion of the energy sector's impact on these four criteria (the economy, security, environment and health) is discussed in detail next.

(1) The Economy

Every sector, by definition, affects the economy. Energy is somewhat unique as its influence is felt so pervasively in both direct and indirect ways. The direct and obvious impact of energy is felt by companies involved in the production and sale of energy itself. Examples would be coal miners, oil exploration companies and solar farm owners whose primary revenue source is energy production. Other groups that sell products or services to these energy producers are impacted in a fairly direct manner as well. For example, oil-field service companies and industrial-equipment suppliers are all economically tied to those companies that produce the energy.

There are other companies that make products heavily dependent on energy as a key input. These companies are not producing energy or selling products or services to those companies, but are buying the energy input and transforming it for use typically in another sector. For example, natural gas is a key input into producing fertilizer for agriculture.

In an indirect – but very important – way, the consumer sector is influenced by energy. According to Energy Information Administration (EIA) data, the average U.S. household has spent between 4% and 8% of disposable income on energy expenditures from 1960 to 2013. About two-thirds of these costs are electricity- and transportation-related; thus, the price of electricity and gasoline can clearly influence the average consumers' excess cash available to spend on other products and services. As a result, many economists view rising energy prices to be similar to a tax increase and falling energy prices similar to a tax break.

Fluctuating energy prices impact different companies and countries in different ways. A lower oil price clearly is hurtful to oil companies because it means that they will earn less revenue. The trickle-down effect to negatively impacting their suppliers follows the price decline. However, lower energy prices are helpful to consumers as they are left with more money to spend. For any country, the net effect (positive or negative) will vary depending on the composition of its economy.

Clearly, energy is a vital part of any economy. Quantifying the exact contribution is not easy but stock market valuations can serve as a useful shorthand methodology. Adding the value of the energy, industrials, utilities and materials sectors shows that 23% of the total market value is reasonably influenced by energy in a direct manner. Consumer discretionary and staples constitute another 23% of the market that is somewhat influenced by energy. As such, one can make a strong case that energy impacts nearly 50% of the U.S. economy.

Figure 7: Energy Impacts a Huge Portion of the Economy Directly and Indirectly

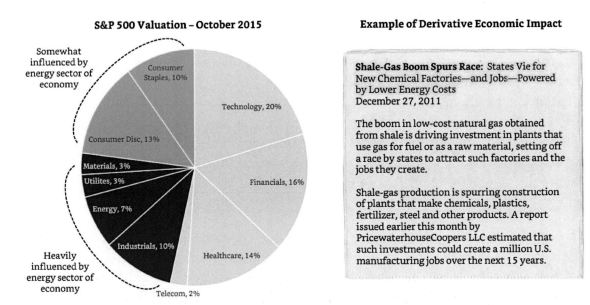

Source: Bloomberg (left) on Global Industry Classification (GICS); The Wall Street Journal (right)

(2) Security

Energy is integral to any country's national security. It is fuel for cars and trucks, electricity and heat for homes, and a critical input into the manufacturing and industrial sectors. Disruptions in any of these areas pose a large risk to society. While many individual citizens do not fully appreciate the risk, their military and government leaders are acutely aware – especially if their country is a net importer of energy.

The wake-up moment for the U.S. happened during the Arab Oil Embargo in the early 1970s. Many Arab nations were angry that the U.S. supported Israel during the 1973 Yom Kippur War. Not able to fight at the level of the U.S. military, they turned to their greatest point of leverage – oil. In October 1973, OPEC raised the price of oil dramatically and agreed to continue to cut production until its political objectives were met.

Figure 8: The Arab Oil Embargo of 1973 Was a Watershed Moment for Energy Security

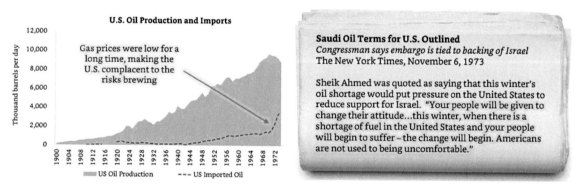

Warning neighbors not to steal your gasoline (4/1973)

Shell gas station line in Chicago (1/1974)

Portland, Oregon gas station with no more gas (11/1973)

Source: Energy Information Administration; Wired.com; Grayflannelsuit.net

By early 1974, it was reported that 20% of gasoline stations in the U.S. had no gasoline and the U.S. started various rationing programs to deal with the issue. American citizens, many of whom were naïve to these risks, now faced both skyrocketing prices and limitations on when they could buy gasoline. When they were allowed, many faced multi-hour wait times to fill up. International allies, facing similar embargoes, began to disassociate themselves with U.S.

foreign policy. Anyone that did not realize the importance of oil to security had become acutely aware of it – fast.

While this risk varies by country and is constantly changing, it is always of importance. As an example, the clipping in Figure 9 is from a speech that the United Kingdom's ambassador to the U.S. made in 2006. That year was a strong one for the U.S. economy, nearly two years before the Global Financial Crisis. China's growth was roaring ahead and its consumption of oil and other resources was deemed to be insatiable. The result: Demand outstripped supply for nearly all commodities and prices were spiking.

A short time after this speech, the energy world would change in a big way. The Global Financial Crisis hurt demand just as new methods of extracting oil and natural gas from shale were bringing incremental supply online. These new methods took U.S. oil production to levels not seen in decades, which led to a clear decrease in oil imports. As imports of oil have declined, the risk to national security from disruption of supply has decreased as well.

Figure 9: U.K. Ambassador Speech on Foreign Policy and Energy Security (2006)

Energy: a burning issue for foreign policy
U.K. Ambassador to the United States Sir David Manning, March 13, 2006 at Stanford University

Energy resources have long been a major strategic concern: access to secure sources, control over supply lines: these are issues of national security.

It was in 1947, as the Cold War intensified, that the US Interior Department first called for a new Manhattan project: a $10 billion program that would be capable of producing 2 million barrels a day of synthetic fuels. This was prompted by concern over the U.S.'s potential dependence on oil.

Fifty years ago, the Suez crisis arose because the Suez Canal was the route by which Gulf oil reached Europe. The canal cut the journey to the U.K. to 6,500 miles, almost half that of the journey around the Cape of Good Hope. By 1955, two thirds of Europe's oil flowed through the canal. Why, argued Nasser, should the oil-producing countries receive 50% of the profits from their oil, if Egypt did not receive 50% of the profits from the canal? The canal was Europe's jugular. Hence the warning that Prime Minister Eden gave to the Soviet leaders Bulganin and Khrushchev during their visit to London in the April of 1956. He said: "I must be absolutely blunt about the oil" ... "We could not live without oil and... we have no intention of being strangled to death."

The oil crises of the 1970s forced the West to recognize its dependence on cheap oil; and the reality that those who controlled supply were in a position to exert direct political pressure on the rest of the international community. In the words of Henry Kissinger, the oil weapon, wielded in the form of an embargo, "altered irrevocably the world as it had grown up in the postwar period." Dr. Kissinger, by his own admission, had before 1973 known little about oil. That would rapidly change. In the US the shortfall struck at a fundamental belief in the abundance of natural resources. In a matter of months American motorists saw retail gasoline prices climb by 40% and had to sit in gas lines.

That was what prompted President Nixon to launch Project Independence in 1973, three decades after it had first been mooted under the Truman Administration. In the spirit of the Apollo and Manhattan projects he set out a series of measures for the U.S. to meet its "own energy needs without depending on any foreign energy source" by 1980. Seven years later, in response to a second oil crisis, the 1980 Carter Doctrine declared that "any attempt by an outside force to gain control of the Gulf will be regarded as an assault on the vital interests of the United States of America, and ... will be repelled by any means necessary, including military force." There is more than an echo here of what Anthony Eden was saying a quarter of a century earlier.

And one further historical reminder: In 1990, in the first Gulf War, the West faced the threat of a dictator who was prepared to seize Kuwait. Had he held on to it, Saddam Hussein would have controlled 20% of OPEC production and 20% of world oil reserves. He would have been in a position to intimidate neighboring countries, to be the dominant power in the Gulf.

Source: British Embassy

Does this mean, at least for the U.S., that the risk to national security is fully mitigated? No. While the issue of national security waxes and wanes, it will never end. The negative impact of becoming vulnerable to energy shortages is too great and the sources of energy are too uncertain for the risk ever to be completely resolved for any country. While there has been progress, the U.S. still imported 27% of its oil needs in 2014.

(3) and (4) The Environment and Health

In 1833, an English economist described the Tragedy of the Commons. He told the story of an English village which had common land for which all the townspeople could use, including sheep owners. The challenge resulted in an unintended consequence – each individual sheep owner was incented to have his sheep graze as much as possible as he received the benefit of better fed sheep whereas the entire group incurred the cost of the depleted land. Unfortunately, the result was that all the sheep owners did the same thing and the common area became destitute for everyone in the town.

While the Tragedy of the Commons was described nearly 200 years ago, its challenge is just as prevalent today. Substitute the word "sheep" with "fossil fuels" and the "commons" with "the environment and people's health" and that describes today's challenge of the commons in the energy world. While there have been policy and regulation attempts to deal with this issue, sometimes effectively, the entrenched interests on the other side are formidable. They are, after all, getting something for free and thus are logically willing to spend a lot to maintain that position.

Producing and using energy has both direct and indirect costs. The direct costs are fairly obvious as companies have to incur costs to produce the energy and consumers have to spend money to use it. Indirect costs, such as the impact to the environment and individual citizens' health, are prevalent as well. As the sheep owners were incented to allow their sheep to graze voraciously and let others handle the costs that accrued to the town, various energy companies and countries have similar incentives. Produce as much "cheap" (in the short term at least) energy as possible to drive economic growth and competitive advantage. The costs of the destruction to the environment or citizens' health will be dealt with later, if at all, by someone else.

A simple chart (see Figure 10) can help frame some of the ways in which energy impacts the environment and one's health. One can think of the impact as stemming from either getting or using the resource. For example, mining for coal often results in coal slurry being generated. This is stored in slurry ponds which risk leaching into the water supply. Once that coal is burned by a utility, the resulting emissions of particulate matter, mercury, nitrogen oxides and sulfur dioxides impact air quality.

Figure 10: Framework for Understanding Select Environment and Health Impacts

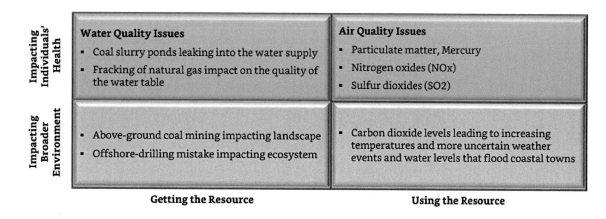

Source: Michael Molnar

While it should be obvious why we want clean air and water, it is often seen at odds with short-term economic growth. An obvious but sometimes forgotten point is that the environment and citizens' health ultimately *does* impact economic growth over the medium- to long-term. The health impacts from burning fossil fuels are very real, even if they can be challenging to directly correlate. See Figures 11 and 12.

Figure 11: Key Air Pollutants and Related Health Impacts

Pollutant	Health Impacts	Sources
Particulate Matter	Short-term exposures can aggravate heart or lung diseases leading to respiratory symptoms, increased medication use, hospital admissions, emergency room (ER) visits, and premature mortality; long-term exposures can lead to the development of heart or lung disease and premature mortality.	Emitted or formed through chemical reactions; fuel combustion (e.g., burning coal, wood, diesel); industrial processes; agriculture (plowing, field burning); and unpaved roads.
Sulfur Dioxide (SOx)	Aggravates asthma and increased respiratory symptoms. Contributes to particle formation with associated health effects.	Fuel combustion (especially high-sulfur coal); electric utilities and industrial processes; and natural sources such as volcanoes.
Nitrogen Oxides (NOx)	Aggravates lung diseases leading to respiratory symptoms, hospital admissions, and ER visits; increased susceptibility to respiratory infection.	Fuel combustion (e.g., electric utilities, industrial boilers and vehicles) and wood burning.
Mercury (Hg)	Exposure can affect the human nervous system and harm the brain, heart, kidneys, lungs and immune system.	When coal is burned, mercury is released into the environment. Coal-burning power plants are the largest human-caused source of mercury emissions to the air in the United States.

Source: Environmental Protection Agency

Figure 12: Report from Physicians for Social Responsibility

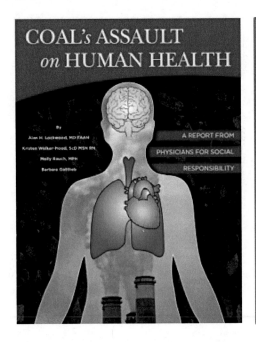

Excerpt from Executive Summary
Coal pollutants affect all major body organ systems and contribute to four of the five leading causes of mortality in the U.S.: heart disease, cancer, stroke, and chronic lower respiratory diseases. This conclusion emerges from our reassessment of the widely recognized health threats from coal. Each step of the coal lifecycle—mining, transportation, washing, combustion, and disposing of post-combustion wastes—impacts human health. Coal combustion in particular contributes to diseases affecting large portions of the U.S. population, including asthma, lung cancer, heart disease, and stroke, compounding the major public health challenges of our time. It interferes with lung development, increases the risk of heart attacks, and compromises intellectual capacity.

Source: Physicians for Social Responsibility

Not all fossil fuels pollute to the same extent. Per unit of energy delivered, coal is by far the dirtiest fossil fuel. It emits substantially more nitrogen oxide, sulfur dioxide, particulates, mercury and carbon than either oil or natural gas. This is one of the reasons that the coal industry is under attack by environmentalists, and why some view natural gas (also a fossil fuel) to be a relatively clean alternative.

Figure 13: Coal Produces More Pollutant Per Unit of Energy Than Other Fossil Fuels

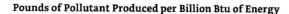

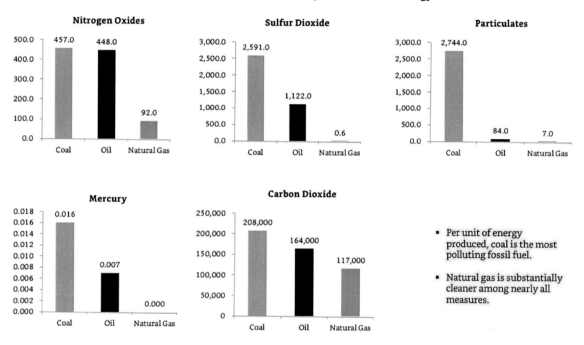

Pounds of Pollutant Produced per Billion Btu of Energy

- Per unit of energy produced, coal is the most polluting fossil fuel.

- Natural gas is substantially cleaner among nearly all measures.

Source: Natural Gas Issues and Trends Report, *Energy Information Administration (EIA). Assumes no post-combustion removal.*

The Real Drivers of Bad Outcomes in Energy

"There are only two mistakes one can make along the road to truth;
not going all the way, and not starting."
- Buddha (~500 BCE)

Are Outcomes in Energy Really that Bad?

The goal of this book is to improve decision-making, and thus outcomes, in energy. This begs a question: Is decision-making in energy that bad? While obviously not all decisions are bad, consider the following 10 examples (we will discuss many of these and others throughout this book):

1. **Amaranth Loses $6 billion in One Month:** Amaranth was a Connecticut-based hedge fund with a solid track record. In August 2006, assets were $9.2 billion. By the next month, assets declined to $3.5 billion and the fund was liquidated as energy trades turned against it.

2. **Venture Capitalists Lost Billions in Solar:** Solar was booming in the mid-2000s as the industry began to take off commercially. Many of the most well-known venture capitalists in the world flocked to fund new solar startups. As the market turned sour on massive oversupply, these investors and others lost billions of dollars in the years that followed.

3. **TXU (Energy Future Holdings) Goes Bankrupt:** In 2007, private equity investors took the Texas utility, TXU, private in a $32 billion deal. Given changing energy markets, TXU (subsequently renamed Energy Future Holdings) declared bankruptcy in 2014 and KKR, TPG and Goldman Sachs wrote down $8 billion of their investment. Even Warren Buffett lost nearly $900 million, stating in his annual letter, "Most of you have never heard of Energy Future Holdings. Consider yourselves lucky; I certainly wish I hadn't."

4. **European Regulations of Carbon Dioxide Have the Opposite Impact of What Was Intended:** The European Union started to regulate carbon dioxide in 2005. Unfortunately, the program's first results ended up rewarding carbon emitters with windfall profits and then incented companies to burn more, not less, coal.

5. **Every U.S. President Since Nixon Has Had a Goal of Energy Independence, Yet None Has Achieved It:** The shortage of gasoline in the early 1970s showed America just how

vulnerable it was to oil imports. Each President since the Arab Oil Embargo has stated a clear goal of energy independence. Countless speeches were given and numerous programs developed, yet none achieved the goal.

6. **Siemens Loses Over $1 Billion Dollars in Solar:** Siemens, the large industrial conglomerate, made a series of acquisitions from 2009 to 2011 in order to get a foothold in the burgeoning solar market. By late 2012, after having suffered losses over $1 billion, it announced it was getting out of the solar business altogether.

7. **Biofuels Heavily Promoted, But Then Industry Implodes:** The U.S. biofuel industry was heavily promoted by President George W. Bush via the Energy Policy Act of 2005. Companies were formed and capital flooded the market to take advantage of this opportunity. Soon, oversupply caused profits and cash flows to decline. Just a few years later, many companies were bankrupt and investors lost billions. As an example, ethanol producer Verasun was worth $25 a share in mid-2006; just a couple of years later it went bankrupt, making its shares worthless.

8. **Fuel-Cell Companies' Valuations Hyped, But Then Collapse:** Fuel cell technology was seen as a great hope for the future of transportation in the late 1990s, helping to wean the U.S. off oil while emitting only water vapor. There were numerous public and private financings of companies during this time as investors tried to cash in on the opportunity. Unfortunately, fuel-cell vehicles never became commercial and sales languished. Both companies and investors were badly hurt as the billions in research and development produced limited results. As an example, Ballard's (BLDP) stock market capitalization declined about $10 billion to less than $500 million as the stock market realized that the hype was not becoming reality.

9. **China Pollution Reaches Unprecedented Levels:** Due to continued growth in coal-fired power generation, China's particulate-matter air pollution (measured as PM 2.5 levels) reached unprecedented levels by 2015. Some cities have recorded PM 2.5 level beyond the maximum of the measurement scale – pollution so bad it is not able to be measured.

10. **U.S. Coal Companies Go Bust, Then Boom, Then Bust Again:** U.S. coal companies were nearly all bankrupt in the late 1990s. Pricing was poor given continued oversupply and thus cash flows and profits were minimal. In the mid-2000s, Chinese demand drove worldwide pricing higher which led many to proclaim "King Coal" was back in business. By 2015, nearly all U.S. coal companies were in financial distress as Chinese demand decreased, natural gas gained share, and regulations drove coal costs higher.

Are outcomes, and thus decision-making, worse in energy than other areas of the economy? Possibly, but it is not a point that needs to be proven. Given the vital importance of the energy sector, poor decision-making has grave consequences and trying to improve is a worthwhile endeavor.

Research Process Conducted

Factually accurate descriptions explaining what happened are often available for bad decisions. "The price of natural gas moved so our investment lost money," would be an example. Unfortunately, these descriptive accounts are not particularly insightful in understanding how to improve in the future.

To search for better insights, I conducted the following research process:

- **Data Gathering:** I started by listing numerous situations in energy and evaluated the path from decision to outcome. Data was gathered through several means: historical news searches, conversations with others in the sector, my experiences advising clients and my own decisions investing capital directly.

- **Decision Analysis:** From this dataset, decisions were evaluated based on the data available at the time of the decision versus simply evaluating the subsequent outcome. The result was a list of numerous situations, rationales for decisions made, and reasons for subsequent outcomes.

- **Search for Patterns:** The final step was to see what patterns would emerge, if any. This took considerable iteration back and forth to the data that was gathered.

Inherently, this process is subjective, not comprehensive, and risks bias. However, the goal was to uncover insights into why bad decisions are made, which could lead to improved decision-making in the future. If that was accomplished, the research process will have succeeded.

The research yielded three key takeaways:

1. **Evaluating Outcomes Versus Decisions:** Most people, myself included, fall prey to judging the quality of the decision based on the outcome achieved versus on the merits of the decision based on what was known at the time.

2. **Describing *What* Versus Understanding *Why*:** The explanations given for a decision were often descriptive, but not insightful. They described what happened but not why it happened.

3. **Two Main Causes of Poor Decisions:** After considerable reflection, there were two clear drivers behind most of the bad decisions. First, the analytical challenge of correctly predicting the outcomes of *complex systems*. Second, the *skewing of human judgment* due to emotional or psychological tendencies.

Takeaway 1 – Evaluating Outcomes Versus Decisions

Most people inherently know that quality decisions do not necessarily mean good outcomes. Yet, humans are hard-wired to overweight the outcome in assessing the quality of a prior decision. This is called **outcome bias** which, even though well-documented, is very difficult to overcome.

The business manager sees profits increase, the hedge fund manager has a stock move in his favor, or the policymaker sees initial results trend as desired and all feel good about the prior decisions made. However, often the outcomes occurred for reasons other than those for which the original decision was based. In other words, you got lucky. Likewise, bad outcomes are reviled and the decisions are nearly always panned as wrong-headed. Sometimes, perhaps many times, this is true. However, while there is a correlation between good decisions and good outcomes over time, not all good decisions lead to good outcomes – nor do all bad ones lead to poor outcomes.

This situation – evaluating outcomes versus decisions – causes two problems. First, a chance for learning and improving is lost. We believe we did a great job and buy into a false narrative to prove that we were right. Second, improperly assessing a situation where a good outcome is achieved by a bad decision can lead to problems in the future. The bad decision-maker can develop a false sense of confidence about his or her abilities and continue the behavior which eventually catches up with them.

Natural gas trader Brian Hunter, a trader of a hedge fund called Amaranth, is a good example. He had outstanding results in 2005, to put it mildly. He earned the firm $800 million trading natural gas and was named a Top Trader (#29 to be exact) in *Traders Monthly* in March 2006. It was disclosed that he was compensated between $75 million to $100 million that year. Unfortunately, just months later, his fortune turned for the worse. From August to September of 2006, he lost over $6 billion of the $9 billion in assets that the entire firm had under management as energy prices moved against him. Amaranth, once a very reputable firm with a long track record of success, imploded and ceased to exist shortly thereafter.

Figure 14: Just Months After Being Named a Top Trader, Brian Hunter Loses $6 billion

Calgary trader, 32, among world's best

Canada's top-earning trader doesn't work on Toronto's Bay Street or for one of the big banks. Instead, he rocks the world's natural-gas markets from his hometown of Calgary, according to the just-released Trader Monthly ranking of best-paid traders.

National Post (www.canada.com) – March 28, 2006

Canada's top-earning trader doesn't work on Toronto's Bay Street or for one of the big banks. Instead, he rocks the world's natural-gas markets from his hometown of Calgary, according to the just-released Trader Monthly ranking of best-paid traders.

Brian Hunter, 32, raked in an estimated US$75-million to US$100-million in 2005, good for a share of 29th spot in Trader Monthly's annual ranking. Mr. Hunter generated US$800-million in profit for his employer, Amaranth Group Inc., making him one of the world's top natural-gas traders, the magazine reported.

Small wonder Amaranth agreed when Mr. Hunter decided he wanted to leave the New York area and return to his home and native land. Amaranth opened an office in Calgary for Mr. Hunter and his team, according to Trader Monthly.

Hot trader led to biggest hedge-fund collapse

Seattle Times – December 17, 2006

...Maounis named Hunter co-head of the energy desk and gave him control of his own trades.

Within 17 months, Hunter would be responsible for $6.6 billion in losses, detonating the biggest hedge-fund implosion ever. Since Amaranth's sudden collapse, investors have questioned the unusual trust Maounis put in his star trader, now 32. They say Maounis gave Hunter too much latitude and that Hunter, trading more than half the firm's assets, was blinded by a bet that had worked like a charm for two straight years.

"Amaranth's demise is not due to some complicated quantitative reason. It's about human failing and frailty," says Hank Higdon, who runs New York-based Higdon Partners, a recruiter for hedge funds and other money-management firms.

Tallying the final days of Amaranth involves huge sums. During one week in September, Hunter's bet on natural gas lost about $4.6 billion. By month's end, the losses totaled $6.6 billion, or 70 percent of Amaranth's assets.

Source: Cited Above

How does this happen? Compensated massively, Brian Hunter was no doubt given a clear signal to continue doing what he was doing. Unfortunately, what he was doing was taking massive risks which, if they went against him, caused unfathomable losses.

This human tendency is very clear from the research. The media often creates a narrative of genius around certain outcomes in energy when luck was simply the driver. The subsequent costs of this faulty thinking can have catastrophic results as Amaranth unfortunately learned.

Takeaway 2 – Explaining "What" Versus Understanding "Why"

The tendency to evaluate a decision based on its outcome means that people often do not thoroughly analyze the decisions that have led to the good outcomes. The decisions leading to a good outcome are assumed to be good, and often false, or deeply exaggerated, narratives that illustrate the savviness of the thought that went into the decision are drafted *after* the fact. Most analysis and reflection are saved for when outcomes are bad. When evaluating these bad outcomes, most of the responses fall into one of two categories:

1. **Something impossible to predict happened**
2. **We were wrong about how we thought it would turn out**

These points are the same, just with a different storyteller. The less humble storyteller highlights the impossible to predict outcome (#1 above). Who can have predicted power prices moving like that? Who could have seen shale gas having such an impact? How could we have known that the Chinese would subsidize energy markets so much? Brian Hunter, the notorious natural gas trader, claimed in an interview that the loss was due to "an unprecedented and unforeseeable run-up in gas prices." This is a classic example of excuse #1 above. How could a natural gas trader who was considered the best at predicting just such movements and was just compensated close to $100 million the year before, be expected to see this? The more self-aware storyteller admits some level of analytical failing (#2 above) as he or she discusses how his or her analysis, interpretation of data, or thesis was flawed in some way.

Regardless of #1 or #2 above, these responses both have one thing in common. They both provide descriptions of what happened with limited insight into why that situation was not more accurately anticipated. Of course, one cannot make perfect decisions and have great outcomes all the time because we live in an uncertain world where all outcomes are probabilistic in nature. That said, by not understanding *why* something was missed and simply describing *what* was missed, an opportunity to learn and improve in the future is lost.

Takeaway 3 – The Two Main Causes of Poor Decisions

These first two realizations – the outcome bias and the focus on understanding *what* happened versus *why* it happened – came quickly from my review of the compiled research list. The next step was to comprehensively detail the "whys" of bad decisions for each situation. After that, the final step was to see if this list contained any patterns that were insightful.

After considerable review, two patterns stood out as key drivers of many bad decisions:

1. **System Complexity:** Energy is a complex system that is constantly changing and contains numerous interdependencies, non-linearity, feedback loops, path dependencies and time delays. Making good decisions is hard because behavior is difficult to predict.

2. **Psychology of Human Judgment:** In many situations, the judgment of decision-makers was skewed due to emotional or psychological reasons. All sorts of cognitive and social biases became apparent. Why did they continue to invest in a losing bet (i.e. loss aversion)? Why did they continue to seek advice from the only party that agreed

with their position (i.e. confirmation bias)? Why did they invest at such a high valuation (i.e. anchoring bias)?

These are not independent factors working in isolation. Human judgment is a key variable *within* existing systems and a major driver in creating *new* system structures (e.g., regulation often creates an entirely new structure). See Figure 15.

Figure 15: The Two Core – and Interrelated – Drivers of Bad Decisions

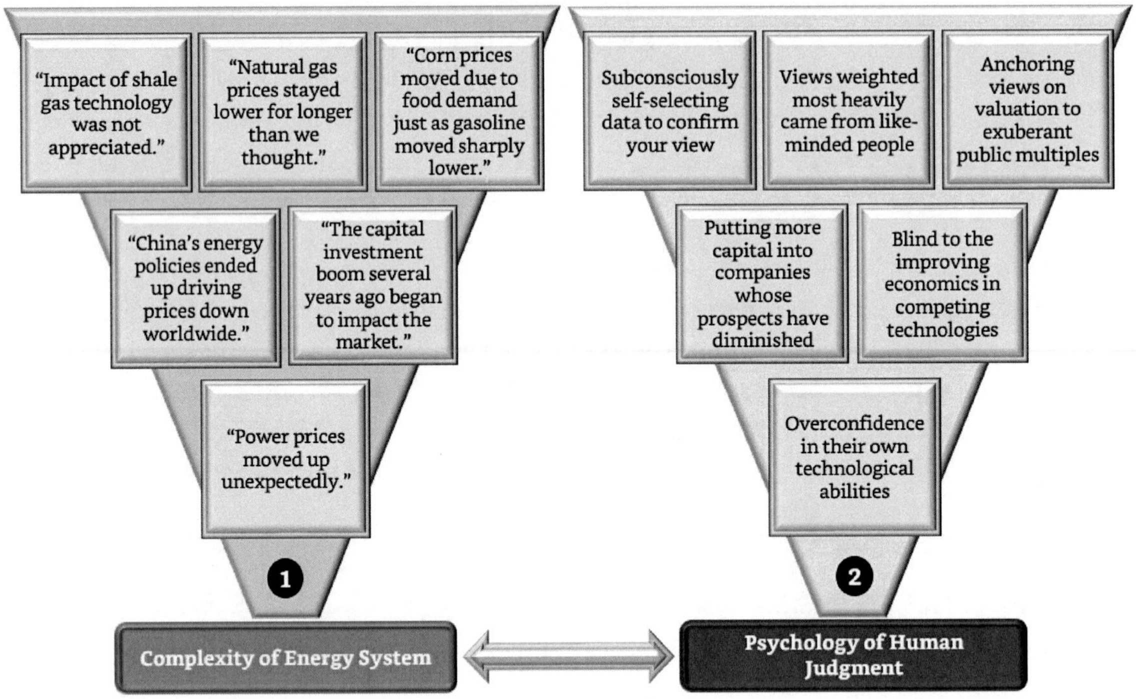

"Impact of shale gas technology was not appreciated."	"Natural gas prices stayed lower for longer than we thought."	"Corn prices moved due to food demand just as gasoline moved sharply lower."

"China's energy policies ended up driving prices down worldwide."	"The capital investment boom several years ago began to impact the market."

"Power prices moved up unexpectedly."

①

Complexity of Energy System

⟺

Subconsciously self-selecting data to confirm your view	Views weighted most heavily came from like-minded people	Anchoring views on valuation to exuberant public multiples

Putting more capital into companies whose prospects have diminished	Blind to the improving economics in competing technologies

Overconfidence in their own technological abilities

②

Psychology of Human Judgment

Source: Michael Molnar

How to Deal with System Complexity and Judgment Biases

Having found an interesting pattern of poor decision-making, the logical next question was what to do about it. Fortunately, the fields of systems thinking and behavioral economics have made significant progress in recent years. Systems thinking is focused on understanding how systems behave by understanding the linkages, time delays and feedback loops involved. Behavioral economics evaluates the psychological biases that we all inherently possess and that can skew our judgment. The following sections of this book are focused on explaining these two fields and applying them to some of the most important topics in energy.

Figure 16: Two Tools That We Will Explore to Improve Decision-Making in Energy

Systems Thinking

What do we mean when we say "systems thinking?" We can use the phrase to refer to a set of tools – such as causal loop diagrams, stock and flow diagrams and simulation models – that help us map and explore dynamic complexity. We can also use it to mean a unique perspective on reality – a perspective that sharpens our awareness of whole and of how the parts within those wholes interrelate. Finally, systems thinking can refer to a special vocabulary with which we express our understanding of dynamic complexity. For example, systems thinkers often describe the world in terms of reinforcing and balancing processes, limits, delays, patterns of behavior over time, and so forth.

Source: Waters Foundation, Barry Richmond

Behavioral Economics

Behavioral economics and the related sub-field, behavioral finance, study the effects of psychological, social, cognitive, and emotional factors on the economic decisions of individuals and institutions and the consequences for market prices, returns, and the resource allocation. Behavioral economics is primarily concerned with the bounds of rationality of economic agents. Behavioral models typically integrate insights from psychology, neuroscience and microeconomic theory; in so doing, these behavioral models cover a range of concepts, methods, and fields. Behavioral economics is sometimes discussed as an alternative to neoclassical economics.

Source: Behavioral economics. (2016, February 6). In Wikipedia, The Free Encyclopedia.

Source: Cited above

Section II

Primer on

Systems Thinking

and

Behavioral Economics

Understanding the Six Characteristics of Complex Systems

"Out of intense complexities, intense simplicities emerge."
- Winston Churchill
British Prime Minister (1874 to 1965)

Most people would agree that the energy world is complex. There are numerous uses and supplies of energy, countless regulations, political situations, and new technologies constantly being discussed. However, system complexity – the complexity identified from the research conducted – is a bit different. It is concerned with understanding how all the relevant variables in that system interact with one another and drive system behavior.

Six characteristics of energy systems drive this complexity: numerous interdependencies, feedback loops, non-linear behavior, system adaptation, path dependencies and time delays. These characteristics create systems that can be very hard to predict, often leading to outcomes never anticipated.

Figure 17: Six Characteristics that Make the Energy System Complex

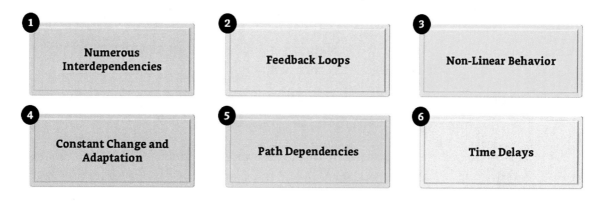

Source: Michael Molnar

(1) Numerous Interdependencies

Complex systems contain many variables that interact with one another. In energy, there are macroeconomic, demand, supply and government variables at work. Each of these groupings can contain countless more detailed variables that influence each other. For example, supply and demand interact to drive the price for a specific energy source. Let's say the price of natural gas changes as the U.S. government allows for more exports. This will make coal, all else equal, a cheaper option for utilities but likely hurt many U.S. industries that use natural gas as a feedstock (i.e., an input to their process). One can see how the complexity in the system can grow quite quickly with seemingly small changes.

Interdependencies are increasing for two reasons, technology and globalization. For example, technological innovation has made it possible to use natural gas and electricity to fuel vehicles. As more supply sources are able to be used in more areas of demand, the interdependency of the system grows.

Also, energy markets, like many other areas of the economy, are more global than ever. Oil, gas, coal and certain renewables can be shipped around the world with relative ease. The result is that changes in end markets or policy in one set of countries will impact other countries' markets as well.

The U.S. push for biofuels starting in the mid-2000s is a good example:

- China's strong economic growth increased the demand for oil worldwide; supply became tight and the price of oil increased dramatically.

- At the same time, the U.S. was concerned about the security of supply because the amount of imports had been continually increasing since the 1970s.

- This led President George W. Bush to enact policies that promoted domestic biofuels; a new industry was created using corn as an input.

- Corn had a new source of demand: transportation. Ten years later, over 30% of the U.S. corn crop was going toward fuel as compared to food.

- This increased demand was a factor in corn prices increasing which in turn drove certain food prices higher in the U.S. and in other countries dependent on U.S. corn; eventually there was pressure for biofuels to be sourced from non-food sources.

Waves of change can flow through markets as seemingly disparate variables influence each other in ways often not anticipated.

Figure 18: Energy Has Numerous Variables that are Interdependent with One Another

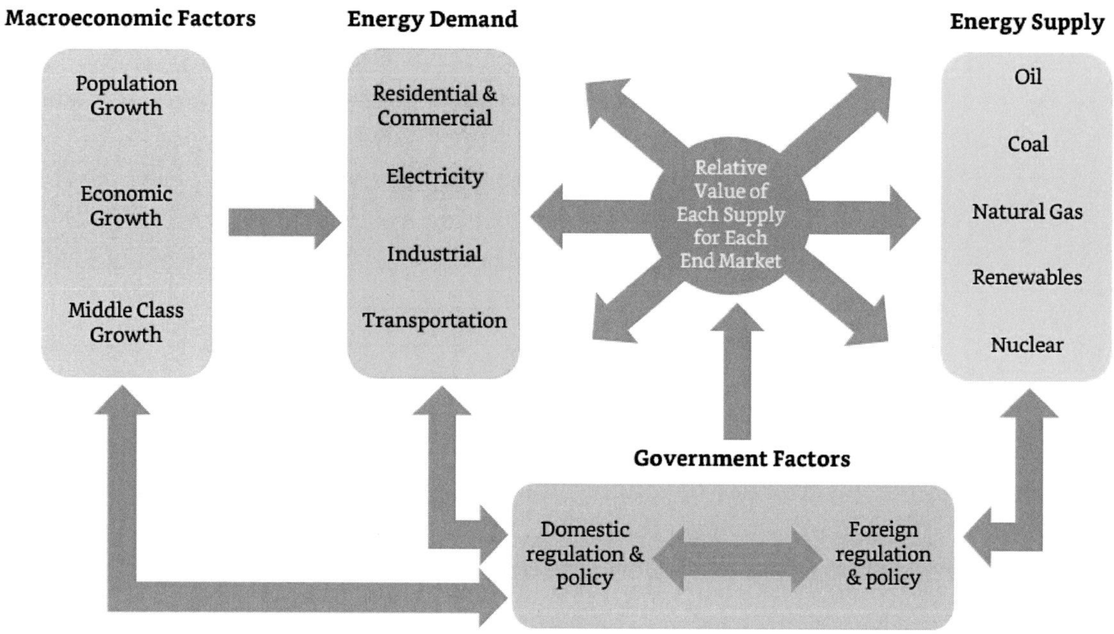

Source: Michael Molnar

(2) Feedback Loops

Feedback loops, where output from one area eventually comes back to influence that same area, is endemic to the energy sector. People tend to think linearly: "A happens to B, B then impacts C. However, complex systems contain a critical final step where C "feeds back" and impacts A.

There are two types of feedback loops: reinforcing (sometimes called "positive") and balancing (sometimes called "negative" or "goal-seeking" feedback loops). Reinforcing feedback loops build on themselves in a repetitive manner. For example, as a population increases, there are more births per year, which adds to population, which then has more births and so on. The result is exponential growth in population – meaning a percentage gain on a larger and larger base – which is exactly what has happened.

The typical example of a balancing feedback loop is a thermostat. There is a desired temperature, say 70 degrees Fahrenheit, which the user programs into the thermostat. The thermostat calculates the difference from the actual to desired temperature and signals the HVAC system to generate heat or cooling as appropriate. The bigger the difference, the more heating or cooling is applied. Eventually, the gap ceases to exist as the temperature approaches 70 degrees and the system stops, now that it has reached its goal, and is in balance.

In the energy world [text obscured] euphoria and investment in solar in the early to [text obscured] acity and R&D (research and development) whic[h text obscured] these lower costs to the end consumer drove de[mand text obscured] an even greater opportunity, which drove even [text obscured] ps experience constraints as nothing can grow [text obscured] supply eventually went into massive surplus re[text obscured] ers were negatively impacted, which drove reduc[text obscured]

The funding of sol[text obscured] back loop. Subsidies improve the relative econo[text obscured] demand. This demand means that the cost to t[text obscured] reases as well. Eventually, as Germany and Spa[in text obscured] ment can be very large. These funding requirem[ents text obscured] inging the system into balance on its own.

(handwritten note: If solar in early 2000's was decreasing in price, why was there a surplus?)

Figure 19: Example of a Reinforcing and Balancing Feedback Loop in Energy

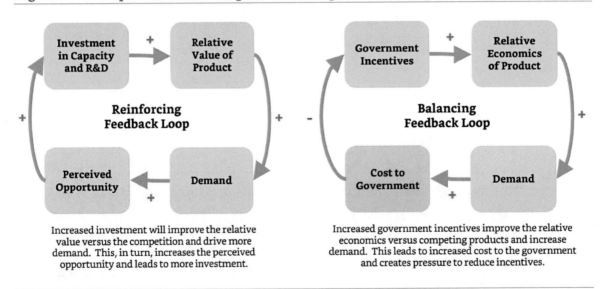

Increased investment will improve the relative value versus the competition and drive more demand. This, in turn, increases the perceived opportunity and leads to more investment.

Increased government incentives improve the relative economics versus competing products and increase demand. This leads to increased cost to the government and creates pressure to reduce incentives.

Source: Michael Molnar

(3) Non-Linear Behavior

By definition, linear behavior is easier to predict and understand than non-linear behavior. If, for example, a company sells 10 more units per year every year, then it is easy to forecast sales in year 10 to be 100 units in that year from a base of zero. If a company sells 25% more each year, it is a bit more challenging. If a company's sales are a constantly changing percentage that, at times, can increase two or three times per year but, at other times, can decrease as much as 80%, predictions become even more challenging.

Non-linearity is inherent in the energy world. Commodity prices, influenced by the forces of supply and demand, are good examples. As both supply and demand fluctuate at varying rates, this drives periods of oversupply or undersupply. Depending on the available substitutes and time delays involved, pricing can move dramatically during such times as evidenced in the price spikes of the mid-2000s.

Oil experienced both oversupply and undersupply from 2007 to 2009. At first, demand was very strong, driven by incredibly strong consumption in China. Supply tightened and, lacking clear substitutes to fill automobiles, prices shot up to $140 a barrel. However, as the Global Financial Crisis hit demand decreased, causing oversupply. As a result, oil prices fell to the mid-$30s per barrel. For such a large market, these are massive moves in the commodity price and highlight the non-linearity that can occur. It is important to note that this time period is not a one-off example, as one can see from the constant non-linear moves in Figure 20.

Non-linear behavior can be driven by factors outside of supply/demand mismatches as well. For example, Spain implemented a very generous subsidy to solar generators in 2006 and 2007. The rate of return for installing solar in Spain was significantly greater than anywhere else in the world and developers rushed to capture the opportunity. By 2008, installations surged to 2.7 gigawatts from 542 megawatts just a year earlier. The government was caught off-guard by this massive ramp and, fearing the costs to these installations, cut the program. The very next year solar installations dropped to just 19 megawatts.

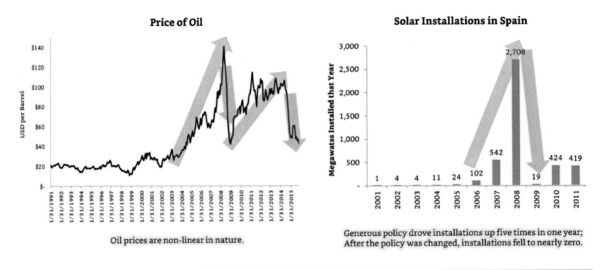

Oil prices are non-linear in nature.

Generous policy drove installations up five times in one year; After the policy was changed, installations fell to nearly zero.

Source: Energy Information Administration (left); Complied by Michael Molnar from multiple solar demand reports and news (right)

(4) Constant Change and Adaptation

Complex systems are not static; they constantly adapt and change. In energy, key areas of change are often related to demand, supply and policy. System behavior, or even the structure of the system itself, will adjust as these variables change.

In the 2000s, China became the worldwide driver of demand for commodities. The infrastructure buildout of railroads, bridges, highways and cities appeared to have no end and the impacts to commodity prices rippled through the world economy. As an example of the magnitude of the buildout, China expanded its power grid by the size of the entire United Kingdom's power grid each year during this time.

Similarly, the supply side is always changing as well. For example, innovation and scaled operations in solar have driven installations from just a few gigawatts each year to over 40 gigawatts (roughly the equivalent of 30 to 60 nuclear plants in capacity terms). Nuclear power was promoted as a source of clean power and a solution to the carbon dioxide problem in the 2000s but, after the Fukushima meltdown in Japan in 2011, became much less desirable by many.

Finally, policy and regulation can change the structure of the system itself. For example, fuel economy standards and acid rain regulations define the rules in their respective markets – and rules drive behavior. Market participants understand this risk, which is why new rules and regulations are such sources of contention.

Figure 21: Demand, Supply and Policy Are Constantly Changing and Adapting

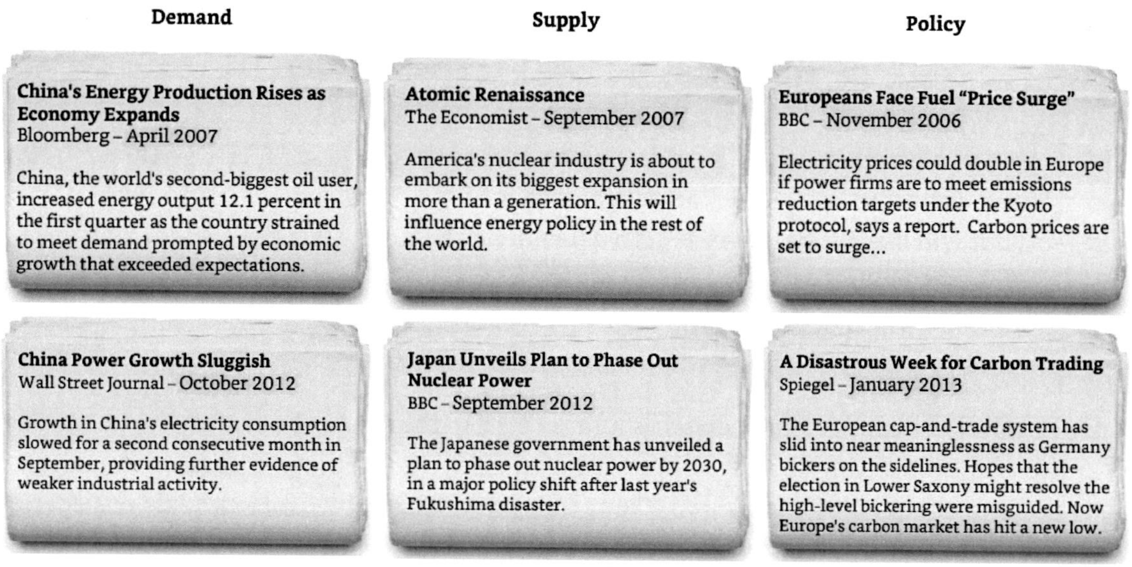

Demand	Supply	Policy
China's Energy Production Rises as Economy Expands Bloomberg – April 2007 China, the world's second-biggest oil user, increased energy output 12.1 percent in the first quarter as the country strained to meet demand prompted by economic growth that exceeded expectations.	**Atomic Renaissance** The Economist – September 2007 America's nuclear industry is about to embark on its biggest expansion in more than a generation. This will influence energy policy in the rest of the world.	**Europeans Face Fuel "Price Surge"** BBC – November 2006 Electricity prices could double in Europe if power firms are to meet emissions reduction targets under the Kyoto protocol, says a report. Carbon prices are set to surge...
China Power Growth Sluggish Wall Street Journal – October 2012 Growth in China's electricity consumption slowed for a second consecutive month in September, providing further evidence of weaker industrial activity.	**Japan Unveils Plan to Phase Out Nuclear Power** BBC – September 2012 The Japanese government has unveiled a plan to phase out nuclear power by 2030, in a major policy shift after last year's Fukushima disaster.	**A Disastrous Week for Carbon Trading** Spiegel – January 2013 The European cap-and-trade system has slid into near meaninglessness as Germany bickers on the sidelines. Hopes that the election in Lower Saxony might resolve the high-level bickering were misguided. Now Europe's carbon market has hit a new low.

Source: Cited Above

(5) Path Dependencies

Path dependency, the challenge to change after a certain path is chosen, is best illustrated with an example. The QWERTY keyboard layout was introduced in 1872 and still dominates today. One of the original design goals was to prevent typewriter jams on mechanical typewriters (and, also, possibly was influenced by the goals of telegraph transcribers). While there is a debate on the initial goals of the keyboard configuration, it is clear that the original objectives are much less relevant in a world of computers and tablets.

There are other keyboard formats that are potentially more accurate and fast, yet the QWERTY format is still the dominant one given that early "path" chosen. This has led to nearly everyone being trained how to type on QWERTY keyboards. Most people do not want to learn a new keyboard and thus most manufacturers will only make their keyboards in QWERTY form. Dvorak, likely a superior layout, never took hold as the history of QWERTY gives it a clear edge. The end result is that most of the English-speaking world types less quickly and accurately than they should.

Autom[...] [...]d. Internal combustion engines (engines
that us[...] [...]had its own oil supply and gasoline was
cheap. T[...] [...]hese types of engines, which made them
more eff[...] [...]e infrastructure of gas stations to be built
across th[...] [...]fix engines when there were problems.
This has[...] [...]r gasoline engines and has made it hard
for new t[...]

This doe[...] [...]not be changed. For example, lighting
transition[...] [...]el shifted from coal to diesel. Change
happens, [...] [...]is involved in the system makeup.

In terms of Path Dependencies, how long till we see electric cars take more market share?

(6) *Time Delays*

Time delays, the period from when a stimulus occurs to the impact being felt, are a key aspect
of complex systems. Simple systems have limited delays: something is done on day one, and
the impact is observable by day two. Complex systems have intricate time delays that can
impact the system months or years later.

Pollution is a good example. It builds up in the atmosphere, air or water over time. One simply
does not burn a ton of coal on Monday and get cancer on Tuesday. This does not make the
impact any less real. The health cost of the horrid air and water conditions in China will
eventually become evident – just with a time delay.

Capacity additions in business are another example. Often, there is a time delay from when a
decision is made to add capacity to when that capacity eventually comes online. For example,
it might take a year to build a large solar polysilicon factory, or one to three years to build a
ship for liquefied natural gas transport, or five to 10 years to build a nuclear plant. This delay
can mean that capacity comes online to a different world than was anticipated when the
decision to add the capacity was made. The resulting impact on the supply-demand balance
can lead to significant problems for the industry in question, as we will discuss later.

Time delays can occur with demand as well. For example, sometimes the adoption curve for a
new technology starts out slow, but builds over time. Distributed solar (putting solar on one's
rooftop) is fairly nascent in the U.S., but has trended up sharply recently as costs decline,
awareness grows, and specific consumer-financing programs are developed.

Final Word on System Complexity in Energy

The six characteristics described in this section highlight the difference between a simple and complex system. Simply put, simple systems do not have these characteristics and complex ones do. Energy markets are a set of complex sub-systems that contain all of these characteristics. Understanding how these systems are structured, the relevant dynamics of behavior, and leverage points that will drive future change, are a big part of what this book is about.

Systems Thinking: Understanding Behavior of Complex Systems

"A new type of thinking is essential if mankind is to
survive and move toward higher levels."
- Albert Einstein
Physicist (1879 to 1955)

What is Systems Thinking (or System Dynamics)?

By definition, simple systems are easy to understand. There are limited variables, few interdependencies, and typically no feedback or time delays. Simple, static analysis will often suffice. However, simple systems are increasingly rare and, unfortunately, simple analysis of complex systems is faulty and leads to problematic decisions and outcomes. Fortunately, systems thinking fills this gap.

The field was created by Jay Forrester at the Massachusetts Institute of Technology (MIT) in the 1950s. He wanted to use his background in science and engineering to help understand behavior and solve problems in complex systems. The field has expanded rapidly over the past 60 years. Systems thinking is now used to evaluate economic systems, internal business processes, strategic decisions, and government policies.

Because the field has grown so much, a concise all-compassing definition of systems thinking is not easy to find. Barry Richmond, a Ph.D. from M.I.T., who was a graduate student under Jay Forrester and created some of the first software programs for the field, has defined Systems Thinking as the following (his words are in italics below):

- **Set of Tools:** *"What do we mean when we say 'systems thinking?' We can use the phrase to refer to a set of tools – such as causal loop diagrams, stock and flow diagrams and simulation models – that help us map and explore dynamic complexity."*

- **Unique Perspective:** *"We can also use it to mean a unique perspective on reality – a perspective that sharpens our awareness of whole and of how the parts within those wholes interrelate."*

- **Special Vocabulary:** *"Finally, systems thinking can refer to a special vocabulary with which we express our understanding of dynamic complexity. For example, systems thinkers often describe the world in terms of reinforcing and balancing processes, limits, delays, patterns of behavior over time, and so forth."*

There is often confusion over the terms "System Dynamics" and "Systems Thinking." Typically, the phrase "System Dynamics" refers to a quantitative application where software is used to help model system behavior. This can be done with programs such as Vensim, Stella or Insight Maker. Variable linkages are mapped, interactions quantified, and the output is a series of numeric data.

"Systems Thinking" is usually used to describe the qualitative approach to mapping the various linkages in the system. Ultimately, the right approach, either quantitative or qualitative, depends on the situation. In this book, we use the terms "Systems Thinking" and "System Dynamics" somewhat interchangeably and focus more on the qualitative aspect of systems thinking in order to map and understand the behavior of systems for the reader.

Typical Problem-Solving Approach Versus the Systems-Thinking Approach

The typical problem-solving approach dramatically differs from a systems-thinking one. Many people are familiar with this conceptual approach: A problem is identified, that situation is analyzed, a decision is made and results follow. It is a clean straightforward framework, but unfortunately, not reality. The world does not flow in such a single-event, independent and linear manner. Russell Ackoff, a pioneering thinker in the area, understood this when he said:

> *"Managers are not confronted with problems that are independent of each other, but with dynamic situations that consist of complex systems of changing problems that interact with each other. I call such situations messes. Problems are extracted from messes by analysis. Managers do not solve problems, they manage messes."*

Systems thinking, not unlike traditional problem-solving thinking, recognizes there is a goal of some sort, which stimulates a decision being made. Systems thinking goes a step further and recognizes that the decision made will change the environment in some way. Other participants react to that changing environment and make decisions. This then changes the environment again, which leads to a continued set of changing circumstances. Finally, there are exogenous (meaning from the outside and not related to you or the other participants) that occur and change the environment. The elements of the system continually interact with each other and drive a behavior over time.

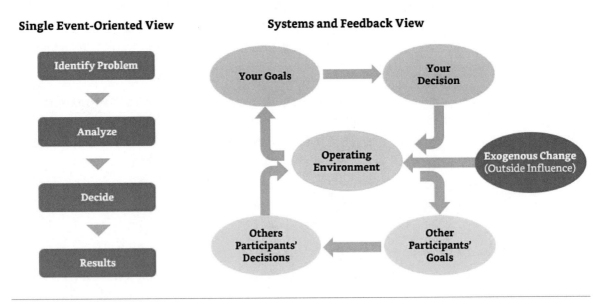

Source: *Michael Molnar*

There are many examples of this in the real world:

- A company that manufactures equipment to use natural gas for transportation experiences a decline in the price of oil (exogenous factor).

- Business sales are rising so capacity is increased; unfortunately, several competitors have done the same and oversupply looms on the horizon.

- A government official implements a policy meant to stimulate the use of certain transportation technologies; weeks later, the related fuel used by the technology supported increases in price and the policy becomes ineffective

- Government officials in country A implement a policy to stimulate a domestic industry; officials in country B react with even more support (e.g., subsidies, tax breaks) as domestic companies complain about country A's unfair support

We will explore the dynamics of many situations like these later in the book.

Example: Romanian Child Birth Policy in the 1960s

Romanian childbirth policies in the 1960s demonstrate the risk of simple thinking applied to complex systems. In the 1960s, the Romanian government wanted to increase a very low birth rate. Several policy changes were made, such as outlawing various forms of contraception, instituting tax incentives for larger families and banning abortion. At a first glance, these policies seem logical to achieve the outcome desired by the government, which was to increase the birth rate from an anemic 15 births per year per 1,000 people (note that typical birth rates by country range between 10 and 50 per 1,000 according to World Bank data).

So what happened? At first, the birth rate increased to 40 per 1,000 people per year. It was deemed a success and seemed to prove the policy worked. However, just a few years later, the birth rate went back down to 20 per 1,000 per year as people found ways to avoid or obfuscate the regulations. Contraception was illegally imported and a black market in "back-alley" abortions gained traction. The initial success was ultimately short-lived and, even worse, there were numerous unanticipated side effects. The "back-alley" abortions led to a tripling of deaths due to complications. Neonatal deaths rose and infant mortality rates increased. Finally, given Romania was a very poor nation, it put a strain on families that had children they could not necessarily afford. This led to large increases in state orphanage populations. Since these orphanages were underfunded, hospital needles were shared which led to an outbreak of disease among children. In short, the policy was a short-term success but a long-term catastrophe.

Poor policy decisions by communist Romania in the 1960s might not seem shocking. But there are many similar examples today. In complex systems, simple analysis of policy, business or investment decisions can lead to bad results. There are many such examples:

- Low-tar cigarettes have driven an increased in intake of carcinogens as people smoke more.

- Energy-efficiency mandates make the cost of use lower to the end user, which leads to people using these items more (e.g., lighting, air conditioning).

- The E.U. carbon-trading policy ended up giving windfall profits to the biggest emitters, then subsequently created an environment that incented utilities to burn coal – the exact opposite its intent.

Figure 23 is a depiction of this concept. It is simple and obvious, but also very true. How many times has a corporate management team been rewarded, often extremely, for decisions that led to the company's eventual demise? Or a government official declares some sort of policy victory only to find out its eventual folly? Or an investor praised as a genius who blows up the next year? As the figure below shows, simple decisions in complex systems can come back to haunt the decision-maker.

Problem Solved?
Often the man on the left will be rewarded in the short-term. Results are better than they were before….

Bigger Problem?
…but many times simple decisions lead to bigger problems in the not-too-distant future.

Source: Michael Molnar

Stocks, Flows and Standard Systems-Thinking Notation

Systems thinking analysis uses a set of common notations and mapping techniques. The most common ones are:

- **Stocks and Flows:** A stock is something that accumulates or degrades whereas a flow is the rate of accumulation or degradation. A bath tub is often used as a simple example. The amount of water in the tub is the "stock" and the stream of water from the faucet is the "flow." While it is a fairly simple concept, what makes systems thinking useful is in mapping the interconnections of stocks and flows, along with time delays and feedback loops to help understand the bigger picture.

- **Auxiliary Variables:** Technically, systems can be mapped using entirely stocks and flows. However, many times it is more clear to use auxiliary variables to highlight the interdependencies involved. This is especially true for the more qualitative systems thinking applications that we will often use in this book.

- **Time Delays:** Time delays are usually notated by two lines across a path of dependence. This highlights that there will be some lag between one variable and another. Time delays are one of the most important drivers of system behavior.

- **Correlation:** The correlation of the causal relationship is often notated with a plus (+) sign or a minus (-) sign to denote positive or negative correlation. The plus sign simply tells the reader that the variables move in the same direction, which may or may not be a considered a good outcome from that person's perspective.

- **Model Boundary:** There needs to be a boundary on the system and these are often shown as clouds. As everything is ultimately interconnected, effective systems analysts are able to judge where the appropriate boundaries of the model should lie. Less experienced systems thinkers will tend to over-model and end up with a needlessly complex model that is confusing to understand and less insightful than hoped.

Figure 24 shows these notations. Inventory is a stock that increases as units are produced, and decreases as units are sold. Auxiliary variables in this simple example are "expectations about future sales" and "market conditions." These arrows show the following logic: The rate at which units are selling, combined with market conditions, influence expectations about future sales. These expectations influence the rate at which management produces more inventory. The plus signs simply mean that the variables move in the same direction. As more units are sold, expectations about future sales increase. As market conditions improve, expectations about future sales increase as well.

These simple systems notations are a bit like playing guitar. By learning four of five chords, one has the potential to play thousands of popular songs that all sound very different. While systems notation is relatively finite and conceptually simple to understand, it can be used to map countless systems to understand how they behave. Also, guitar has various levels of complexity where, for example, one can simply strum a chord or finger-pick complex arpeggios. Similarly, systems analysis can be conducted at various levels. One can qualitatively draw the lines of interconnection or use software to model the interactions using advanced mathematics.

Figure 24: Typical Notations in Systems Thinking

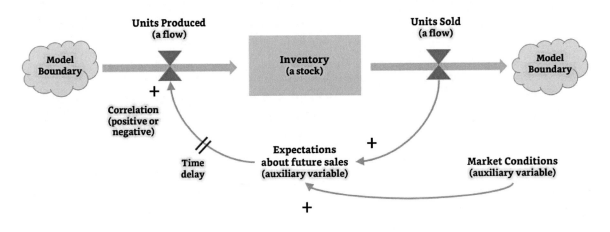

Source: Michael Molnar

Many people are dealing with stocks and flows, but do not recognize it. Financial analysts are a good example. As an analyst assesses a company's prospects, he or she will typically look at accounting statements. A balance sheet is simply a set of the various stocks, assets and liabilities of the business. Income statements and cash flow statements are the flows. Accounting is a very elegant manner by which they are all linked together.

While I was a Visiting Research Fellow at a think tank in the early 2000s, we modeled eBay's financial performance using system dynamics software. It was an effective way to bring financial statements to life. eBay's balance sheet did not contain much information on its key asset, the installed customer base. We modeled the various drivers of the customer base in the software and the resulting output was the accounting statements. This analysis allowed for a much deeper understanding of the opportunities and risks to the business than a simple review of accounting statements or a financial analyst's typical forecast model in a spreadsheet.

Spreadsheets are a very useful tool for modeling companies. However, when there are multiple business drivers, numerous interdependencies, non-linear behaviors and time delays, simple spreadsheet analysis has limitations. A systems dynamics model, either quantitatively built or qualitatively mapped, helps to provide a different level of insight into what is really driving the business and how that business might progress over time.

Figure 25: Accounting Statements Are Simply Sets of Stocks and Flows

Balance Sheet	
Assets	
Cash	75
Accounts Receivable	50
Inventory	75
Equipment	50
Total	250
Liabilities	
Accounts payable	100
Notes payable	50
Total	150
Stockholders' Equity	
Contributed capital	50
Retained earnings	50
Total	100
Total equity and liabilities	250

Income Statement	
Revenues	100
Expenses	
Cost of goods sold	10
Selling, general and admin	8
Research and development	5
Interest expense	2
Total expenses	25
Pretax income	75
Income tax expense	20
Net income	50

Cash Flow	
Cash flow from operating activities	
Cash collected from customers	100
Cash paid to suppliers	-20
Cash paid to employees	-20
Cash paid for interest and taxes	-10
Total	50
Cash flow from investing activities	
Cash paid for equipment	-25
Total	-25
Cash flow from financing activities	
Cash received from loan	100
Cash paid in dividends	-50
Total	50
Net increase / (decrease) in cash	75
Cash beginning of year	0
Cash end of year	75

A balance sheet is a set of "stocks"...   ...whereas income and cash flow statements are sets of "flows"

Source: Michael Molnar

Feedback Loops and Typical System Behaviors

Stocks, flows and auxiliary variables are the building blocks of systems thinking. Linking them together with relevant time delays and feedback loops are where systems thinking comes to life. A feedback loop can be thought of as a circuit of influence. Something happens to A, which impacts B, which then goes back and impacts A. As described in the prior section, there are two types of feedback loops: balancing feedback loops (sometimes called negative or goal-seeking) and reinforcing (sometimes called positive). The typical notation in graphing these loops is to put either an R or B, for reinforcing or balancing, in the middle of the loop.

The combination of feedback loops and time delays are what drive four typical system behaviors:

1. **Exponential Growth**

2. **Overshoot-and-Oscillation**

3. **S-Curve Growth**

4. **Overshoot-and-Collapse**

Exponential Growth

Figure 26 depicts the reinforcing-loop dynamics of network economics, where businesses become more valuable as their network grows. In a membership-based business model, for example, non-members become members at some rate. This, by definition, makes the offering more attractive to non-members as the key value of a network is a large installed base. This stimulates more non-members to become members and the loop continues. eBay's business model is centered around just such a dynamic.

The outcome, or system behavior as it is commonly stated, is exponential growth. Exponential growth means that a stock is growing by the same percentage cumulatively. Numbers can grow quickly as percentage gains are applied to a growing base. It is the same concept as compound interest in a bank account. Linear growth, in contrast, grows by the same number of units each period.

An example can help to illustrate the difference. Exponential, or compound, growth of 5% a year for 10 years on a starting number of units of 100, yields 163 units at year 10. Linear growth of 5 units per year for 10 years means there are 150 units (100 starting plus 50) at year 10. As we shall see, the human mind is often challenged in correctly predicting exponential growth or decline given various cognitive biases. Understanding what drives exponential growth or decline, as well as our mind's limitations in evaluating it, is an important part of making better decisions in energy.

Until reinforcing loops hit a constraint, growth is exponential as shown in Figure 26. "Carrying capacity" is a term often used to highlight such a constraint. In our example, the carrying capacity would be the maximum number of possible members. Eventually as this company grows, the constraint would become more of an issue. Until then, however, growth can continue exponentially.

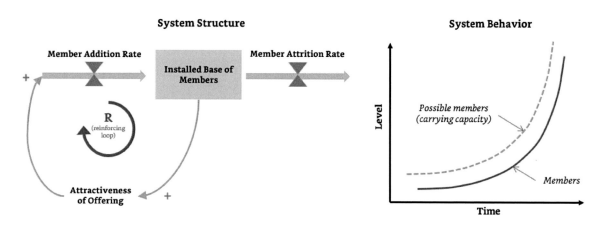

Source: Michael Molnar

Overshoot-and-Oscillation

Balancing feedback loops are another type of feedback. This loop "self-corrects" and the resulting system behavior is much different than reinforcing loops. Figure 27 shows a simple example in housing development. There are two stocks: "buildings under construction" and "housing available." As buildings under construction are completed, they increase the housing available. This will decrease the number of people looking for a home that cannot find one, which is to say that they are negatively correlated. Less people looking for homes means expected operating profit from new construction will be lower as there are less people who need homes (positive correlation). These expectations influence the desire for new development, which feeds the construction rate and the buildings under construction. The system in this example balances as operating profits decline and the spigot of new construction is turned down.

Balancing loops often oscillate around the carrying capacity due to time delays inherent in the system response. If the time delay for supply to adjust is long, there will be more extreme oscillations; stocks are built up much higher than needed, which means they will have to decrease sharply when adjustment finally happens. As we will see in discussing booms and busts, these oscillations are an inherent part of what drives severely cyclical industries.

Figure 27: Balancing Feedback Loop and Goal-Seeking System Behavior

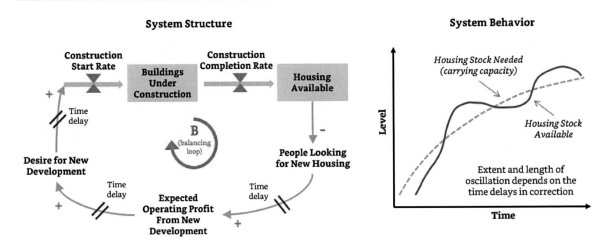

Source: Michael Molnar

S-Curve Growth

When reinforcing loops, balancing loops, and carrying capacity constraints interact with one another, S-curve growth is the result. eBay's network economics can help illustrate this concept. Growth can be exponential early on, as discussed. But as the installed base grows, it approaches a capacity limitation of the amount of new members possible. As new members join, this in effect decreases the population of possible new members. This eventually leads to a lower member-addition rate and growth flattens as the balancing feedback loop takes hold. The resulting growth looks like an "S," hence the name "S-curve."

Understanding the timing of the exponential growth and balancing loop taking hold is important for investors. Wall Street loves to push high-growth stories. Typically, the company is growing fast in a market that is pitched as nearly "limitless." Valuations may be high but they are justified by the growth, or so the story goes. These situations usually result in stock prices that can move higher in the short term as exponential growth surprises to the upside, but then are followed by terrific crashes as the balancing loop takes hold and growth does not meet the market's lofty expectations.

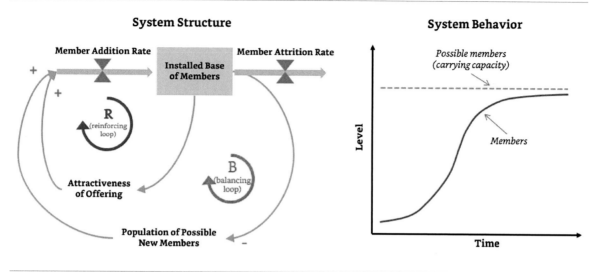

Source: Michael Molnar

Overshoot-and-Collapse

Each of the previous system behaviors ran into a constraint of static carrying capacity. While carrying capacity is often fairly static, there are situations where the carrying capacity itself becomes depleted. The resulting behavior is called "overshoot-and-collapse."

Deer population growth presents a good example. Deer populations, like many populations, have a reinforcing feedback loop dynamic. More deer growing at a similar birth rate per deer equals larger populations of deer. If the food supply is not growing at a similar rate, the deer can diminish the food supply to dangerous levels. Deer can literally eat themselves to mass hunger and starve to death as a result.

Many environmentalists worry about a similar analogy with the human population. Global population is growing exponentially and there is some limit to the capacity (i.e. food, resources) for the world to handle larger and larger populations. The time delays in recognizing the growing problem are the key difference between the situation being "overshoot-and-oscillation" versus "overshoot-and-collapse." The longer the time delay, the more likely the collapse scenario.

While nearly everyone can envision the deer situation, many simply cannot envision a similar situation with humans. There are differences, mainly around the ability for humans to anticipate the problem and then drive improvements in technology and efficiency to handle it better. While these are critical differences, humans would be well-served by recognizing the similarities in the dynamics as well.

Figure 29: Time Delays in the Balancing Loop Drive Overshoot-and-Collapse Behavior

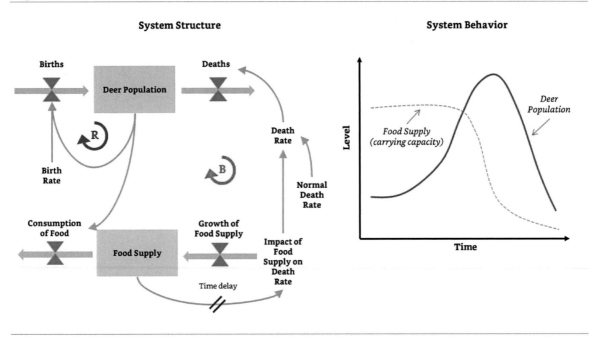

All examples of "overshoot-and-collapse" need not be as dreadful as mass starvation of deer or human hardship. In fact, there are times when it is the *desired* effect as is the case in the wine industry. Winemaking involves fermentation of grape juice into alcohol and carbon dioxide in a controlled environment. Yeast (analogous to the deer in our prior example) are the consumer of the grape juice (the food supply). It keeps expanding until it consumes nearly the entire supply of grape juice. Eventually, the yeast consumes itself into extinction and only the "pollution" is what is left. The pollution here is alcohol, or wine in this case.

Summary of Four Types of Typical System Behaviors

While each system is unique, there are often consistent structural patterns and resulting system behaviors. Outcomes that might seem random are likely some combination of the four structures and system behaviors described in this section. For example, a vexing situation might be nothing more than S-curve growth that has entered its decline period and then evolved into an oscillating cycle. Below is a summary of the four system behaviors with commentary around when they often occur.

Figure 30: Summary of Four Typical System Behaviors

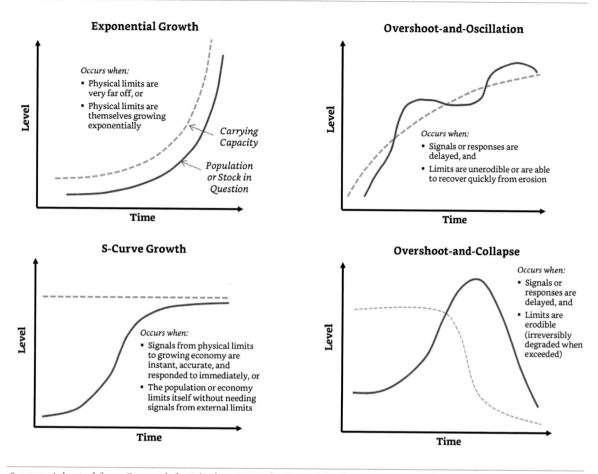

Source: Adapted from Beyond the Limits, *1992, by Dana Meadows, Jorgen Randers, Dennis Meadows*

Commodity System Structures

The world of energy, both traditional and so-called alternative energy, is a commodity market for the most part. Unlike an industry like retail, where a brand might be the primary reason consumers pay 50% or 100% premium, energy is seen as homogenous and thus often competes on price. Simply put, a gallon of gasoline is seen as being the same from Exxon or Shell and a kilowatt hour of electricity is a kilowatt of electricity, nothing more. Some people forget this when discussing alternative energy. An energy company CEO whom I know, phrased it well when he told me, "Alternative energy is simply a specialized input for a commoditized output."

While each commodity system is unique, there are certain similarities in their system structures. Commodity systems are influenced by three feedback loops:

1. **Capacity Loop:** The capacity loop is the creation of new capacity to make more product, which is done in anticipation of the sales to be achieved from the capital investment. For example, an oil company drills new wells or a solar company expands its manufacturing facility.

2. **Utilization Loop:** The utilization loop is influenced by the expected profitability of increasing utilization of existing capacity. If pricing is good, factories and mines will run longer and vice versa.

3. **Substitution Loop:** The substitution loop is a function of the price of substitutes and the relative value of one product versus another. As pricing for one commodity moves up, another becomes more valuable on a relative basis and will be substituted in, if possible.

Two time delays are important to understand:

1. **Substitution Delay:** The potential for other products to be substituted for the traditional product can occur, but often with a delay. For example, the price of oil is said to be inelastic in the short term as automobiles are all generally designed to run on gasoline. If the price of gasoline stays high for a long time, consumers might demand different fuels or technologies. This process takes time to impact the system as manufacturers have to design, manufacture and market such new cars. The extent of the delay will vary by that particular market's dynamics; for example, coal-to-gas switching in power generation is on a significantly shorter time delay than alternative fuel transportation.

2. **Capacity-Build Delay:** The second time delay in commodity structures is the building of new capacity which is typically stimulated by expected future pricing. Once planned, new capacity can take anywhere from a few months to a decade to come online, depending on the industry and the situation. For example, in the power-generation industry, a nuclear plant can take many years to come online but a solar factory can be built in just months.

Figure 31: Typical Commodity System Structure

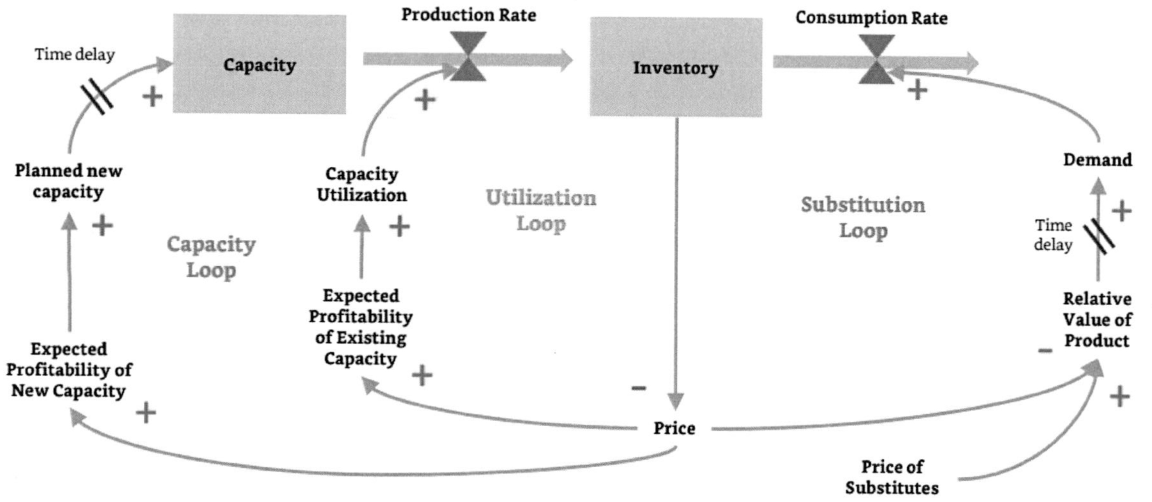

Source: Michael Molnar

Quantitative Example of the World3 Model

While most of our analysis in this book will be qualitative in nature, it is helpful to have a quick look at a more mathematical approach using system dynamics software. Figure 32 is a depiction of the "World3" model that was made famous in the 1972 book, *The Limits to Growth*. Many credit this book and model with starting the modern discussion around the carrying capacity of the earth and the consequences of unfettered population growth in a world dependent on fossil fuels.

In Figure 32, one can see just how many variables there are in the model. I have highlighted one flow to show how mathematical relationships can be quantified in software programs (in this case, InsightMaker). Most software allows for a high degree of complexity such as data table lookups and if/then statements – all meant to simulate reality in a way to provide the type of insights desired for the problem at hand. The output (i.e., the system behavior) is shown on the top right hand side in the figure below. This simulation shows humans vastly overshooting their carrying capacity and facing future declines. Remember that the point for most system dynamics models is not to come to a single forecast, but to learn about the range of future scenarios that are possible.

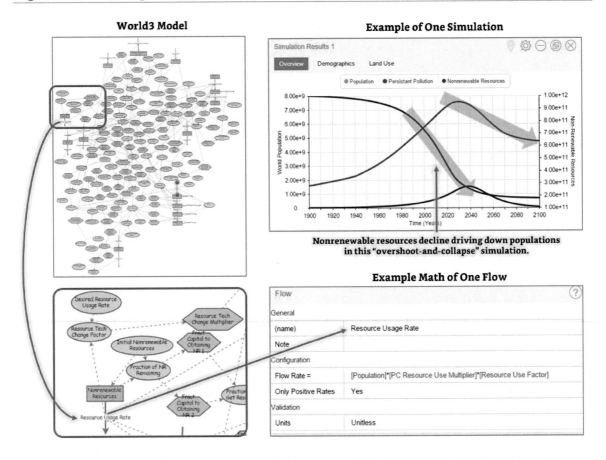

Nonrenewable resources decline driving down populations in this "overshoot-and-collapse" simulation.

Source: InsightMaker, Model by Scott Fortmann-Roe

Qualitative Example on the 2008 Housing Bust

Qualitative analysis, often called systems thinking, is equally useful. This often involves mapping out the system as a means to understand or communicate the dynamics taking place. Qualitative analysis can be supplemented with other traditional forms of quantitative analysis as well. Whether one uses a more quantitative, qualitative or hybrid approach simply depends on the goals for the task at hand.

One example of a hybrid approach is work I did on housing as a sell-side analyst at Goldman Sachs. I covered the homebuilders in the years leading up to the market crash in 2008. Before the crash, there were countless bull and bear arguments such as:

- *"As long as interest rates are low, then housing stays strong."*

- *"It's a confidence game; Right now, confidence is strong and so housing will stay healthy."*

- *"The higher divorce rate supports more need for housing stock than ever before."*

- *"There are many people who simply want a second home as a vacation home."*

- *"This is all speculation and will bust."*

The list was endless. Most of the arguments had some merit, but very few possessed a strong systems view of the structure of the housing market. So we mapped the variables that were driving the system. This allowed a more comprehensive view and analysis of how this market would progress.

An approximation of the system map we generated is reproduced below in Figure 33. A trained systems thinker would be appalled with the casual nature of linkages formed and notations used. However, our purpose at the time was to qualitatively talk through the housing cycle and communicate our view, which we then followed up with more traditional quantitative analysis.

We specifically highlighted the importance of market participants' expectations on both the supply and demand side of the equation. There was a clear risk that if expectations changed, it could quickly reverberate through the system. Another insight: Most people need to be able to sell their existing home in order to buy a new one. This was a dynamic that was not being discussed at the time, but it became a critical factor when the market became troubled. In fact, several years later, challenges in selling a home to buy another one was a topic that CEOs of the homebuilders were actively discussing (See the article in Figure 34).

Figure 33: System Map Used in 2005/2006 To Describe our Negative View on Housing

Housing Demand

Housing Supply

- # Households that Need a Place to Live
- Expected Price Appreciation
- Capital Gains on Old House
- Income, Job Security
- Mortgage Payment
- Affordability of Housing
- Expected Profitability of Housing as Investment

- Primary Residence Purchasers (vs renting)
- Speculative Purchasers and Second Homes

- **Demand:** # People in Market to Buy
- Units Sold at What Price
- **Supply:** # Homes in Supply (on market)

- Existing Homes for Sale (85% of sales)
- New Homes Built (15% of Sales)

- Desire to Sell
- Usable, Existing Housing Stock
- Ability to Get Entitled Land
- Desire to Build and Ability to Finance

- Expected Sales Price
- Moving, Other Needs
- # of Existing Units
- Unusable Stock
- Available Land
- Ability to Entitle Land
- Credit Strength & Availability
- Expected Profitability

Source: Approximation of Chart Used in Goldman Sachs Homebuilder Initiation, "Tougher Cycle Ahead," November 2005. Authors: Chris Hussey and Michael Molnar

Figure 34: New Home Sales 1963 to 2014

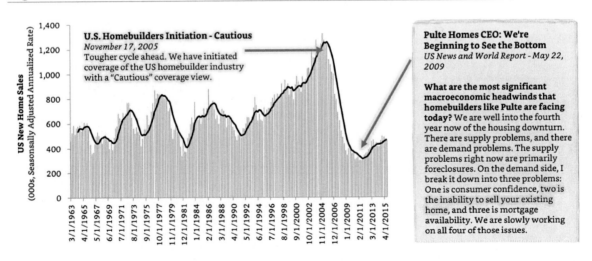

U.S. Homebuilders Initiation - Cautious
November 17, 2005
Tougher cycle ahead. We have initiated coverage of the US homebuilder industry with a "Cautious" coverage view.

Pulte Homes CEO: We're Beginning to See the Bottom
US News and World Report - May 22, 2009

What are the most significant macroeconomic headwinds that homebuilders like Pulte are facing today? We are well into the fourth year now of the housing downturn. There are supply problems, and there are demand problems. The supply problems right now are primarily foreclosures. On the demand side, I break it down into three problems: One is consumer confidence, two is the inability to sell your existing home, and three is mortgage availability. We are slowly working on all four of those issues.

Source: United States Census Bureau

Does the time series of new home sales in Figure 34 look familiar? It is an example of "overshoot-and-oscillate" behavior described earlier. The chart highlights how steep cycles can be, and how different cycles can be to one another. Before the crash, there were numerous arguments for a secular change in the market that would lead to a new "normal." These arguments turned out to be incorrect but confidence and sentiment can count for a lot. This sentiment led to a delay in the correction mechanism, which meant housing became massively oversupplied and resulted in a very sharp adjustment in the other direction to bring it back into balance.

Key Benefits of Systems Thinking

Systems thinking can be applied to numerous areas: foreign policy, war, business strategy, hunger, civil unrest, recessions, depressions, crime, stock prices and more. There are several key benefits. **First, systems thinking allows for more insight to predict outcomes.** Of course, perfect foresight is not possible. But the ability to better understand how trends are developing within the system and have insight into its future direction is greatly improved by understanding the structures and likely resulting behaviors involved.

Second, mapping out the system structure can help evaluate leverage points to more effectively change system behavior and outcomes. This is helpful for policymakers who are hoping to affect change or to the business managers and investors trying to evaluate it. Dana Meadows, a pioneer in systems thinking, summarized various leverage points in her book, *Thinking in Systems*. The chart below was adapted from her list and highlights the typical points of most leverage (system goals) and least leverage (flow rates). However, it is important to understand that the impact of a leverage point is always situation-dependent. There are many times that leverage points that fall on the "least leverage" part of the continuum can have a large impact; it simply depends on the particular situation.

Figure 35: Leverage Points of Change in a System

	Leverage Point / Examples	Commentary
① Least Leverage	**Flow Rates** *Hiring or firing rate, tax or spending rate*	• People directly affected care immensely, but it rarely changes the overall system behavior • Impactful when they are moved into a range that triggers another leverage point – e.g., a flow change that adjusts the impact of a reinforcing loop
②	**Stock Buffer Size** *Level of debt, level of inventory*	• Example: A lake is a large "stock" with a small "flow" whereas a river is the opposite; rivers are inherently more volatile and overflow more given the smaller buffer • Can be very impactful to change the buffer size, but also many times is simply not possible to do
③	**System Structure** *Stock A driven by Flows B, C*	• Structure of interconnections is hugely important, but can be hard to change at times • Example: the baby boom in the U.S. pressured elementary school system, then high school, then colleges, then jobs, then housing and soon retirement – impossible to change once started
④	**Time Delays** *Planning-to-delivery delay, pollution occurring to impact*	• Delays are sources of oscillation in balancing feedback loops • Major point of leverage, but cannot often be changed; if that is the case, changing the growth rate is likely the next best option
⑤	**Balancing Feedback Loops** *Freedom of Information Act, pollution taxes*	• Applying change to any component of a balancing loop can change the strength of entire loop • Often the leverage here is found in preventing participants from obfuscating the balancing loop from happening (i.e. anti-trust laws, removing subsidies)
⑥	**Reinforcing Feedback Loops** *Changing birth rates, changing interest rates*	• Reducing the gain of a reinforcing loop is often more impactful than strengthening a balancing feedback loop • By slowing down a reinforcing loop, the system has time for balancing loops to function well
⑦	**Information Flow** *Air pollution reporting, calorie labeling*	• Adds a new loop to the system; missing information flows are a major source of poor behavior • Example: the U.S. embassy reporting PM 2.5 levels (air pollution) in China drove the Chinese government to report and now the public is applying pressure for change
⑧	**Rules** *Physical laws (thermodynamics), social rules (constitutions, laws)*	• Major driver of how systems work, which is a big reason lobbyists are paid to influence them • Example: acid rain regulation changed the rules for how the power industry operated and drove substantial change in fuel sources and use of abatement technology
⑨ Most Leverage	**Goals** *Economic growth, quality of life*	• Changing the purpose can be hard, but clearly impactful as systems are designed around them • Important to have participants' goals not trump system goals; this is a major tension in capitalism where successful capitalists often want to limit competition

Source: Adapted from Donella Meadows (Thinking in Systems); Michael Molnar

Third, the ability to simulate and learn is very valuable. One can model and perform countless scenarios to predict what might happen. As real-life experience can be expensive, these learnings are often very valuable. U.S. President Eisenhower once stated, "Planning is everything. The plan is nothing." This is analogous to the benefits of modeling in my view: The model is nothing, but the modeling is everything in terms of learning and understanding.

Finally, systems thinking provides a means to communicate as described in the housing example that I used to share with clients. Policymakers can use systems thinking to communicate why they are structuring policy a certain way. Mapping the system is often much more intuitive for people to understand versus a series of disparate formulas or regression analysis.

Behavioral Economics: Understanding How Judgment Forms

Judgments, Decisions and the Interplay with Systems

Systems are made up of many different variables, not the least of which are people and the decisions they make. People are involved in energy systems as policymakers, business executives, investors and private citizens. Unfortunately, as we will discuss, the mind has inherent biases that can skew humans to have poor judgment; and bad judgment is a harbinger of a bad decision.

People's judgments and subsequent decisions impact systems in two ways. First, judgments by people are felt as key variables within existing system structures. For example, expectations about future profitability of new capacity are often a key judgment which is made as executives decide whether and how much to build.

People's judgments can also be a determinant of the structure of the system itself. For example, the policymakers that decided to regulate emissions of acid rain judged that something needed to be done and acted. Regulations like these create new sets of rules and variables (in this case, the price of emissions) and by doing so create a new system structure.

How is Judgment Formed? Understanding Your Two Minds

We can all remember times that our judgment seemed logical, analytical and effective. Data is gathered, analysis is performed, judgment formed, and a reasonable decision is made. However, if we conjure up a bit of self-awareness, there are other times where we were considerably less thoughtful. Our judgments seem rushed, based on spurious information, or were formed without us really "thinking." The result is often a bad decision that we look back on with some degree of embarrassment.

Evaluating how judgment forms is more nuanced than analyzing system structures. Systems structures can be thought through, evaluated, and debated with a certain level of facts and logic. Judgment is more difficult to evaluate with such precision. Yet, most people would agree that there are two aspects of one's mind at work – one that appears more thoughtful at times and one a bit less so.

This reasonably obviously point has had some considerable debate among economists. Much of classical economic theory portends that individuals are non-emotional mathematically efficient decision-makers. People carefully assess options, obtain relevant data, analyze it and make the economically most rational choice. Twenty years or so ago, another camp in economics – those living in the real world and possessing an understanding of psychology and marketing – began to question these views. These so-called behavioral economists contend that there are a host of reasons, often psychological or behavioral in nature, why individuals do not always make the rational mathematically optimal choice. Through considerable research, they have shown that people possess biases in forming quality judgments.

There is no reason to overcomplicate the issue. The mind forms judgments, sometimes more rationally and sometimes less so. We will call Mind 1 the rational one, and Mind 2 the behavioral one. At times, the rational mind dominates and, at times, the behavioral mind dominates. Most times, it is very hard to differentiate as both minds influence judgment simultaneously. When the behavioral mind dominates, it does not mean that the outcome is necessarily a bad decision, but there are clear risks of biases entering judgment due to the influence of Mind 2.

Figure 36: The Two Minds That Influence our Judgment

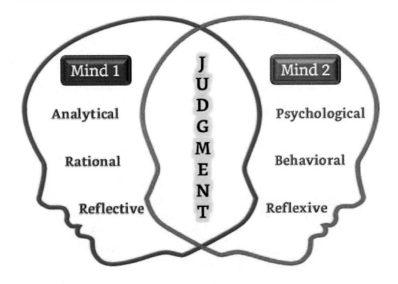

- Judgment is the forerunner to a decision (meaning people form a judgment and then make a decision)
- Judgment at times is analytical, reflective and rational; other times it is psychological, reflexive and behavioral
- Humans have inherent biases of judgment that can cloud good judgment

Source: Michael Molnar

Two behavioral economics' pioneers have described similar concepts. Richard Thaler in his book, *Misbehaving,* uses the terms "Econs" and "Humans." "Econs" are those mathematically optimizing perfect decision-makers often described by classical economists, and "humans" are, well, normal people. Daniel Kahneman in his book, *Thinking Fast and Slow,* describes

"System 1" and "System 2." System 1 is the automatic part of the mind that is constantly forming judgments often unbeknownst to us. System 2 is more reflective and controlled thinking. The particular words used to describe these aspects of judgment formation are not nearly as important as recognition that judgment can be influenced in two distinct manners.

Framing the Types of Judgment Biases

There has been considerable research on the biases that creep into our minds and skew judgment. Richard Cialdini, a psychology professor at Arizona State University, wrote the highly acclaimed book called, *Influence*, in 1984 which showed great examples of how we are easily influenced in irrational ways. Paco Underhill, an anthropologist by training, highlighted how people make purchasing decisions in his work, *Why We Buy: The Science of Shopping* (1999), which is standard reading for many in the retail world. Amos Tversky and Daniel Kahneman, psychologists by training, pioneered research in behavioral economics in the 1970s, receiving a Nobel Prize in 2002. Richard Thaler, an economics professor at the University of Chicago, performed some of the most influential research showing the importance of psychology on decision-making. There are countless others and the field continues to grow.

This research has identified countless biases, by some measures over 100, that cloud good judgment. While comprehensive, a list of 100 discrete biases is not altogether helpful. Therefore, I have segregated those most relevant to our research into the following four groups (See Figure 37):

1. **Data or Probability Biases:** Biases in the way we gather or interpret data or probabilities

2. **Calculation or Decision Biases:** Biases resulting in illogical calculations or decisions

3. **Social Biases:** Biases driven by inherent social tendencies or needs

4. **Memory Biases:** Biases that hinder learning and improvement

The list below is by no means comprehensive, but simply the most common biases emerged during the research we conducted. Many of these biases interact with one another so it is important to not always think that each bias is always a discrete event. The following four sections discuss each of the biases in some detail. The descriptions are fairly short as the crux of this book is about applying these concepts to energy versus proving their existence which has been done via significant academic research already.

Figure 37: Categories of Select Judgment Biases

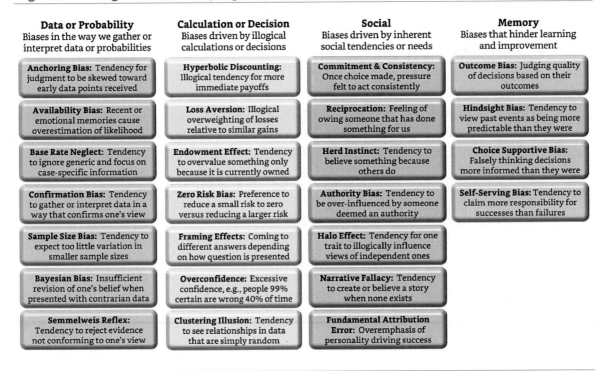

Data or Probability Biases in the way we gather or interpret data or probabilities	**Calculation or Decision** Biases driven by illogical calculations or decisions	**Social** Biases driven by inherent social tendencies or needs	**Memory** Biases that hinder learning and improvement
Anchoring Bias: Tendency for judgment to be skewed toward early data points received	**Hyperbolic Discounting:** Illogical tendency for more immediate payoffs	**Commitment & Consistency:** Once choice made, pressure felt to act consistently	**Outcome Bias:** Judging quality of decisions based on their outcomes
Availability Bias: Recent or emotional memories cause overestimation of likelihood	**Loss Aversion:** Illogical overweighting of losses relative to similar gains	**Reciprocation:** Feeling of owing someone that has done something for us	**Hindsight Bias:** Tendency to view past events as being more predictable than they were
Base Rate Neglect: Tendency to ignore generic and focus on case-specific information	**Endowment Effect:** Tendency to overvalue something only because it is currently owned	**Herd Instinct:** Tendency to believe something because others do	**Choice Supportive Bias:** Falsely thinking decisions more informed than they were
Confirmation Bias: Tendency to gather or interpret data in a way that confirms one's view	**Zero Risk Bias:** Preference to reduce a small risk to zero versus reducing a larger risk	**Authority Bias:** Tendency to be over-influenced by someone deemed an authority	**Self-Serving Bias:** Tendency to claim more responsibility for successes than failures
Sample Size Bias: Tendency to expect too little variation in smaller sample sizes	**Framing Effects:** Coming to different answers depending on how question is presented	**Halo Effect:** Tendency for one trait to illogically influence views of independent ones	
Bayesian Bias: Insufficient revision of one's belief when presented with contrarian data	**Overconfidence:** Excessive confidence, e.g., people 99% certain are wrong 40% of time	**Narrative Fallacy:** Tendency to create or believe a story when none exists	
Semmelweis Reflex: Tendency to reject evidence not conforming to one's view	**Clustering Illusion:** Tendency to see relationships in data that are simply random	**Fundamental Attribution Error:** Overemphasis of personality driving success	

Source: Michael Molnar

(1) Data or Probability Biases

Biases in how we gather or analyze data or probabilities are some of the most common.

Anchoring bias describes how the mind will put too much weight on data received early or at the time of decision relative to its actual importance. Irrationally, this spurious information can skew judgment in material ways. Daniel Kahneman in *Thinking Fast and Slow* described an experiment performed. People were asked two questions: "Is the height of the tallest Redwood tree more or less than 1,200 feet? What is your best guess about the height of the tallest Redwood tree?" Another group was asked the exact same question but 180 feet was the number in the first question versus 1,200 feet. The difference in the answers were striking. The group that had 1,200 feet in the first question had an average answer to the second question of 844 feet. The second group, the ones with 180 feet in the first question, had an average response of 282 feet. This is a classic example of anchoring, where merely stating a number in the first question skews one's judgment in answering the second question.

While there are countless other experiments showing similar results, one only needs to visit a shopping center to see this effect. Many retailers discount to the "suggested retail" price. For many retailers, this "discount" is constant, meaning every week nearly all items discounted. If something is always 40% off, why continue to perpetuate the view that anyone ever pays the "suggested retail price?" The answer lies in the anchoring bias. Doing so makes customers feel good about getting a deal as they anchor their view of savings to that "suggested retail price." The strategy of eliminating this and having "everyday low pricing" has been tried, but it is often met with resistance; whether people admit it or not, it does not feel as good a deal. For example, J.C. Penny tried moving away from discounting in 2011 and quickly reverted back just two years later after a decline in sales.

Figure 38: Marketers Tug on Consumers' Anchoring Bias When They Discount

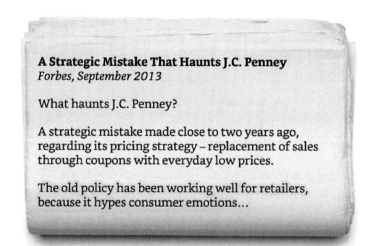

Source: Forbes; Gap.com

On Wall Street, investors are often overly influenced by so-called consensus earnings numbers. Once a number (e.g., "Company ABC is estimated to earn $1.50 in earnings per share") is heard it has a substantial effect on judgment. Even those who pride themselves on understanding what consensus should be (e.g., good stock pickers) often do not understand just how influential anchoring is on their own judgment.

Availability bias is where a prior experience that is readily available in one's memory, often because it is emotionally memorable or recently occurred, skews one's judgment. For example, investors in the stock market will often feel more confident predicting the future direction of a stock if they have had a good experience investing in it previously. Traders will often make comments to the effect of, "I know how this stock trades" and feel a sense of confidence in an investment thesis based on prior good experiences with that particular stock. However, the thesis that will drive the future direction of the stock is based on factors that often have nothing to do with what drove the stock in the past. The trader's mind is simply conjuring up the emotionally pleasing memories of past success and skewing one's current judgment.

The Ebola outbreaks in 2015 were another example. For those in the United States, the risk of contracting the disease was infinitesimally small. Yet, there was considerable fear given the substantial media attention. For example, numerous New Yorkers interviewed discussed the fear they had contracting Ebola by riding the subway – no doubt due to recent media reports triggering the availability bias. There are many such examples. People think there is a much greater probability of an airline crash if one just happened and fears of terrorism increase right after news reports, for example.

Base rate neglect occurs when preconceived stereotypes overshadow probabilities. For example, variations of the following experiment have been performed by academics. A researcher describes a man named who is very athletic, tall and in his mid-20s. They ask a series of people if that person is more likely to be a professional baseball player or an accountant. Inevitably, people massively overweight the man's physical description and answer "baseball player" even though chances are much higher that he is an accountant simply due to the fact that there are many more accountants than baseball players in the world.

Confirmation bias is the mental push to search for, and believe in, information that supports our existing views. It happens all the time on Wall Street when a position moves against an investor and that investor ends up asking others, with known similar views, for their view. Their minds are seeking to quell the discomfort and search for evidence proving they are right and the market is wrong. The result is a false sense of confidence that can cause them to be slow to react to the truth.

For anyone doubting this bias, simply tune in to Twitter or Facebook and see the comments people make. For those who believe in right wing principles, their posts are often littered by Fox News, *The Wall Street Journal* and Anti-Obama memes. For those that are left-leaning, their posts often contain content from MSBNC, *The New York Times*, and anti-Bush memes.

Sample size bias is the tendency to underappreciate the variability in small samples. The following example was detailed in the book, *Thinking, Fast and Slow*. Several years ago, research showed that smaller schools were more successful that bigger ones. The study showed that of the 1,662 schools in Pennsylvania, six of the top 50 schools were small which was four times what one would normally expect according to the study's analysis. The conclusion was that smaller schools were getting better results. The Gates Foundation invested $1.7 billion to implement aspects of these findings, including splitting larger schools into smaller ones.

Closer inspection of the data revealed something else, however. While it was true that there was an abnormally high number of small schools in the top group, there was also a large number of small schools that were among the *worst* schools in the state. This is due to the fact that small sample sizes have large variability. Underestimating that variability and drawing specious conclusions is common.

Wall Street "research" does this all the time with what is known as "channel checks," where calls or visits are made throughout the sales chain to get a feel for what is going on. For example, an analyst will call or visit, say, 10 retail stores to get an understanding of how sales are trending into the holiday season. It is very common for erroneous conclusions to be formed. What may seem to be a pattern is simply the math of a small sample size and lacks any true insight.

Conservatism (sometimes called Bayesian) bias is the tendency to insufficiently adjust one's view as new information becomes known. Thomas Bayes, an English minister and mathematician who lived in the 1700s, developed the math that dictates how people should update their views of probabilities as new information comes to light. This math, called Bayesian Statistics, allows for quantification of conditional probabilities: Given that X happened, what is *now* the probability of Y occurring. The specifics of the math are beyond our scope here, but countless studies have shown that individuals do not adequately adjust their beliefs as new information becomes known. Real-life examples include CEOs failing to adjust strategy to changed market conditions or investors reacting too slowly to new information.

The **Semmelweis reflex** is the tendency to reject information that is contradictory to one's existing belief. It is similar to confirmation bias in that it is driven by humans' desire to avoid cognitive dissonance, the mental stress incurred by holding opposing views in one's head. It is different, however, in that confirmation bias seeks information to confirm one's view, while the Semmelweis Reflex rejects information that has already been made known to you. It is named after Ignaz Semmelweis who was a Hungarian physician who lived in the 1800s. He had the idea, which was novel at the time, for doctors to consistently wash their hands in order to prevent disease. Physicians during this time did not believe this held any merit and, because they had not done it in the past, rejected this recommendation. His ideas were only accepted decades after his death as data continued to prove the merits of this best practice.

(2) Calculation or Decision Biases

Calculation or decision biases occur when the mind is driven to illogically calculate an outcome or make a decision. Some of these biases are similar to the prior group, but they are still different enough to be worth segregating.

Hyperbolic discounting is a fancy word for something we all inherently know. People tend to prefer more immediate payoffs than payoffs over time, even if the payoffs over time are a better economic bet. The conundrum of energy-efficiency investments is a good example. For an investment upfront, long term cost savings often make it a worthwhile investment. Yet many times these investments are not made given the upfront capital cost. We will discuss this in more detail later.

Loss aversion has been studied extensively in the past few decades. Prospect theory, developed by Daniel Kahneman and Amos Tversky in 1979, showed that people do not necessarily think rationally about gains versus losses. One should be indifferent between a gain of $100 and a loss of $100 but the mind tends to weight losses twice as much as gains, which leads to an aversion for losses. This inherent aversion to losses is something Wall Street deals with every day; for example, investors often hold onto losing stocks for too long to irrationally avoid crystallizing the loss.

The **endowment effect** is the tendency to overvalue something simply because we already own, or are endowed, with it already. Researchers have shown this with people who have tickets to concerts or sporting events. For example, assume you have snagged tickets to a hot show for, say, $50. Given the show is sold out, the secondary market price to buy or sell these tickets is $500 per ticket. Many people who would never pay $500 feel totally fine going to the event as they only paid $50. The logical thing to do would be to sell the ticket as the opportunity cost of going is $500, but most people do not. They end up valuing it more simply because they already own it.

There is a Wall Street maxim that states, "You buy your positions each day," which is a recognition of the risk of the endowment effect. It should not matter if you own a position or not, the right question is: "Would you buy it today?" If yes, then keep it. If not, sell it. As with all biases, the endowment effect can be hard to avoid as it is part of our mental makeup. Traders are often no better and "fall in love" with positions all the time.

Zero-risk bias is our tendency to focus on reducing small risks to zero versus decreasing larger ones lower – even though many times the rational decision is usually to do the latter. Nuclear power is an interesting, albeit highly debatable, example. No doubt nuclear issues like those that occurred at Fukushima in Japan are awful and most citizens would like to see this risk reduced to zero. At the same time, nuclear power is a secure source of power not dependent on foreign nations and very clean in terms of carbon dioxide and most pollutants. The preference to reduce this very small risk to zero has resulted in many countries phasing out nuclear entirely. Yet that likely increases very real problems with other pollutants. This example highlights two things. First, many of these biases work together. Nuclear power is something that inherently provokes strong emotions and the availability bias can skew judgment.

Second, energy – like most complex issues – is about tradeoffs among imperfect options. Biases such as zero risk bias can result in poor decisions of the various trade-offs involved.

Framing effects are a fascinating bias that build on the insight that humans are loss averse. Consider the use of credit cards at gas stations in America. When this new payment form came about, customers were originally charged a premium. After all, there was a charge assessed by the credit-card company to the merchant, so in turn it made sense to charge customers a bit more for this service as well. Customers, however, were very upset at this additional cost. Gas station owners did something simple, but creative, to solve the problem. They simply changed the "regular" price to the higher amount and then offered a "discount" for users of cash, whereas credit-card owners would pay the new "regular" price. Merely framing the same economic decision differently resulted in a dramatically different outcome as almost immediately customers felt much better about using their credit cards.

Nowhere is **overconfidence** more endemic than in top business schools or Wall Street. As an experiment, one of my professors in graduate school had each person in the class rate their intelligence to the rest of our business school class on a scale of one to five (three was average). Upon tallying our responses, the average was around 4.25 to 4.5 – we clearly all had a strong view of ourselves. While we all were quite quantitative and realized the average must be 3.0, we apparently were all a bit too confident in our individual abilities.

Numerous studies have shown similar bias, where people indicate they are 99% certain of something, but end up being wrong, say, 40% of the time. The Wall Street concept of "conviction" is a good example of this bias. Having conviction is deemed to be a positive, showing just how strongly he or she believes in a trade or investment. Unfortunately, it leads to vapid confidence in subpar ideas, which can lead to financial losses.

Finally, the **clustering illusion** is the mind's tendency to see patterns when none exist. An example is during World War II when the Germans were bombing London. Certain areas were hit multiple times while other areas were not hit once. Many people concluded, not illogically at first glance, that German spies were in the areas not hit. However, after the war when the bombings were analyzed statistically, they were found to be totally random. Similar to the sample size bias, the mind has a tendency to want to see patterns when none may exist.

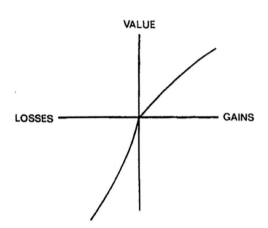

Prospect Theory Value Graph
Losses Valued 2x That of Gains

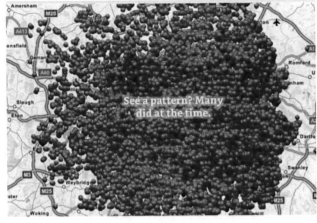

Bombing Sites in Central London
October 7, 1940 to June 6, 1941

Source: Prospect Theory: An Analysis of Decision Under Risk (Kanheman, Tversky, 1979); Bombsight.org

(3) Social Biases

Humans are social animals who constantly interact with one another. As a result, we have inherent social needs and tendencies that can skew our thinking. One such bias, **commitment and consistency** is our tendency to desire to be consistent with prior commitments. This is not necessarily a bad trait but, at times, it can make us think in illogical ways. Robert Cialdini, in his groundbreaking book *Influence*, detailed the research of two Canadian psychologists who asked gamblers before and after betting about their confidence in the outcome. Gamblers were shown to be markedly more confident just after placing the bet, even though nothing had changed. This is commitment and consistency at work. After making the commitment to the bet, they had an inherent desire to be consistent, which skewed their thinking into being much more confident in the outcome. This plagues good decision-making as it can slow reactions to a changing environment.

Reciprocation is an inherent feeling of being indebted to someone who has given us something. This inherent bias to reciprocate is very strong as shown by the difference in the rate of contributions to charities that have given a "free" gift to people (without asking for it) versus those that have not. The indebted feeling those that received the free gift causes more of them to give than otherwise would – even when the gift is often deemed a piece of junk that the recipient had no desire in receiving.

The **herd instinct** is the tendency for people to think like others as it is more psychologically comforting than being alone. If one is wrong but following others, there is comfort in numbers. If one is wrong and alone, it can feel horrible. This is a driver for companies having similar strategies and investors holding the same investments. Sometimes those that believe they are contrarians only take the contrarian point of view once they have found enough people that hold that contrarian view. This perhaps is a "mini-herd instinct" but still highlights the pull of this psychological need.

Authority bias highlights how humans are inclined to be obedient to authority figures. Many times, this makes sense. The individual in the police uniform should be listened to and the person in the lab coat does know a lot about medicine. However, there are all sorts of times this bias skews judgment when it should not. We overweight someone as an expert on television because they are wearing a doctor's coat, even though the small print on the screen says he is an actor. We believe the famous celebrity endorsing a product when it is illogical to do so. We overweight someone's opinion with a fancy title even when their title is irrelevant to the topic on which they are speaking.

A great, and sad, example of this in energy was depicted in the documentary, *Merchants of Doubt*. It showed how certain powerful interests hired public relations firms to create doubt on key topics such as cigarette smoking and climate change. One such hired gun depicted in the film, Marc Marano, clearly understands the power of perceived authority. In an interview he stated, "Well I'm not really a scientist…although I play one on television sometimes," and laughed. Sad, but unfortunately very effective due to the authority bias.

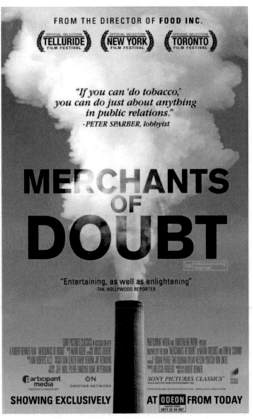

Source: Camel Cigarettes; Merchants of Doubt movie poster

The halo effect is our tendency to irrationally suppose one specific positive trait is indicative of non-related potential positive traits. For example, tall or good looking people are often judged to be better at their jobs than they are. Yes, they are good looking but that has no bearing on their job performance. CEOs who have done a good job in one industry often are perceived to be a good fit for a role in another company or industry which might not make sense. Many times a protégé of a successful person is viewed as having the traits of their mentor when they might have substantial less skill. These inferences are not completely irrational, but the halo effect can drive judgment to leap to conclusions without doing the necessary diligence.

The **narrative fallacy** is based on the long history of storytelling among people. People are storytellers by nature. For generations, much of our early history and collective intelligence was passed down through parables. Unfortunately, this sometimes creates situations where we create a story or narrative when none exists.

Wall Street loves storytelling. Many times banks will put out "research" with all sorts of analysis equating the current situation to decades ago and drawing conclusions. "Twenty years ago, interest rates moved this way and industrial stocks moved that way," for example. These are interesting, but not always insightful as so many other factors were at play. I remember when I was a sellside analyst protesting an analogous historical reference that was about to be published, a senior member of the team's reply was indicative. He said, "Listen you might be right, but clients love historical stories referencing today's situation regardless." He was right. Clients love debating a story when they should be more focused on the crux of the current predicament.

Finally, **fundamental attribution error** is our tendency to overemphasize the impact of personality over situational factors in assessing what drove an outcome. CEO competency is often viewed in such a manner. For example, during the boom times of the early 2000s, CEOs of homebuilders were deemed savvy for having made prior decisions that capitalized on the rewards of the current cycle. While some decisions were savvy, it was general economic activity and consumer confidence that primarily drove the boom. For many CEOs, it was a matter of being in the right place at the right time. One of the few exceptionally self-aware executives at a major homebuilder said it best during the last year of the boom, "When this market goes south, make no mistake...no one will be able to give away land much less sell it for a profit." He was right. Situational factors ended up trumping all in the end. Many deemed savvy just months before were facing critical questions about their strategy just months later.

(4) Memory Biases

Biases do not stop when decisions are made. They can continue in how we remember what happened. Unfortunately, these memory biases hinder future learning and improvement.

Outcome bias, evaluating the quality of a decision based mainly on the outcome, is fascinating as most professionals understand this bias but make no effort to counteract it. We simply are biased to feel that a good outcome is the result of a good decision. While they are clearly correlated, plenty of good decisions result in bad outcomes and vice versa. As demonstrated by the case with Brian Hunter, the trader who lost $6 billion in just a few weeks, it is dangerous to recognize this too late.

Hindsight bias is where we tend to think we knew it all along (when we were right), or that a situation that occurred was clearly predictable (when others were wrong). The 2008 U.S. housing bust was obvious, right? The technology bubble in the early 2000s was clear too, yes? These both became obvious in hindsight but not as the situations were developing. Determining what should have been known at the time is not always easy.

Have you ever been in a situation where someone is taking credit for a decision that turned out well, but for different reasons than they anticipated? This is the **choice supportive bias** at work. People have a tendency to falsely believe they were more informed than they were at the time, essentially taking credit for the times they were lucky versus wise. We have a need to be right and, when the outcome is positive, the mind's tendency is to believe we were smarter than we were. People will often create a story in their head that decisions were made for a different reason than they were to fulfill this need.

Finally, **self-serving bias** is another tendency we often recognize in others but not always in ourselves. This is our innate tendency to take credit for success, but not for failure. We inherently need to be to be right, and admitting failure creates significant cognitive discord. Yet, not admitting failure inhibits a chance for learning. Charlie Munger, Warren Buffet's partner, once said, *"I like people admitting they were complete stupid horses' asses. I know I'll perform better if I rub my nose in my mistakes. This is a wonderful trick to learn."* Few people truly get this point.

What to Do When Playing Offense or Defense

How best to deal with these biases of judgment? Context matters, specifically if you are on the offense or defense in a particular situation. "On offense" means you are trying to persuade others of something. "On defense" means that you are the one that someone is attempting to persuade or influence.

A prime example of someone on offense is a marketer. A somewhat cynical, but not altogether inaccurate, job description is that marketers are tasked with creating a perception that is greater than reality. Discounts to suggested retail prices (anchoring), framing the decision to buy insurance on products where it makes no sense (framing/loss aversion), paying actors to pretend they are doctors to sell goods on television (authority bias) and strategically pricing certain goods lower to give the perception that all prices in the store are a good deal (halo effect) are all such examples. Marketers are masters of understanding and exploiting biases of judgment.

However, biases on offense can also have a more constructive social purpose. The concept of *paternal libertarianism* promoted by Richard Thaler is a good example. The concept is simple: There are certain decisions people should be making, but often are not. Are there ways to frame questions or decisions in ways that nudge them in the right direction (the paternal part) while also maintaining the freedom for them to decide whatever they wish (the libertarian part)?

An example is 401(k) retirement planning. This is something that nearly all people should be doing if they have the option. However, it was historically structured as an "opt-in" selection for workers when they joined a job. Opt-in meant that when people joined a new employer they had to check a box to join the 401(k) program and, if nothing was checked, they were not enrolled. Paternal libertarianism takes the view that enrolling in the 401(k) is clearly the right decision, so there should be an "opt-out" framing instead. In that scenario, the default option is to be automatically enrolled in the plan, unless you proactively opt out. The result: Many more people are saving for retirement in their 401(k) plans which is the right decision for them and society as a whole.

The game plan on offense breaks down at a high level as follows. First, identify the goal. Is it to sell more product, change employee behavior or influence policy makers? Then, evaluate what biases exist or could exist to skew judgment. Finally, develop a program to trigger those biases or avoid the biases from becoming triggered, whatever one's goal may be. As discussed, this can be nefarious or altruistic in its intention, unfortunately or fortunately.

Defensively, there are three steps to be effective:

1. **Awareness and True Recognition of the Power of Biases.** The very first step is a recognition and awareness of the influence of biases on our judgment. However, mere awareness is not enough and, unfortunately, this is where most people stop. The power of these biases is so inherent in our mental makeup that even those who have studied it for years are still massively influenced by them. I have studied behavioral biases for more than 15 years and each day I am amazed at how my own judgment is skewed by the simplest of influences. Step one is both an awareness *and* a respect for their mental pull no matter your awareness.

2. **Understanding When Biases Pose the Most Risk.** This will depend on the situation. Shopping for a car? Beware the sales tactics that may trigger numerous biases. Making an investment? Beware the points in your decision process where your mind will likely deceive you. Knowing when biases pose a risk is critical as they can easily sneak into judgment unnoticed.

3. **Processes to Cut off the Influence.** The final step is to have some process to cut off the power of the bias. Robert Cialdini in his book *Influence* coined the term, "click whrrr" as a sort of mental cue to help counteract bad thinking. Mentally, hear a clicking sound when you recognize the presence of a bias and then a "whirring" sound to begin your process of counteracting its effect on you. So if someone gives you a gift for "free" with the goal of persuading you to donate money, immediately hear a "click" and know judgment is being skewed. Then hear a "whirring," which is your cue to mentally remind yourself that it is a gift and that you are under no obligation to give something in return.

These processes to cut the power off will vary tremendously by the task at hand. For example, investing in stocks often follows some sort of process: Evaluating a universe of possible investments, analyzing several, making a decision to invest, and then managing the portfolio. At each stage, there are biases influencing us and processes can be developed to stop the biases. There is no single right answer but, in order to counteract behavioral biases, one needs a strong awareness along with a process or set of rules designed with the peculiarities of the people involved.

The Biggest Gap in Good Decision-Making

In its simplest form, a good decision has two requirements. One, requisite knowledge of the subject matter and, two, good judgment. **The first component, requisite knowledge, is fairly simple. One needs to know something about the subject in question.** You can have great judgment but not fully understand a particular subject and therefore make a poor decision. The word "requisite" means "that which is required or necessary for a particular purpose" and so it will vary by situation. For example, the knowledge needed by an individual citizen to buy a pair of shoes is different from the required knowledge needed by an institutional investor allocating hundreds of millions of dollars into the development of a hydropower plant.

The second requirement, superior judgment, requires having solid control of Mind 1 and Mind 2. Mind 1, the analytical and rational mind, needs to have the analytical tools necessary for the task at hand. If you are valuing a company, you need to have skills in evaluating accounting, analyzing cash flows, and performing valuation analysis, for example. At the same time, good judgment requires a level of awareness of our inherent biases and processes by which to manage them (Mind 2).

Are people good at all aspects, bad at all three, or a mix? It depends on the person and situation. However, there are some insights to be gained by looking at these three aspects of good decision-making along four groups: individual citizens, business people, policymakers and institutional investors.

On average, individual citizens often lack the knowledge to make effective decisions in complex areas outside their normal areas of interest and work. This makes sense as they have jobs and families to attend to and are not often thinking about a topic such as energy all the time. There is also a considerable amount of poor education on general science issues as evidenced by a survey that showed 26% of Americans believing that the sun revolves around the earth (National Science Board Survey, 2014). For these Americans, many of which have strangely confident views of topics in energy, their judgment is lacking in knowledge and is massively influenced by psychological factors.

Individual citizens, on average, also are typically weaker on average analytically than the other cohorts and are subject to behavioral influences in the way they form judgments. In short, while there is a wide distribution of skills among individuals, the group has a lot of gaps to good decision-making on average and specifically when it comes to energy.

Government often, but not always, has specialized teams on policy areas for topics such as energy. Usually, this means that those teams possess the requisite level of knowledge for the policy being evaluated. Analytically the skills often vary but on average the work is often decent. Behaviorally, judgment is often skewed sharply.

Finally, business and investors often have good requisite knowledge. This makes sense as they are often focused on a particular area such as energy or industrials. For a similar reason, analytical skills are often quite sharp as well but they can fail in complex situations. However, behavioral aspects of judgment are often very weak. There are times that the analytical skills are so sharp that there is a hubris that allow biases to creep in even more as the arrogance of one's perceived intelligence makes them blind to Mind 2's shortcomings.

There are two takeaways:

1. First, while there is a distribution of skills by group on average, **behavioral biases are a clear gap among all**.

2. Second, while bias management is the biggest and most consistent gap to each, I would argue it is **often the area of least focus**. For example, business and investors are focused on improving their knowledge base and analytical techniques constantly. Yet, very few have any focus on systematically understanding their behavioral biases. Ironically, behavioral biases are often the cause of their worst – and most costly - decisions.

Figure 41: Typical Decision-Making Skill Level by Category By Group

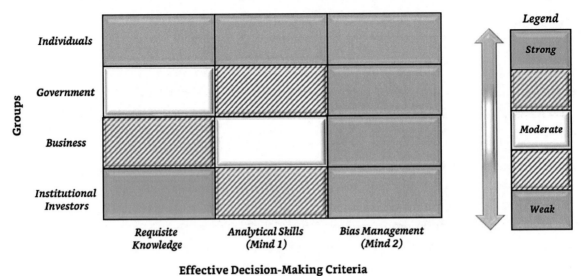

Source: Michael Molnar

Section III

Applications

To

Energy

Case Study Applications

"The greatest enemy of knowledge is not ignorance,
it is the illusion of knowledge."
- Stephen Hawking
Theoretical Physicist (1942 to Present)

The sections that follow take several of the most important topics in energy and analyzes them with a systems thinking and behavioral economics lens. There are four broad areas discussed, each with specific case studies as detailed below:

- **The Pollution Challenge**
    - Understanding Acid Rain Regulation's Success in the U.S.
    - The Real Risk of "Overshoot-and-Collapse" Due to Global Warming
    - The Headwinds to Success of Energy-Efficiency Regulations

- **Potential Game-Changing Technologies**
    - Solar – Exponential Industry Growth, Psychological Investor Errors
    - Fracking and the Changing Nature of Supply in Oil and Natural Gas
    - U.S. Energy Independence – The Challenge and Fracking's Potential
    - Electric Vehicles and Windows of Opportunity

- **Business Cycles and Business Models**
    - Time Delays, Skewed Judgment and Boom-Bust Cycles
    - Reinforcing Feedback Impacting the Business Model; the Utility Death Spiral
    - Reinforcing Feedback Inherent to the Business Model; the Yieldco Example

- **The Politics of Energy**
    - The Structure of U.S. Energy Policy and the Ineffective Dynamics it Causes
    - China's Quest for Growth and Its Related Consequences
    - Fluctuating Energy Prices, Civil Unrest, and Shifting World Powers

The topics were chosen for both their importance in the current energy environment as well as the applicability of their learnings elsewhere.

Decoding the Pollution Challenge

> *"If the earth must lose that great portion of its pleasantness which it owes to things that the unlimited increase of wealth and population would extirpate from it, for the mere purpose of enabling it to support a larger, but not a better or a happier population, I sincerely hope, for the sake of posterity, that they will be content to be stationary, long before necessity compels them to it."*
> *- John Stuart Mill*
> *Political Economist (1806 to 1873)*

Given the perceived risk to economic growth, government actions to addressing pollution are often slow and inadequate. The costs of inaction on citizens' health and, ironically, economic growth, is, at best, negative and, at worst, dangerous. Understanding the system structure of how pollution impacts short- and long-term growth, the feedback that creates regulations, and the consequences of delaying action helps frame the issue better than the simple "growth versus the environment" debate that often takes place.

First, a success story: **U.S. acid rain regulations** that began in the early 1990s helped to change the path of a disturbing increase in sulfur dioxide and nitrogen oxide emissions. Because of the success of regulations, acid rain is barely a discussion among the public anymore. Understanding what happened and the drivers for success are helpful learnings to be applied elsewhere.

A more vexing problem, **carbon dioxide emissions**, are discussed next. Various psychological and political challenges make timely regulatory action less likely. This risks an "overshoot-and-collapse" scenario where aspects of the world environment are permanently damaged.

Finally, **energy-efficiency** mandates are evaluated. While well-meaning and somewhat effective, two headwinds limit their effectiveness. Various judgment biases often drive slower-than-anticipated levels of initial investment in efficiency. And once the investment is made, the so-called "rebound effect" begins to diminish the savings.

Understanding Acid Rain Regulation's Success in the U.S.

Brief History of U.S. Environmental Milestones

Before evaluating acid rain regulation in the U.S., some history of the U.S. environmental movement is helpful. The U.S. underwent very strong economic growth in the first part of the 20th century. This growth drove increased fossil-fuel usage which, in turn, resulting in considerable environmental damage.

As standards of living improved due to economic growth, the public started to become more concerned about environmental issues. By the 1950s and 1960s, public concern about the quality of air and water began to increase substantially, which culminated in the first Earth Day in 1970. That same year, President Nixon formed the Environmental Protection Agency (EPA). From these times to the present day there have been a constant flow of news – some positive, some negative – and regulations as shown in Figure 42.

Figure 42: Select Milestones in U.S. Environmental History

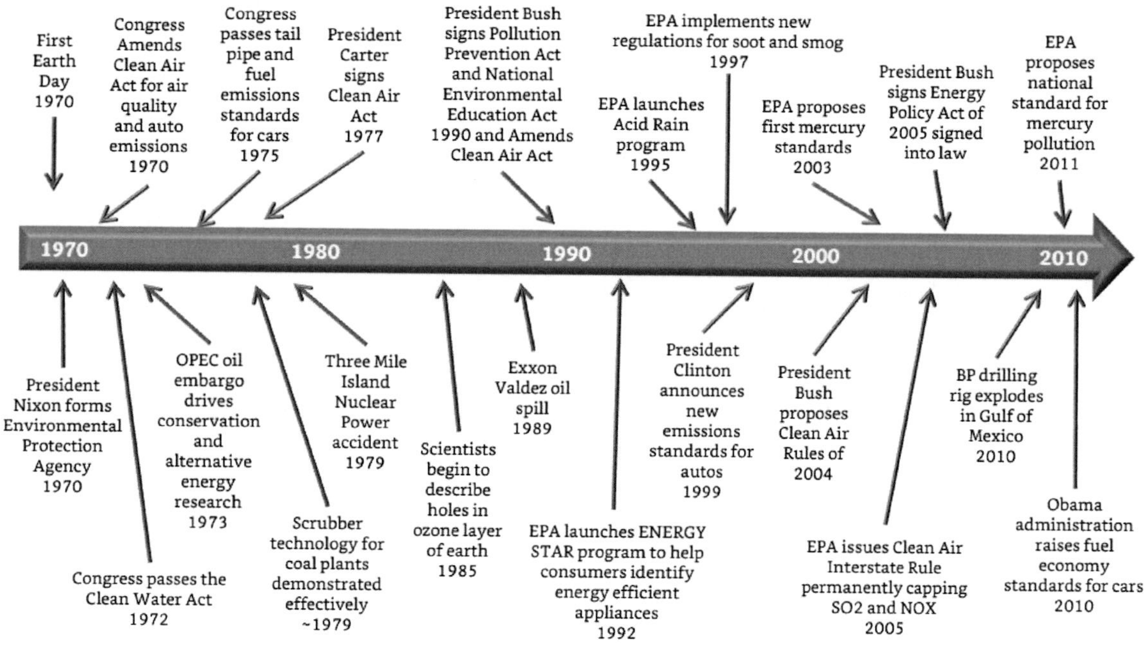

Source: Environmental Protection Agency; NBC News; Michael Molnar

- 83 -

Descriptive Analysis of What Happened with Acid Rain

U.S. acid rain regulations implemented in the mid-1990s are a good case study on effective environmental regulation. Acid rain occurs when nitrogen oxides (NOx) and sulfur dioxides (SO2) are released into the atmosphere, often by burning fossil fuels for power generation or transportation. These gases form acidic compounds which then can be deposited back to earth in wet climates via rain or mist – hence the laymen's term, "acid rain." There are many negative impacts: Streams, rivers, soils and trees are damaged as their acid levels increase, building materials are degraded, and public health and air visibility are compromised.

Coal contains a large amount of nitrogen oxides and sulfur dioxides relative to other fuel sources. Per billion of Btu (a unit of energy) generated, coal contains 2,591 and 457 pounds of pollutant of sulfur dioxide and nitrogen oxides compared to 1,122 and 448 for oil and 0.6 and 92 for natural gas. As the U.S. economy grew, coal consumption increased from 400 million tons per year in 1960 to 1 billion tons per year by 1990. As one would expect, this increased coal usage led to higher sulfur dioxide and nitrogen oxide emissions and the result was increased problems with acid rain.

Figure 43: Acid Rain Was a Major Problem in 1990 in the U.S.

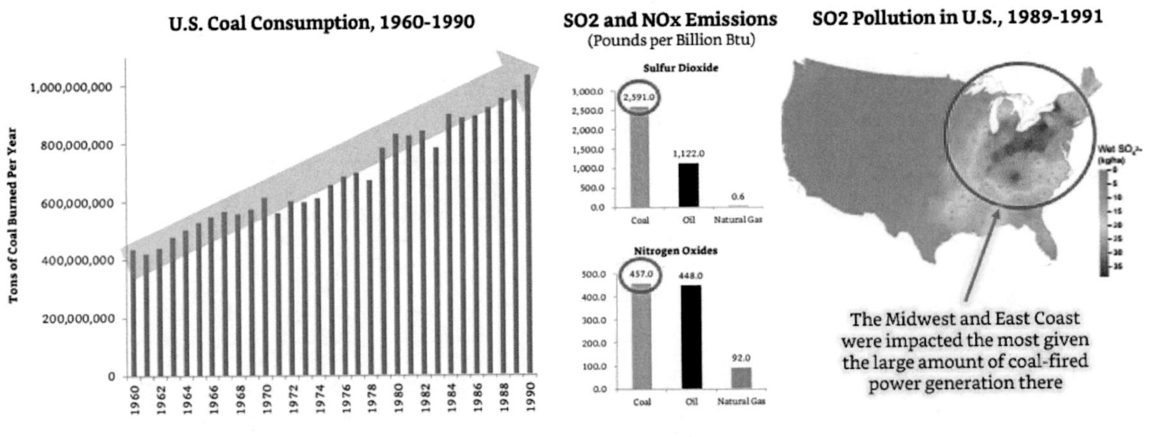

U.S. Coal Consumption, 1960-1990

SO2 and NOx Emissions (Pounds per Billion Btu)

SO2 Pollution in U.S., 1989-1991

The Midwest and East Coast were impacted the most given the large amount of coal-fired power generation there

Source: Energy Information Administration

Public pressure drove the U.S. government to finally take action. The result, a regulation called "cap-and-trade" in the 1990 Clean Air Act, effectively put a price on pollution. The approach taken was novel, effectively setting a cap on the overall market emission level, allocating allowances to polluters, and then creating an allowance trading program. The flexibility of the allowance structure, versus a program that mandated all plants act in the same way, allowed for the same benefits but at a potentially reduced cost.

How? Theoretically, market participants would figure out the least expensive way to reduce the pollution. Plants that had high costs to reduce the emissions could buy allowances whereas those with low costs to do so would be incented to implement that technology and sell the allowances.

The results were very good as the original goal to reduce emissions levels to 50% below 1980 levels by 2010 was achieved by 2007, three years ahead of schedule. The cost of implementation, which was expected to be in the range of $1.9 billion to $7.5 billion per year, ended up being $1.2 billion to $2 billion per year (Source: E.P.A., *Cap and Trade: Acid Rain Program Results*). Finally, the cost-to-benefit ratio was estimated by some to be 40-to-1, meaning there were $40 of benefit for each $1 spent (Source: "A Fresh Look at the Benefit and Costs of the U.S. Acid Rain Program," *Journal of Environmental Management*). While calculating benefits to such issues as human health and the environment is always subject to some debate, it needs to be done and the extraordinarily positive ratio highlights the economic value of this investment for the United States.

Figure 44: The Results of the U.S. Acid Rain Program Have Been Impressive

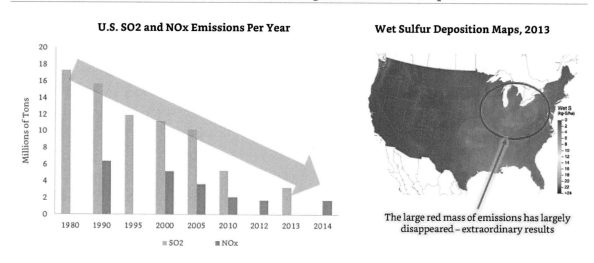

Source: Environmental Protection Agency; National Atmospheric Deposition Program

Given the success of the acid rain program, it is important to understand the drivers of that success in order to apply the learnings elsewhere. The simple descriptive analysis that many economists would give is that the cost of emissions was finally priced and the policy was structured in a way to be both effective and efficient. This is factually correct, but perhaps not that insightful. Why were there delays in the government's response? What was the trigger, if any, to finally acting? What are the learnings that can be applied to other issues in pollution?

In general, utilities act rationally. Regulated utilities (those that are given monopoly rights over a region and therefore are subject to certain regulatory rules) meticulously calculate how to make the most money according to the rules of the system that are in place. As utilities are natural monopolies, they are highly regulated and the rules are often much more clear than in other industries. For example, regulated utilities get their capital-expenditure plans approved by the local regulator who determines a "fair" rate of return on those expenditures. This is translated into the rates that are charged to citizens in that area. In practice, there is additional complexity but this level of knowledge is sufficient for our purposes here.

By pricing sulfur dioxides and nitrogen oxides, the rules of the system changed. Utilities were presented with a clear decision to either implement abatement technology (e.g., scrubbers to capture the pollutants before they are emitted into the air), change their coal source to something lower in sulfur, or buy allowances that allowed them to pollute. As the allowances ratcheted down over time, this latter option would become less available, or at least more expensive. Without this change in system structure, utilities would have simply kept burning high-sulfur coal and emitting pollution.

Several dynamics were in place as detailed in the system map in Figure 45:

- **Exponential Coal Power Plant Growth:** Economic growth in the U.S. drove more coal plants to be built given the relative cost effectiveness of coal for much of the 1900s. The result was exponential growth in coal consumption and emissions.

- **Acid Rain Problems Grew as Unregulated Coal Use Increased:** Given limited regulations on the pollution generated by coal usage, the amount of coal – and related pollution – continued to increase. As the amount of sulfur dioxides and nitrogen oxides in the atmosphere continued to build, they began to be deposited more and more in regional lakes and streams making many of them void of life.

- **Eventually, Public Pressure Drove the Government to Act:** A balancing information loop eventually took hold. Scientists issued alarming reports and journalists produced investigative reports, making the public more aware of the problem of acid rain. This eventually led to the U.S. government regulations.

While participants in systems have emotions, systems themselves have no inherent emotion. Pollution started to build, and would continue to accumulate until a balancing loop or constraint was met.

The balancing loop of public pressure was felt, but with a delay. There can be a long time delay from the time of actual pollution, to perceived pollution, to regulatory action, to the impact of those regulations. The length of this delay can be the difference between an "overshoot-and-oscillate" and "overshoot-and-collapse" scenario, the latter of which means that irreversible damage occurs. For acid rain, while there are likely some long-term impacts, the reaction was quick enough to avoid catastrophe.

Figure 45: Mapping the Dynamics of the Acid Rain Program and Eventual Solution

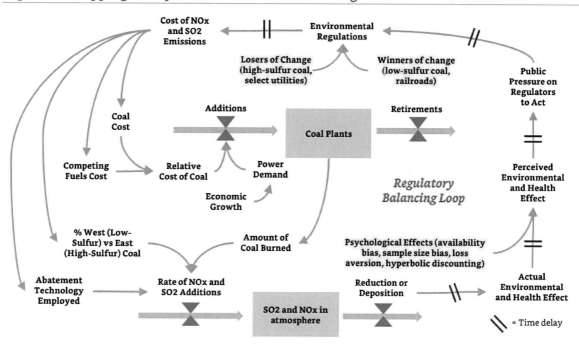

Source: Michael Molnar

As public pressure was a key factor, it is important to understand how that judgment was influenced. Three psychological biases likely played an important role:

- **Availability Bias:** The coining of the phrase "acid rain" – intentional or not – likely helped to trigger the availability bias. People have an emotional reaction when they envision acid raining down on them and their communities. If the problem was referred to as "the nitrogen and sulfur deposit effect," the emotional impact would have been much less.

- **Sample Size Bias:** People saw tangible evidence in many communities where local lakes and rivers were devoid of life. Many people no doubt took this small sample size and – consciously or subconsciously – came to the conclusion that many more lakes were contaminated than probably were.

- **Loss Aversion and Hyperbolic Discounting:** There are two biases at work: loss aversion (valuing losses two times that of equal-sized gains) and hyperbolic discounting (valuing the present irrationally more than the future). The perception was that acid rain was creating losses in the environment and public health *now*, which psychologically was likely very painful. This is a very different psychological impact than the issues with carbon dioxide, where people often feel like they have to force themselves to incur an economic loss now for an uncertain gain in the future.

Psychological biases in forming rational judgments do not necessarily lead to bad decisions, they simply bias our views one way or the other. Availability bias, sample size bias, hyperbolic discounting and loss aversion were all at work in the minds of the public in the 1990s. The public's judgment and anger pressured politicians to implement new regulation.

Figure 46: Articles Highlighting the Turning Point in Public Opinion on Acid Rain

Acid Rain Study Shows Its Harm to Environment
The New York Times
March 15, 1986

WASHINGTON, March 14— The National Academy of Sciences said today that it had found conclusive evidence that the burning of coal and other fossil fuels causes environmental damage. The finding was in a report on acid rain that the academy called "the most comprehensive to date."

The report, which uses records stretching as far back as the 1880's, demonstrates that the burning of coal, gasoline and other fossil fuels in the Eastern part of the country caused lower visibility, acidified lakes, dead fish and other adverse environmental effects.

The Turning Point on Acid Rain
The New York Times
March 23, 1986

The web of nature is so resilient that it tears only under the roughest insults. That's why biologists concerned about acid rain have had so hard a case to prove. Rain made acid by industrial pollution doesn't eat visible holes in leaves or poison fish in a single downpour. The mildest of toxins, its damage is subtle and accumulates over decades. The hundreds of lifeless lakes now found from Florida to Maine are only the most obvious symptoms of a whole seaboard under severe environmental stress.

...

Mr. Reagan said he fully accepted a new report by Drew Lewis, his former Secretary of Transportation and special envoy to Canada on acid rain.

...

The Northeastern states want Midwest utilities to install expensive scrubbers to trap their gases, or else burn low-sulfur coal. Coal miners in Eastern states, who produce mostly high-sulfur coal, fear losing 40,000 jobs to the low-sulfur mines of the West. This clash of powerful interests has favored advocates of inaction.

With the President's acknowledgment of the acid rain problem, procrastination is no longer so justifiable. A wider constituency now favors control because the first signs of acid rain damage are beginning to appear in the West and Southeast. Congress at last has the chance of finding a way to reconcile opposing factions and protect lakes and forests across the country.

Source: New York Times

There was one last factor that was political in nature, but very important. With most changes, there are subsequent winners and losers. As expected, the losers will do nearly anything to prevent the change and the winners will help move the change along – either overtly or covertly.

Figure 47 highlights several news articles from the time. The article at left details how a large coal user stated that Bush's proposed legislation would "wreck" the U.S. economy. Do you remember the economic calamity this regulation caused? No? That's because it did not happen. What it meant was that it would wreak havoc on its business as they would have to purchase more expensive coal, buy allowance credits, or implement pollution-abatement technology. In short, the company was about to be charged for its free ride in the Tragedy of the Commons and it did not like it (see page 15 for the Tragedy of the Commons discussion).

Figure 47: Articles Highlighting the Changing Landscape for the U.S. Coal Industry

Largest Coal User Criticizes Bush's Acid Rain Proposal The New York Times August 18, 1989 The nation's largest user of coal said yesterday that President Bush's acid rain proposal could wreck the American economy, and contended that it was "one of the harshest, least flexible and most costly bills ever introduced in the Congress."	**Low-Sulfur Coal in the Battle on Acid Rain** The New York Times April 12, 1986 Low-sulfur coal reserves, 43 billion tons in the East and 190 billion tons in the West, assure our country of an economical supply of clean fuel for centuries... The coal industry would create an additional 100,000 mining jobs over the next 10 years... - HARRY L. STOREY President, Alliance for Clean Energy	**A New Geography For the Coal Industry** The New York Times November 25, 1990 THE rumble of change is being heard in the coal fields of America. Utilities are exploring the costs and availability of lower-sulfur coal. Miners in central Appalachia and the western United States are contemplating big gains in production. Railroads expect a surge in shipments. And the high-sulfur mines of the Midwest and northern and southern Appalachia are looking at leaner times.

Source: New York Times

While high-sulfur coal producers and users stood to lose, the Acid Rain Program was likely to benefit several other constituents quite well. First, the owners of low-sulfur coal mines saw the clear potential for their coal. Coal did not have to decline in total consumption, just the mix of high- versus low-sulfur would change. This would be a bonanza for certain coal companies which were happy to remarket themselves as "clean." Various coal organizations that would benefit started to support changes in regulation. Many of these so-called "clean energy" organizations were nothing more than low-sulfur coal-supported lobbying organizations (see middle article in Figure 47).

Figure 48: U.S. Coal Production by Region, 1949-2012

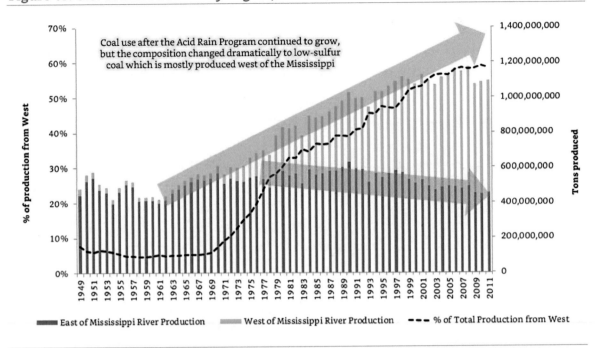

Source: Energy Information Administration

Second, low-sulfur coal was mainly in the Northwest United States in places like Wyoming. The coal had to be transported to the Midwest and East, making the railroads a clear beneficiary. Coal that cost $10 a ton could increase by $20 to $40 a ton to ship, a bonanza for the railroads, another a powerful political group that could exert its influence.

Finally, industrial companies that sold pollution-abatement technology would have a new market. Likewise, engineering and construction companies that would install the equipment stood to gain as well. *Today's environmentalists should take note: The "enemy of your enemy" is your friend. Changing the world of energy is not "go-it-alone" hero work all the time.*

The Real Risk of "Overshoot-and-Collapse" Due to Global Warming

Understanding the Causes and Risks of Global Warming

From 1870 to 2013, the levels of carbon dioxide (CO_2) in the atmosphere have increased nearly 40%, from 288 ppm (parts per million) to 395 ppm. The biggest sources of CO_2 over this time period have been the burning of fossil fuels and land use (cutting down trees). While land and oceans are considered sinks as they absorb CO_2, they have not been able to keep up with the increased emissions as populations and economies grow in a fossil fuel-dominated world.

Sources and sinks of CO_2 are measured in terms of gigatonnes of CO_2 ($GtCO_2$), where one gigatonne equals one billion tonnes. Data on our recent history, from 2004 to 2013, show that the world has emitted 35.7 $GtCO_2$ (gigatonne of CO_2) per year with the land and oceans only able to absorb 20 $GtCO_2$. The net result is that 15.7 $GtCO_2$ per year continue to amass in the atmosphere. As 7.81 $GtCO_2$ equals roughly one ppm, this means that we are adding about two ppm per year on average.

Figure 49: Annual Additions & Subtractions to CO_2 Balance; Summary of 1870 to 2013

Average GtCO2 per Year, 2004-2013

	CO2 per Yr	+/- per Yr
Sources of CO2		
Fossil Fuel and Cement	32.4	1.6
Land-Use Change	3.3	1.8
Total	35.7	
Sinks of CO2		
Land Sink	(10.6)	2.9
Ocean Sink	(9.4)	1.8
Total	(20.0)	
Net Addition	**15.7**	**0.4**

Note: 1 gigatonne = 1 billion tonnes

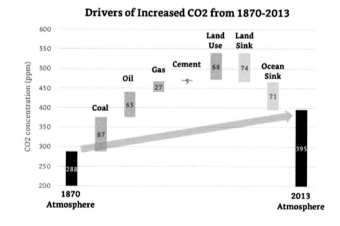

Source: Global Carbon Project, 2014

The risk posed by rising carbon dioxide levels in the atmosphere is due to the greenhouse effect. Solar radiation from the sun passes through carbon dioxide, but thermal radiation (i.e., heat) only partially passes back. The remaining trapped heat increases temperatures on the earth. If global temperatures rise too much, there are numerous risks, including severe weather events such as droughts, hurricanes and permanent flooding of coastal towns.

As one would expect, the data shows that temperatures have indeed been trending up with these increased levels of CO2 in the atmosphere. Carbon dioxide has increased from 318 ppm (parts per million) in 1958 to 397 ppm in 2014. This is not surprising given world growth during this time and the subsequent increase in fossil fuels usage.

To evaluate the global temperature change, it is helpful to compare a longer time series to a base-period average to smooth out individual-year volatility. Taking 1951 to 1980 as the base period, one can see the trend in the temperature changes over time in the chart below. The trend is clearly higher with 2014 registering the biggest increase over the base period on record at +0.75 degrees Celsius.

Figure 50: CO2 and Temperature

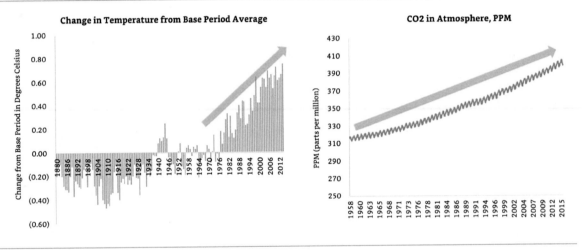

Source: NASA

Proper climate science is more complicated than the simple charting and analysis above. For those seeking something deeper, it is worth evaluating the Intergovernmental Panel on Climate Change's (IPCC) extensive research on the topic. The IPCC, formed in 1988, is a group of scientists organized by the United National Environmental Programme and the World Meteorological Organization to "provide the world with a clear scientific view on the current state of knowledge in climate change and its potential environmental and socio-economic impacts." Its conclusions are clear: Global warming presents a very real risk to the Earth. The sensitivity analysis from its climate models is shown below. Over 400 ppm starts to trend toward potentially 2 degrees Celsius warming (or 3.6 degrees Fahrenheit).

Figure 51: IPCC Estimated Temperature Changes and Different Levels of CO2

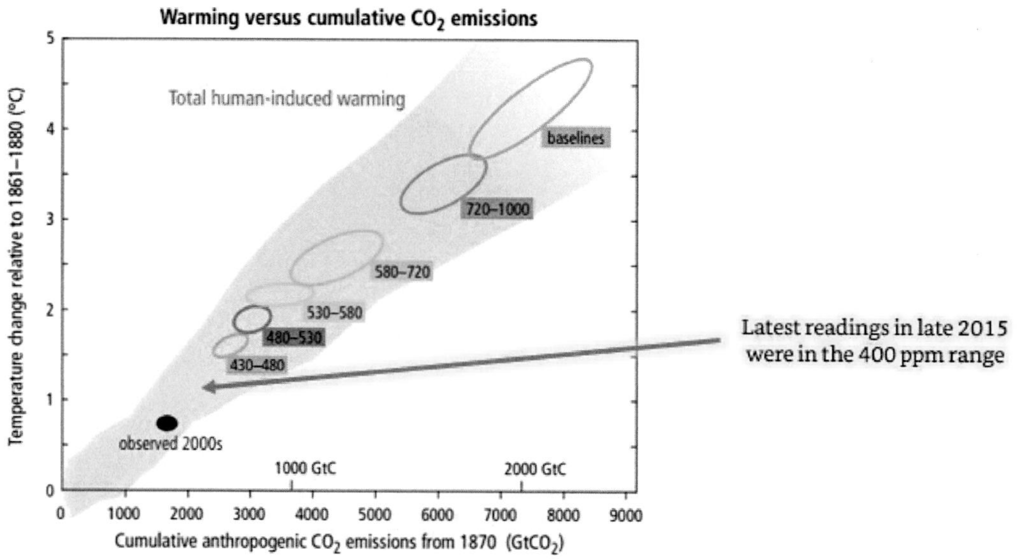

Warming versus cumulative CO₂ emissions

Total human-induced warming

baselines

720–1000

580–720

530–580

480–530

430–480

observed 2000s

Latest readings in late 2015 were in the 400 ppm range

Temperature change relative to 1861–1880 (°C)

Cumulative anthropogenic CO₂ emissions from 1870 (GtCO₂)

1000 GtC   2000 GtC

Source: IPCC 2014 Report

While the IPCC models are much more robust, it can be helpful to do a back-of-the-envelope calculation as well. In 2014, there was a measured +0.75 degrees Celsius increase above the 1951 to 1980 base period. During this time, there was a 77 ppm increase in CO2 taking the midpoint of the base period. This equates to a 0.01 degree move for each 1 ppm of CO2 increase in the atmosphere. So a 100 ppm increase in CO2 to over 400 ppm would mean that roughly 1 degree more would be added to the 0.75 to get a 1.75 degree Celsius impact. This is roughly where the IPCC comes out as well.

What levels of temperature increase are deemed "safe?" While many climate scientists have previously stated a desire to limit the increase to 1 degree Celsius, that seems less practical given how much CO2 has been put in the atmosphere and temperature increases already incurred. Therefore, many currently are hoping that global temperature increases can at least be limited to less than 2 degrees Celsius.

The risks of going above 2 degrees Celsius (or 3.6 degrees Fahrenheit) vary by type of impact and across geographies. Risks include rising sea levels hurting coastal towns, increased intensity of hurricanes, changing precipitation, and more intense heat waves and droughts. These risks will impact different parts of the world in different ways. Places like Russia and Canada could potentially see some early benefits as ice melts, but places like the Marshall Islands might cease to exist as sea levels rise. Overall, however, the impacts are very harmful for the world. To make matters worse, the risks are likely non-linear – so as CO2 increases the temperature increases might be even more than expected.

Figure 52: Assessing the Type, Probability and Potential Impact Around the World

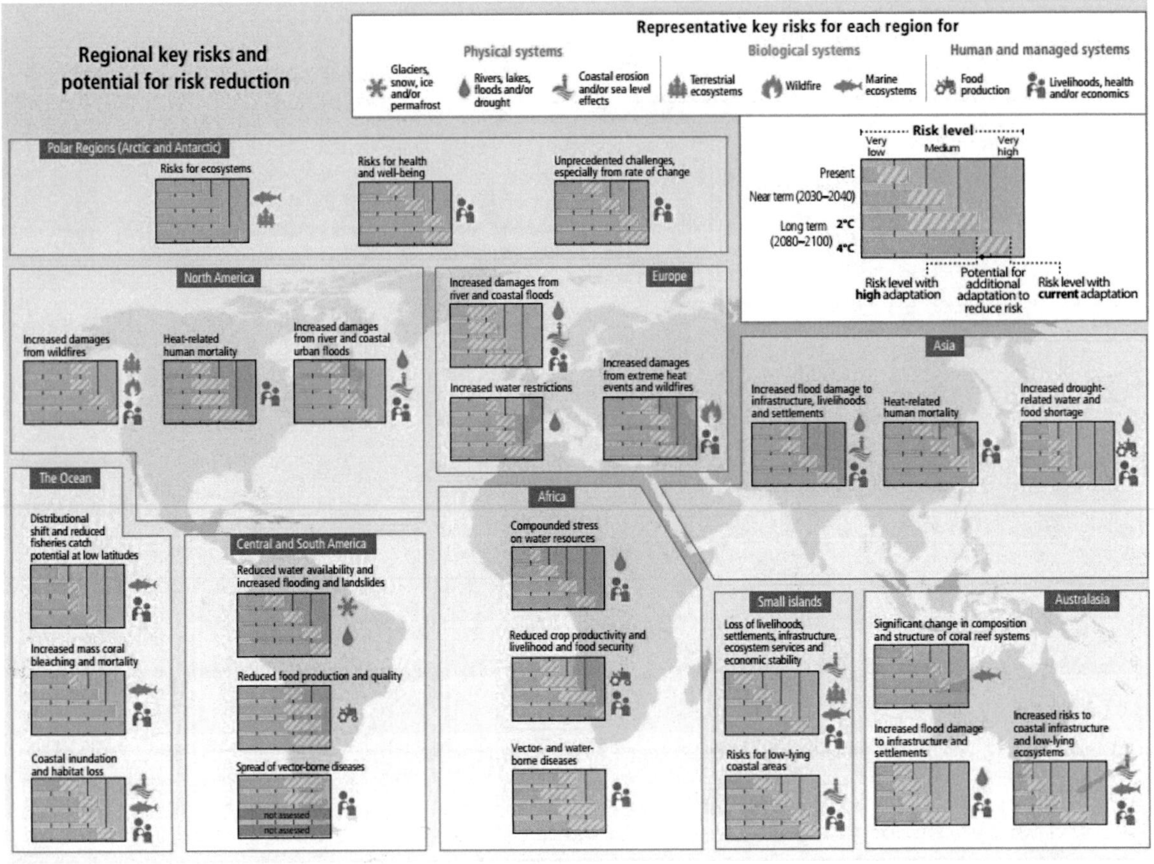

Source: IPCC 2014 Report

The Critical Delays in the Growth and Regulatory Response Loops

CO2 levels present the toughest "overshoot-and-collapse" risk that the world has faced. Many scientists attempt to explain carbon dioxide levels as a bathtub filling up (burning fossil fuels, cutting down trees) and draining (absorption by the oceans and land), which is exactly how many system dynamics professionals describes "stocks" (see page 44). If the stock (e.g., level) of CO2 continues to rise, the impacts could have a materially negative economic and human impact that is not easily reversible.

Figure 53 maps two critical loops related to the CO2 problem:

- **Regulatory Response Loop:** This entire loop is on a continued set of delays. CO2 in the atmosphere impacts global temperatures, actual temperatures impact perceived temperatures, perceived temperatures drive global action, and regulatory action impacts the emissions rates – but with delays at each step.

- **Growth Impact Loop:** CO2 increases the temperature which, in turn, creates a series of negative climate effects that all occur with a time delay as well. The effects will then impact economic growth.

Figure 53: Delays in the Regulatory Response and Impact to Growth Pose Clear Risks

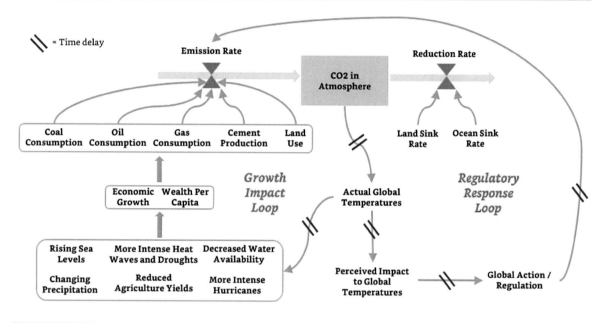

Source: Michael Molnar

The system does not care why the delay occurred. It simply reacts non-emotionally. More CO2 means higher temperatures and increased sea levels, extreme weather events, heat waves, and droughts. The fear among many scientists is that the regulatory response delay will lead to a an "overshoot-and-collapse" scenario where many parts of the environment are permanently impacted. For example, once sea levels rise and certain coastal towns and islands are flooded, the damage is hard to reverse.

Climate change is a probabilistic question. No one can say with 100% certainty that it will happen and, if it does, what the actual impacts will be. That being said, the following logic means that the probabilities are clearly highlighting a significant risk:

- **Logical Causal Argument of the Risk:** There is a causal relationship between CO_2 and temperature increases, which is the greenhouse effect.

- **Data Highlights It is Happening:** CO_2 levels in the atmosphere have increased as have global temperatures.

- **Risks Are Clear:** Increasing temperatures logically pose a risk – not the least of which are rising sea levels permanently flooding coastal cities.

- **Scientific Consensus:** The scientific community is in massive consensus that increased CO_2 levels in the atmosphere are causing increased temperatures and pose a grave risk to the world (as evidenced by the IPCC reports).

Given these factors, the debate should center on what should be done – and at what cost – to limit the disruption. However, there are certain groups that – while in the minority – are very vocal with a different agenda. These so-called "climate deniers" generally own assets that will be impaired if the current system is changed or are paid by those people whose assets will be impaired. Their intentions are merely to obfuscate the facts and drive confusion as the longer the delay, the better the value of their assets.

The Skeptical Science website is a great resource for getting fact-based answers to common skeptic arguments (their motto is "getting skeptical about global warming skepticism.)" They have listed five common tools that climate deniers often use:

1. **Fake Experts:** Dubious experts, fake scientists or think tanks paid to have a view; these "experts" inundate certain media outlets that have alternative agendas.

2. **Logical Fallacies:** A typical example: "CO_2 regulation is government overreach, if you hate big government, you can't favor CO_2 regulation."

3. **Impossible Expectations for Research:** By only highlighting the uncertainty in research, they attempt to confuse or delay action (no amount of research can provide 100% certainty of anything).

4. **Cherry-picking Data or Situations:** Only highlighting the few contrarian reports generated often by dubious sources and not recognizing the clear scientific consensus.

5. **Conspiracy Theories**: A typical example: "China made this all up to hurt American competitiveness."

While climate deniers can be frustrating given their dubious motivations, it is equally frustrating to see well-intentioned policies that end up doing more harm than good. Biomass policy in Europe, discussed next, is a good example of such a situation.

Poor CO2 Policy #1 – Back to the Age of Wood

While renewable energy often paints a mental picture of solar panels and windmills in people's minds, a large portion of it is supplied by wood (i.e., biomass) in Europe. This is ironic as the Age of Wood we discussed earlier in this book (see page 8) was mankind's first source of energy. Somehow, hundreds of years later, it became a possible solution to the vexing problem of CO2 levels in the atmosphere.

To be fair, there was a logic to burning wood being "renewable." Planted trees store carbon as they grow; they are part of the "land sink" in our carbon accounting shown previously. So while burning a tree releases carbon, planting one stores it. Therefore, as long as trees keep getting planted, the net carbon impact is neutral. Some proponents even make the argument that if carbon capture on the CO2 released when burning wood is done, the process then becomes carbon negative. In theory, this is true. In practice, the results have been unimpressive.

Regardless, at the time policy developed in Europe, many environmentalists were appeased with this argument for carbon neutrality. Utilities and other coal facility owners were happy as they could use their existing facilities and simply add wood to the mixture to make the fuel source say 80% or 90% wood and 10% to 20% coal. The existing facility was used and it would now be "green" as long as European regulators agreed wood was green. Given support from many sides, European regulators ended up agreeing that biomass (e.g., wood) was renewable and thus qualified for generous subsidies.

This policy created a system structure that had some perverse, but reasonably predictable, outcomes. First, U.S. wood waste – byproducts from producing such things as building products – was sought by European customers. This was a reasonably good use of waste wood that would otherwise likely rot in a dump. However, the supply of waste wood is dependent on the general economy and those industries that generate the waste such as housing and construction. Soon, the aggressive climate targets in Europe drove demand for wood waste to levels beyond the stock of wood waste in the U.S.

However, European utilities desire to burn wood remained given the subsidies in place. As a result, U.S. forests started to get chopped down and shipped to Europe to meet demand. This led to increases in the price of wood, hurting U.S. businesses that depended on this type of wood for their business.

As one would expect, some wood companies hired "experts" to produce "research" showing the benefits of burning wood. However, it clearly defies common sense to chop down trees in the U.S., process them into wood pellets, truck them to the coast, ship them across the ocean, and then truck them to European utilities – all to burn them in the name of saving the environment. *One does not need a Ph.D. in Economics to realize that is senseless.*

Figure 54: Europe's Classification of Wood as Renewable Drove a Series of Side Effects

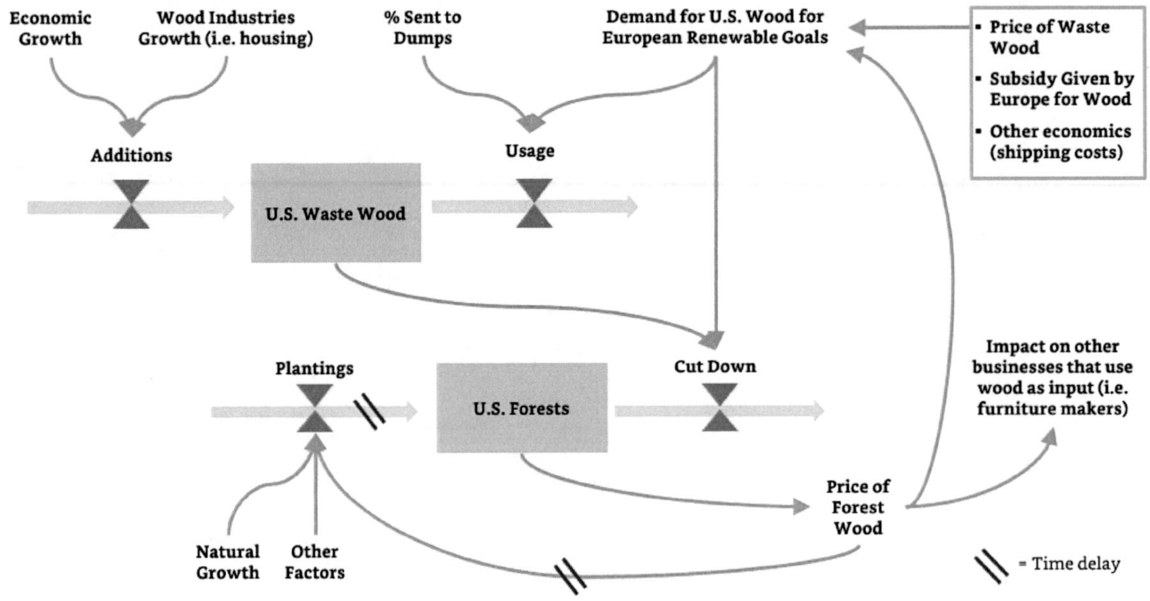

Source: Michael Molnar

The case study highlights the following takeaways:

- **Rules Are Critical:** Rules are a major catalyst for changing systems behavior, for the better or the worse. When European regulators classified all wood as renewable, it drove a very clear sequence of subsequent behaviors and effects.

- **Poor Subsidy Design Can Create Bizarre Outcomes:** Generous renewable subsidies were offered in an attempt to create an energy mix the E.U. desired. The side effects, unfortunately, were not anticipated. For example, some projections have U.S. non-waste wood (e.g., forests) as the major source of wood for this program in coming years.

- **International Regulations Can Impact Domestic Non-Related Businesses:** This case study demonstrates how policies in one region of the world can impact non-related businesses in another region. For example, furniture makers and other manufacturers that use U.S. wood as an input probably never anticipated their biggest risk would be European regulators counting wood as renewable.

Poor CO2 Policy #2 – The European Union's Emissions Trading Scheme

Getting government policy right is hard. Political, economic and social factors can be challenging obstacles to overcome for even the most skilled politician. However, what about a policy that ends up incenting the exact behavior policymakers are trying to stop? Furthermore, what about a policy that ended up granting billions of dollars to the companies that the policymakers were trying to regulate? That is what happened when the European Union attempted to regulate carbon emissions.

I have a lot of respect for the E.U. moving early to regulate carbon emissions. When moving early, admittedly, mistakes can happen. Still, the question remains: How did such well-meaning people create a policy that led to such poor results? Our goal is not to blame, but to understand in order to prevent future debacles.

The E.U. started its carbon emissions program in 2005. It based the program on the highly successful "cap-and-trade" policy that was so successful controlling acid rain in the United States. Under these programs, emitters such as manufacturers or utilities are looked at in total and a cap is placed on total emissions available for the group. Allowances to pollute up to the year's cap are then distributed to the emitters in some manner; for example, based on their percentage of the emissions total for the years preceding the regulation. These caps are reduced in subsequent years in order to drive lower total emissions over time.

The logic is that such a structure allows for market participants to find the cheapest solution for pollution possible. One company might feel good about its ability and the related cost to control their pollution and choose to invest to reduce CO_2 directly (and sell its allowances). Another may choose to simply buy permits that allow it to emit.

While logical and with precedent, the initial results were embarrassingly bad. The biggest polluting companies got multibillion-dollar windfalls, coal became the most economic fuel source, and there was little reduction in CO_2. The Europeans in charge of designing the policy would argue that "Phase 1" was a "learning phase" and that subsequent phases will go better. This might be true but, given the extent of the poor results, one cannot simply say "we are learning" without a clear understanding of how to improve. Especially when, I would argue, the poor results were predictable.

Figure 55: Articles Highlighting the Ineffectiveness of the E.U. Carbon Regulations

EU carbon trading system brings windfalls for some, with little benefit to climate
The New York Times
December 9, 2008

The European Union started with the most high-minded of ecological goals: to create a market that would encourage companies to reduce greenhouse gases by making them pay for each ton emitted into the atmosphere. Four years later, the carbon trading system has created a multibillion-euro windfall for some of the continent's biggest polluters, with little or no noticeable benefit to the environment so far.

Carbon Trading: ETS, RIP?
The Economist
April 20, 2013

In Europe itself cheaper carbon makes heavily polluting coal more attractive than cleaner gas. This is encouraging power generators to switch from gas to coal, and to build more coal-fired power stations than they would otherwise do. According to World Resources Institute, a think-tank in Washington, DC, European countries are planning 69 new coal plants, with a capacity of over 60 gigawatts, almost as much as France's nuclear-power capacity.

Source: Cited above

There were both analytical and psychological deficiencies at work. Analytically, there was a gap in understanding how the system structure would be influenced by exogenous factors such as U.S. coal and natural gas trends. The following sequence of events happened, but clearly were not anticipated:

1. **Shale Drilling Drove Down Gas Prices:** U.S. technological improvements in extracting natural gas from shale drove substantial supply of gas in the U.S., which drove down pricing.

2. **Coal-to-Gas Switching in U.S.:** Given the better economics, U.S. utilities switched to natural gas from coal.

3. **U.S. Coal Looked to Europe for New Markets:** U.S. coal producers sought to make up revenues through exports. As more supply flooded Europe, coal prices dropped.

4. **Coal Became More Economic Than Gas in the E.U.:** At the same time, natural gas prices in Europe stayed high as they are price-linked to oil and local in nature. Regulators ended up giving away (rather than auction) too many permits, which ended up driving the price of carbon dioxide to very low levels.

The end result, ironically, was that the European utilities were strongly incented to burn coal and the biggest emitters actually received windfall profits from the permits given to them.

Figure 56: Factors Both In and Out of Europe's Control Drove Very Poor Outcomes

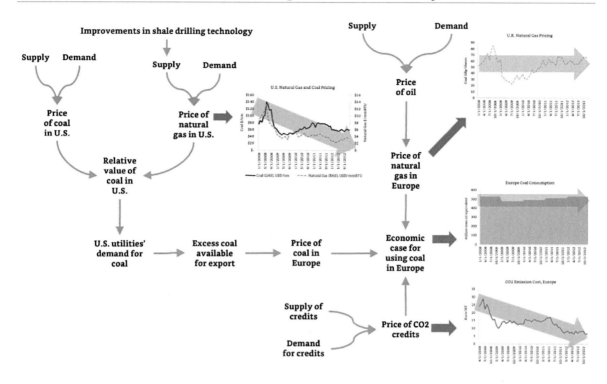

Source: Michael Molnar; Bloomberg

Beyond the analytical misstep of not understanding the system dynamics, there were likely psychological factors that skewed judgment:

- **Availability and Anchoring Bias:** The Europeans likely looked at the success of the U.S. Acid Rain Program's cap-and-trade structure and thought it could be successful with CO2. No doubt it has potential, but one can only assume that they over-generalized the ease of success based on anchoring to the outcomes in the acid rain program. This may have been a driver in not having better judgment on such critical items as setting a floor for emissions prices (so they don't fall to extremely low levels) and auctioning permits rather than giving them away.

- **Herd Instinct:** There was, and still is, a view that the public will not accept a tax on carbon. Therefore, nearly all policymakers, economists, and businesspeople have followed the herd to such regulations as cap-and-trade programs, which are much more difficult to implement. Unfortunately, this is a missed opportunity as nearly all economists agree that a tax is the most effective policy.

E.U. regulators likely followed the herd in this same way and implemented a complicated cap-and-trade program. Unlike the U.S., the E.U. already has very high gasoline taxes so there was a precedent for such a tax-based policy in the transportation market. This first so-called "learning phases" would have been much more interesting had the E.U. implemented the tax and broke from the herd.

Figure 57: Europe Already Taxes Gasoline Substantially More Than the U.S.

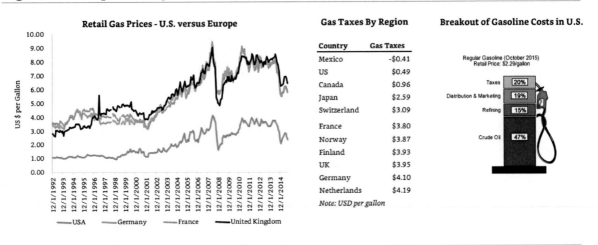

Source: Bloomberg; Energy Information Administration; AFDC

Will the World React Fast Enough?

When facing the risk of an "overshoot-and-collapse" scenario – one in which delaying too long permanently destroys something needed – time delays in responding are critical. Nearly 30 years ago in 1988, James Hansen from NASA testified before Congress that it was 99% certain that the global warming trend was not a natural variation, but caused by the buildup of carbon in the atmosphere. Unfortunately, there has been lot of media attention but no real action. Handshakes and international conferences do not count if they do not decrease the amount of CO_2 in the atmosphere. The data shows it has continued to climb and there are no signs that will change.

There are five factors, three psychological and two political, that are driving a significant delay in response time:

1. **No Availability Bias Triggered Until Too Late:** Unlike the term "acid rain," the terms "global warming" and "climate change" are incredibly ineffective on an emotional level. "Acid" is painful but "warming" is what New Yorkers seek when they go to the

Caribbean on vacation in the winter. A comedian I saw a few years ago joked, "If they wanted to get people's attention, they should *not* have called it global warming – that sounds nice as I want to be warm. They *should* have called it global herpes – that'll get people's attention!" While funny, this is not a minor point as emotions are needed to trigger public pressure on government to act.

Also, tangible evidence – such as the lifeless lakes which Americans saw during the acid rain crisis – are harder to see with CO2. People vaguely have an idea that severe weather events are likely driven by CO2 – and could increase in the future – but the connection is unclear and therefore less emotional. This likely means that the availability bias will only be triggered once the evidence is so clear in the physical environment (e.g., coastal towns under water) that the public cries out for a reaction. Unfortunately, this may mean that the world is in store for a long period of significant pain as the delay in action will have been very long.

2. **Framing and Hyperbolic Discounting Makes Action Now Feel Like a Bad Deal:** The decision is often framed as a huge payment (i.e., a loss) now to avoid some unknown loss in the future. That is an ineffective framing of the situation, the work of economists and not marketers. Judgment is impaired in two ways. One, we feel losses two times as much as gains as discussed (i.e., loss aversion). Losses are hard to bear, especially for an uncertain gain the future. Two, we are biased in terms of hyperbolic discounting where we irrationally overweight the present versus the future. No matter what the scientific studies, logic or math shows, it just does not feel like a good deal to most individuals.

Reframing the argument is possible as shown in the June, 8, 2016 edition of *The Economist* magazine. In discussing some of the costs of climate change, it said, "*Private insurers say that last year was the second most expensive in American history for disaster related to climate change, costing them $139 billion. But private insurance paid only a quarter of the costs, leaving taxpayers to cover the rest. By comparison, funding renewable energy property seems rather cheap.*" These types of framings are rare, however.

3. **"Losers" Are Winning the Communications Game:** For any change, there are winners and losers. In the bid to limit carbon emissions, fossil-fuel companies stand to lose billions. Therefore, it is logical that they will resist change with substantial resources. They understand the communications game well and are fighting with communications plans based on psychology and emotion.

People intent on obfuscating the truth know this fact. Frank Luntz, a Republican strategist, actually detailed his thoughts in a leaked memo that was a textbook example of how to skew judgment by exploiting cognitive biases. Luntz understands emotions impact on judgment, having said "Eighty percent of our life is emotion, and only 20 percent is intellect. I am much more interested in how you feel than how you think." I have clipped pages from the leaked memo below with boxes in red highlighting the biases they are exploiting. It is an impressive, albeit perhaps not ethical, example of applying many of the behavioral concepts detailed in this book. He even added sections on "Words that Work" to help the politicians with canned but effective messages.

Figure 58: Frank Luntz, Republican Strategist, Understands How to Skew Judgment

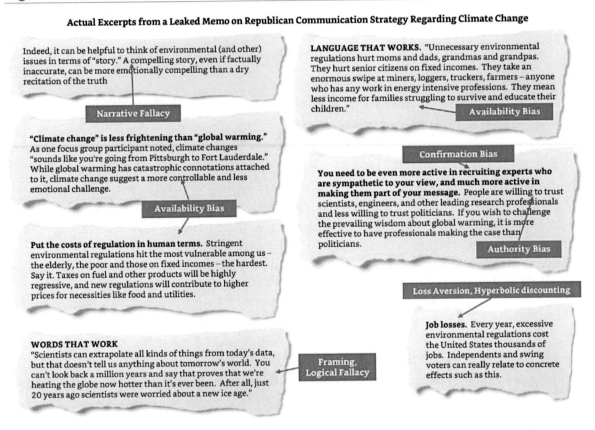

Actual Excerpts from a Leaked Memo on Republican Communication Strategy Regarding Climate Change

Indeed, it can be helpful to think of environmental (and other) issues in terms of "story." A compelling story, even if factually inaccurate, can be more emotionally compelling than a dry recitation of the truth

Narrative Fallacy

"Climate change" is less frightening than "global warming." As one focus group participant noted, climate changes "sounds like you're going from Pittsburgh to Fort Lauderdale." While global warming has catastrophic connotations attached to it, climate change suggest a more controllable and less emotional challenge.

Availability Bias

Put the costs of regulation in human terms. Stringent environmental regulations hit the most vulnerable among us – the elderly, the poor and those on fixed incomes – the hardest. Say it. Taxes on fuel and other products will be highly regressive, and new regulations will contribute to higher prices for necessities like food and utilities.

WORDS THAT WORK
"Scientists can extrapolate all kinds of things from today's data, but that doesn't tell us anything about tomorrow's world. You can't look back a million years and say that proves that we're heating the globe now hotter than it's ever been. After all, just 20 years ago scientists were worried about a new ice age."

Framing, Logical Fallacy

LANGUAGE THAT WORKS. "Unnecessary environmental regulations hurt moms and dads, grandmas and grandpas. They hurt senior citizens on fixed incomes. They take an enormous swipe at miners, loggers, truckers, farmers – anyone who has any work in energy intensive professions. They mean less income for families struggling to survive and educate their children."

Availability Bias

Confirmation Bias

You need to be even more active in recruiting experts who are sympathetic to your view, and much more active in making them part of your message. People are willing to trust scientists, engineers, and other leading research professionals and less willing to trust politicians. If you wish to challenge the prevailing wisdom about global warming, it is more effective to have professionals making the case than politicians.

Authority Bias

Loss Aversion, Hyperbolic discounting

Job losses. Every year, excessive environmental regulations cost the United States thousands of jobs. Independents and swing voters can really relate to concrete effects such as this.

Source: Frank Luntz leaked memo vis MotherJones.com

There are some who doubt the impact of communications strategy, feeling that people have strong enough science backgrounds to allow them to see through such tactics. For those with these views, consider the following data from the National Science Foundation.

The National Science Foundation was created in 1950 with one of its goals as the following: *"to serve as an independent body of advisors to both the President and the Congress on policy matters related to science and engineering and education in science and engineering."* In its report, Science and Engineering Indictors – 2014, it detailed the results from a myriad of questions asked to the public on science. For example, when asked, "Does the Earth go around the Sun, or does the Sun go around the Earth," only 74% of respondents answered correctly. Meaning 26% of Americans surveyed believe the Sun revolves around the Earth.

What's the point? In general, Americans (and rest of the world for that matter), do not know much about science. Their judgments are based on emotions as their knowledge is weak. Even for those with good knowledge, as we have seen in our discussion on behavioral economics, the pull of Mind 2 is also exerting its influence as well. In short, communications strategy matters.

These three psychological challenges increase the delay in the public pressure "balancing feedback loop" from taking hold. There is potential for these headwinds to be changed and controlled. The term "climate change" can be re-marketed showing more real and tangible effects. The situation can be re-framed from feeling like a loss today for an uncertain gain in the future, to a wise investment today that has a big payoff in the near term. Communication experts focused on obfuscating the facts can be countered with equally effective programs detailing the other view.

The last two headwinds, four and five below, are political in nature but just as daunting:

4. **Winners Versus Losers Ratio:** Remember, acid rain regulations did not create losers out of the whole coal industry. In fact, total tonnage kept growing. High-sulfur coal mine owners lost, but there was a series of winners: low-sulfur coal mine owners, railroads, and industrial companies that had pollution control equipment. Unfortunately, carbon regulations impact nearly all fossil-fuel companies to some degree as all are significant CO_2 emitters as shown in Figure 59.

Figure 59: CO2 Emission Levels by Type of Coal and Type of Fossil Fuel

		2013 Production	Sulfur (pounds per million Btu)	Mercury (pounds per trillion Btu)	CO2 (pounds per million Btu)
Northern Appalachia	High-sulfur	76	2.72	11.7	204.7
Central Appalachia	Mid-sulfur	66	0.93	7.6	206.4
East Interior (IL)	High-sulfur	126	2.69	6.4	203.1
Wyoming - North	Low-sulfur	130	0.37	7.1	214.3
Wyoming - South	Low-sulfur	243	0.28	5.2	214.3
Total for Production, Average for Rest		641	1.40	7.6	208.6

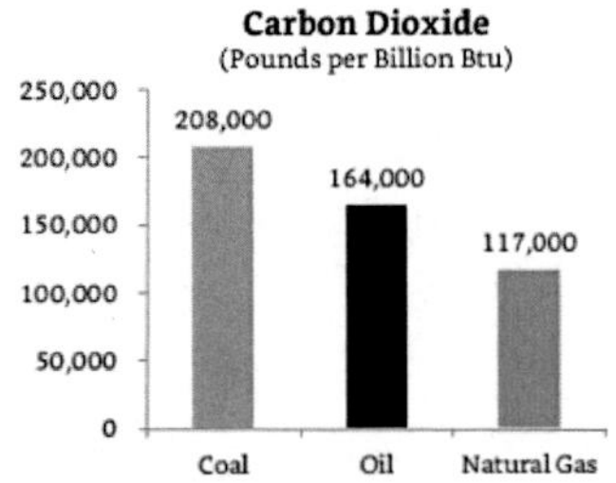

Carbon Dioxide (Pounds per Billion Btu)

Coal: 208,000 | Oil: 164,000 | Natural Gas: 117,000

While there are types of coal that are low sulfur, deviations for mercury and CO2 are much less so. Likewise, natural gas and oil are less CO2 intensive, but still will stand to feel some pain if CO2 is regulated (oil more so than natural gas).

Source: Energy Information Administration Annual Energy Outlook

While there will be many losers from CO2 regulation, there will be winners as well. Yet, until there is clarity on regulations these winners are not clear. For example, will the regulations price carbon directly or simply continue to subsidize certain "cleaner" forms of energy? How exactly will the pricing mechanism work? It's less clear who the winners will be.

5. **Level of International Trust and Cooperation Needed:** Unlike acid rain, CO2 is a more global issue. The U.S. and Europe put the vast majority of the CO2 in the atmosphere over the past 100 years, and China and India are adding to it now. So what is exactly fair in terms of regulating current emissions? The Chinese and the Indians will argue that the U.S. and Europe are primarily responsible because they received the biggest economic benefits, so they should pay more. The Americans and Europeans argue that if China and India do not do anything, their remedies will have no impact. Both are correct and the situation could be resolved with negotiation. However, the level of coordination and trust to execute such a plan is daunting. The incentive to cheat is massive as other countries bear your costs of noncompliance. Both factors make this a very challenging headwind to overcome.

Figure 60: CO2 Emissions by Geography, 1959-2013

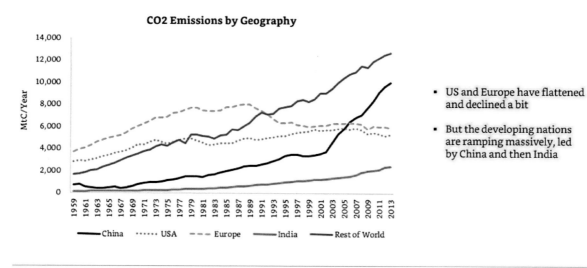

Source: Global Carbon Project 2014

So Where Does This Leave Us?

What is most likely to happen? In my view, we risk an "overshoot-and-collapse" scenario where the carrying capacity of the Earth is permanently damaged due to a long delay in response. Specifically, this means that temperature increases will drive sea levels higher and coastal towns and islands will be flooded. More extreme weather events will economically hurt the areas impacted and lives will be lost.

Some may push back and talk of the "momentum" in climate talks and handshake agreements. There is momentum in the right direction and that is a positive trend. However, the system does not care about momentum. The system is an emotionless set of interactions – and all the system knows is more CO_2 is going into the atmosphere each year. Make no mistake, a balancing loop will eventually take hold. The only question is whether it is proactively driven by humans, or reactively by nature.

My base view is that the world will only react with meaningful regulations (i.e., binding, enforceable) once the negative impacts from global warming are being felt firsthand, making them undeniable to even the biggest skeptic. By then, the stock of CO_2 in the atmosphere will be immense and its repercussions will be felt for many years to come.

The Headwinds to Successful Energy-Efficiency Regulations

Understanding Government-Driven Energy Efficiency

One of the ways governments have tried to control pollution is through energy-efficiency regulations. Energy-efficiency regulations come in many forms. In the U.S., the three major ones are building codes, appliance standards and fuel-economy regulations for transportation. All have considerable complexity, but strive for the same thing: mandating a level of efficiency in using resources, whether it be electricity, gasoline or natural gas. There are three challenges with energy efficiency: information gaps, hyperbolic discounting, and the rebound effect.

Figure 61: Select Examples of Energy-Efficiency Regulation

The Energy Independence and Security Act (EISA) of 2007	NAECA 2015 – What You Need to Know	2013 Building Energy Efficiency Stands for Residential and Nonresidential buildings California Energy Commission	EPA and NHTSA Set Standards to Reduce Greenhouse Gases and Improve Fuel Economy for Model Years 2017-2025 Cars and Light Trucks
The Energy Independence and Security Act (EISA) of 2007 was passed with the intention of moving the United States toward greater energy security, partly by increasing the standards for product efficiency. Section 321 of the Energy Independence and Security Act (EISA) establishes increased minimum energy efficiency standards for general service lamps. EISA does not ban incandescent light bulbs, but its minimum efficiency standards are high enough that the incandescent lamps most commonly used by consumers today will not meet the new requirements. Once implemented, the Act will essentially eliminate 40W, 60W, 75W, and 100W medium screw-base incandescent light bulbs. Source: www.lightingfacts.com	On April 16, 2015, new water heater energy factor (EF) requirements took effect as the result of updates to the National Appliance Energy Conservation Act (NAECA). These requirements call for higher energy factor (EF) ratings on virtually all residential gas, electric, oil, and tankless gas water heaters, completely altering the water heater landscape. NAECA 2015 also affects some light-duty commercial water heaters. The Energy Factor (EF) indicates a water heater's overall energy efficiency based on the amount of hot water produced per unit of fuel consumed over a typical day. The higher the EF, the more energy efficient the water heater. Source: Bradford White	The 2013 Building Energy Efficiency Standards focus on several key areas to improve the energy efficiency of newly constructed buildings and additions and alterations to existing buildings... The most significant efficiency improvements to the residential Standards are proposed for windows, envelope insulation and HVAC system testing. The most significant efficiency improvements to the nonresidential Standards are proposed for lighting controls, windows, unitary HVAC equipment and building commissioning. Source: California Energy Commission	EPA is establishing national GHG emissions standards under the Clean Air Act, and NHTSA is establishing Corporate Average Fuel Economy (CAFE) standards under the Energy Policy and Conservation Act, as amended by the Energy Independence and Security Act (EISA). The final standards are projected to result in an average industry fleetwide level of 163 grams/mile of carbon dioxide (CO_2) in model year 2025, which is equivalent to 54.5 miles per gallon (mpg) if achieved exclusively through fuel economy improvements. Source: EPA

Source: Cited above

Judgment Headwinds – Information Gaps, Loss Aversion and Discounting

Imagine a hypothetical investment where your bank offered you a 5% return on your money if you put it into a special investment program with limited risk? What about 10%? 30%? 50%? 300%? Assuming it was not a fraud, you would likely have interest in getting such a high return for low risk. This is what the rational optimizing view of traditional economics would indicate, as well as common sense. Energy-efficiency appliances offer just that, yet consumer adoption is often muted and slow

There are several reasons why older, less efficient products are not replaced at speeds economists often predict. First, individuals simply do not have the knowledge or information needed in many instances. How can I compare my existing appliance's operating costs to new, more efficient ones? This is an **information gap** and is clear to anyone who has, for example, recently changed a water heater at their home. Recognition of the information gap was a driving force behind mandated labeling of energy usage on automobiles and appliances with things like EnergyStar ratings. These are meant to close the gap and are a very good idea.

Figure 62: Examples of Required Labeling to Help Obtain Necessary Information

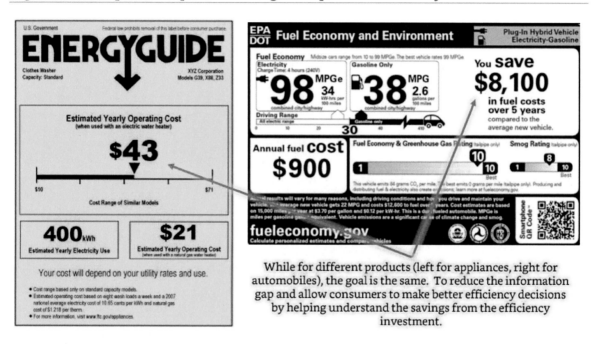

While for different products (left for appliances, right for automobiles), the goal is the same. To reduce the information gap and allow consumers to make better efficiency decisions by helping understand the savings from the efficiency investment.

Source: Federal Trade Commission; Car and Driver Magazine

Once consumers have reasonably reliable information, a rate of return on the investment can be calculated. Say you pay $1,000 for a more efficient appliance but get savings of $100 a year for 20 years. That equates to a 7.8% return on your investment in the appliance (See Figure 63). Research published in the *Frontiers of Energy Research Journal* calculated the implied discount rates (i.e., rates of return) on many energy-efficiency projects. The midpoint of the ranges of return given were extraordinary for some. For example, a refrigerator's implied rate of return was 170%.

Figure 63: Energy-Efficiency Math (left) and Implied Discount Rates Per Study

	Rate of Return Analysis			Implied Discount Rates Per One Study			
Year	Cash (Paid) / Saved	Economic Value			Low	High	Midpoint
0	-1000		Thermal insulation		2%	32%	17%
1	100	Rate of Return	Space heating		2%	36%	19%
2	100	7.8%	Air Conditioning		3%	29%	16%
3	100		Refrigerators		39%	300%	170%
4	100		Lighting		7%	17%	12%
5	100		Automobiles		2%	45%	24%
6	100						
7	100						
8	100						
9	100						
10	100						
...20	100						

Individuals have three challenges in making good decisions:
- Getting the information needed for the analysis at left
- Ability/skill to do the analysis at left
- Hyperbolic discounting bias which results in high discount rates as shown above

Source: Michael Molnar (left); "Energy-using durables – why consumers refrain from economically optimal choices," by Renate Schubert and Marcel Stadelman, (right)

There are two behavioral reasons explaining why the uptake on such profitable investments are not made as often one would think. First, it has been shown that people are **loss averse**, valuing losses at roughly two times the level of similar gains. The initial capital outlay is therefore judged to be a larger, more painful loss than the subsequent gains.

Second, it has been shown that people apply **hyperbolic instead of exponential discount rates**, meaning they value today more than tomorrow in an irrational manner. Exponential discounting means that a similar rate is applied for each time period and so for several time periods in the future, valuation falls in a consistent manner. Hyperbolic discounting means that people will drop the value of something (in their heads) dramatically for a short delay, and then less so for time periods farther out. This means the rate at which they discount is not consistent. For example, if offered $100 today versus $200 in one year's time, many studies have shown that people choose the $100 today. However, if offered $100 in five years but $200 in six years, many of those same people shift their preference towards waiting the one extra year for the incremental $100. In reality, it is the same offer, just five years into the future.

These behavioral biases are somewhat alleviated by the energy-efficiency labeling requirements. This helps to give people a rough idea of the savings per year, which allows them to perform a simple payback calculation. So while a rate-of-return calculation will seldom be done by a layman, most will understand that the incremental $4,000 in costs will be paid for in two years given the annual savings of $2,000 per year – and that often sounds like a decent deal. However, hyperbolic discounting and loss aversion are inherent parts of our cognitive makeup and can be difficult to overcome.

Feedback Headwinds – The Rebound Effect

While the decision to make an energy-efficient purchase is skewed by psychological factors, government-mandated energy-efficiency regulations create an additional headwind called "the rebound effect" once that investment is made. By mandating efficient products, the number of units of energy used per application is less. For example, you accomplish your goal of say heating water with less electricity. This means that, all else equal, your costs are less as you used less. If your costs are less, one tends to think less about efficiency and use more. This is seen all the time where people will leave the air conditioner or lights on more if the cost is not material. The net effect, called the "rebound effect," eats into the savings achieved by mandating energy efficiency in the first place. The extent of this rebound effect is debated, but various studies have shown that it can consume up to 20% to 60% of the benefits.

Figure 64: Simple System Structure and Behavior of Energy-Efficiency Programs

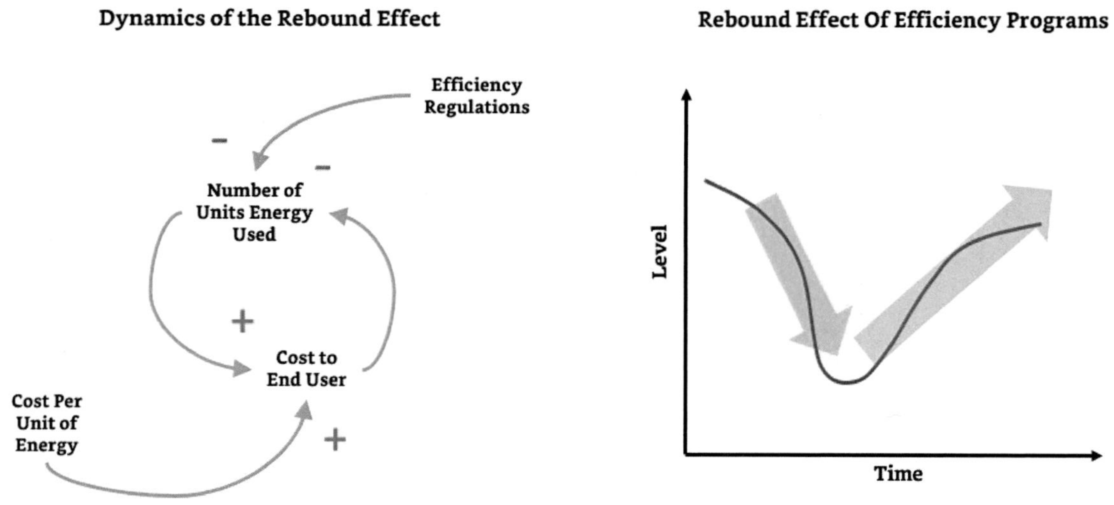

Source: Michael Molnar

Are Efficiency Regulations a Bad Idea?

Energy efficiency, doing the same with less, is not a bad goal. However, it is important to understand that *mandating* energy efficiency through regulations is the result of either a lack of political will or ability to price energy appropriately. If energy was priced appropriately, meaning including the cost of pollution and other externalities, mandating efficiency would not be needed. Consumers would pursue it in their own selfish interest of saving money.

Decoding Potential Game-Changing Technologies

"Maybe I can do somethin'... maybe I can just find out somethin', just scrounge around and maybe find out what it is that's wrong and see if they ain't somethin' that can be done about it."
- Tom Joad
From "The Grapes of Wrath" by John Steinbeck (1939)

Technology has changed the world in countless ways – from the automobile to the Internet to mobile telephony. Energy faces countless technological changes looming on the horizon. In this section, we discuss three technological advances that have the potential to disrupt energy markets.

Solar has grown tremendously over the past 10 years, from one gigawatt installed in 2004 to over 40 gigawatts in 2014. Yet, despite this exponential growth, investors have done quite poorly. The drivers of the industry's exponential growth are mapped along with a discussion as to the psychological drivers of poor investor returns.

Fracking, a drilling technique that allows for more production of oil and natural gas, has changed world energy markets. Two important topics are discussed. First, fracking's ability to fundamentally change the dynamics of supply by allowing faster responses to market conditions and – inadvertently – mitigating some of the psychological biases that often lead to undersupply and oversupply is discussed. Second, fracking's potential to make the U.S. energy independent by supplying more domestically produced oil is evaluated, along with its related risks.

Finally, the dominance of the internal combustion engine is facing its biggest test yet – **electric vehicles**. The challenge of breaking into a so-called "path-dependent" market is discussed. Fuel-cell technology, the previous attempt to break into this market in the early 2000s, is analyzed and the lessons learned are applied to the electric-car market today.

Solar – Exponential Industry Growth, Psychological Investor Errors

The Dynamics of Growth

While solar power was invented decades ago, it began only to ramp commercially in the early 2000s with the push for more clean energy at a time of very high fossil fuel prices. The progress in only a decade is remarkable, with annual solar installations growing from nearly zero megawatts to about 40 gigawatts per year. The cost of power generated by solar became consistently cheaper each year and thus installations and capacity grew exponentially.

Figure 65: Solar Installation Growth

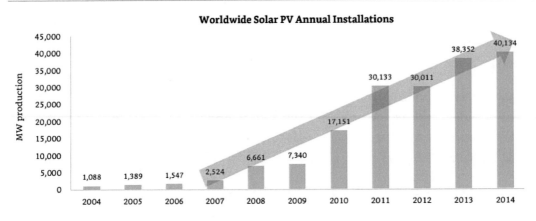

Source: Bloomberg

Exponential growth was driven by two key factors. First, the cost decline reinforcing loop took hold as the industry scaled. As energy prices were high and volatile, U.S. was importing a lot of oil, and the risk of global warming was becoming more accepted, there were demands for new forms of energy and solar was supported with various subsidies. Sensing an opportunity, investors began to put capital into promising companies and talented entrepreneurs began to enter the sector in droves. This allowed these companies to scale their operations, which was a major driver of cost declines as high fixed costs were absorbed into a bigger output. Finally, as installations grew, the entire value chain became more efficient. Improvements in solar racking, labor efficiency and financing all drove costs lower. The effect was a reinforcing loop of cost declines.

Figure 66: The Scale Effect on Cost Declines in Solar

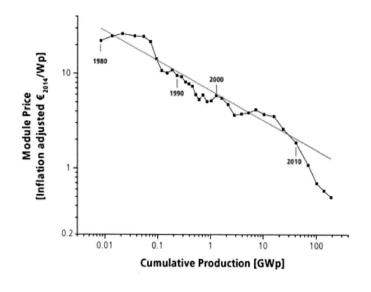

The Fraunhofer Institute for Solar Energy in Germany calculated that each time cumulative production doubled, the price of solar went down by 19.6% for the last 34 years (per their November 2015 report)

Source: Fraunhofer Institute

Second, less impactful – but growing in importance – is the political power loop shown in Figure 67. As solar installations grow, the number of businesses and workers increase. This, in turn, leads to a more powerful political force that can lobby for solar. As energy markets have significant government intervention on the demand (mandated energy efficiency) and supply (subsidies) sides, having a powerful seat at the table is critical. While the voice of solar compared to the entrenched fossil-fuel industry is still minor, it has grown and had success in having subsidies continue to be funded.

These dynamics are mapped below in Figure 67. The data is impressive:

1. **Polysilicon Costs:** Polysilicon is an important input for many types of solar modules. While initially there was a shortage of polysilicon in 2008, subsequent supply additions and technological improvements drove the cost from over $300/kg in 2008 to $21/kg in 2014.

2. **Modules Costs:** Solar modules are the key part of a system that converts sunlight into power. The cost of modules declined from $4/watt in 2008 to $0.60/watt by 2014.

3. **Inverter Costs:** Inverters are key parts of the electronics of solar systems. Their costs declined from nearly $0.50/watt to below $0.25/watt as well.

4. **Delivered Cost of Power:** The result of these and other cost declines resulted in the delivered cost of power declining from $0.40-$0.50/kWh to $0.12-$0.15/kWh. The exact costs depend on the geography and type of installation but the trends are the same – massive cost declines as the reinforcing loops drove costs lower.

Figure 67: The Dynamics of Cost Declines in Solar

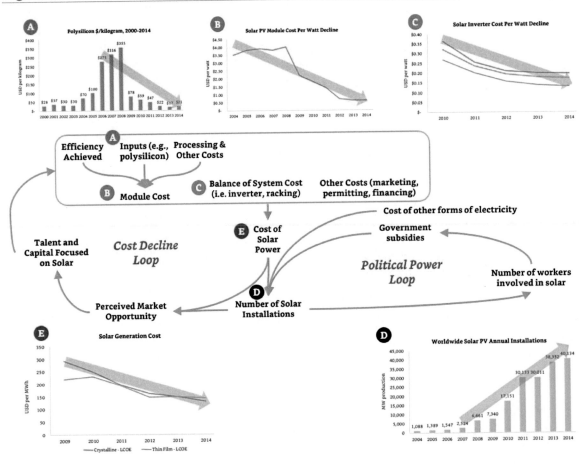

Source: Michael Molnar; Bloomberg

As installations of solar grew, companies that produced the modules that generated the electricity saw their market capitalization soar. The biggest darling of them all was First Solar (FSLR) whose market capitalization peaked at $20 billion in 2007. Venture capitalists poured hundreds of millions of dollars into startups that would become the next "First Solar" and corporates invested in their own internal programs as well. Times were very good.

Then things got bad – very bad – as supply began to outpace demand which drove pricing down sharply. This led to lower profits for the industry and re-ratings in valuations. Bankruptcies followed and investors took massive losses. How does something like this happen to arguably a such as sophisticated group of people (the investors)?

Figure 68: The Downturn in Solar Was Remarkably Bad for Investors

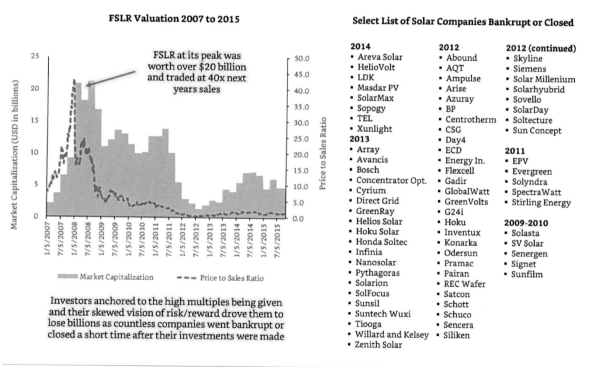

Source: Bloomberg (left); Greentech Media (right)

Information or knowledge gaps were not the cause. The investors involved were very sophisticated and had access to consultants and advisors to fill in knowledge gaps when needed. Analytical skills were not the core problem either. These investors have done tons of deals in the past and were well-versed in how to structure a deal and value a company.

The culprit was Mind 2 and the behavioral skewing of judgment at nearly every part of the investment process. Many venture capitalists likely suffered from an acute case of **overconfidence and the halo effect**. Their prior successes, many of them having funded some of the most well-known software and internet companies in the world, were remarkable. Such success can create an overconfidence that similar success will be had in their next venture. Unfortunately, investing in energy is much more capital intensive and has a series of dynamics that were often not appreciated.

Once companies were formed, they were funded at incredibly high valuations. Many investors succumbed to the **anchoring bias** when assessing what valuation multiple to apply. So-called relative valuation (versus absolute, which is looking at the company in isolation based on its cash flows over time) is done all the time and, in theory, should be mathematically equivalent. However, investors were getting comfortable with eye-popping valuations of 20x, 30x, and 40x sales simply because that is where other companies were trading as well.

These valuations implied massive cash flows and extraordinary returns on capital for many years into the future which was at odds with what most likely was going to happen. No energy company typically earns returns on capital at the level that was implied by these valuations. Thinking otherwise is an example of **base rate bias**, where the human mind ignores the base rate and focuses on information only applicable to certain cases. To be fair, venture capitalists are paid to find special companies that will not be "average." However, even with that caveat, any investor needs to think about risk/reward and these valuations were implying significant risk and limited reward.

Investors also misjudged the Chinese impact on the market supply. Chinese companies, nearly always with substantial government support, scaled massively. Their growth contributed to the huge oversupply situation which hurt pricing and profits for all solar companies worldwide.

What investors missed at first, and then did not appropriately judge once it became known, was that the system structure changed when the Chinese entered the market. No longer was the typical commodity market in place where once pricing fell below marginal cost, supply would decrease reasonably quickly as facilities were forced to shut down. Solar was part of the Chinese government's strategy for becoming world leaders in clean energy and generating jobs for its people. This dynamic resulted in much longer than normal **time delay** of that supply coming out as the government was willing to do a lot to ensure that the Chinese companies would survive. In a long down-market with negative cash flows, the venture capitalists balance sheet would pale in comparison to the Chinese government support toward their domestic champions.

Why were investors reaction so slow relative to these market conditions? Two biases seemed to work in tandem, the **Semmelweis Reflex** (bias to reject information that is not conforming to your view) and **Bayesian/Conservatism** (tendency to underestimate the amount of change). I used to tell clients, "listen, that Chinese competitor didn't get your Western MBA so the whole marginal cost thing isn't working the way you think" but was met with substantial pushback as this was not how commodity markets often worked. As new information came to light about the motivations of the Chinese, the adjustments by most investors was still too conservative. They simply could not believe that supply would continue to come out of China at such a rate and for so long.

Finally, once investments were made even with the market in a very bad spot, many investors continued to fund losing companies that had incredibly slim chances of success. Why? It was a combination of the **endowment effect** and the pull of the **consistency and commitment bias**. Once decisions are made – in this case an investment – it is very hard to think clearly about the current situation; in this case, the risk/reward to investing more capital. Investors were endowed (i.e., owned) with the company and had strong views on just how special they were relative to the competition. They felt a strong need to be consistent with their prior decisions. However, if these same investors were given the opportunity to first invest at that later point (versus already having been an investor), I doubt they would have funded them. The right decision was to shut down much earlier or try to sell.

The Psychology of Losing Money - Corporates

Unfortunately, losing money in solar was not relegated to venture capitalists as corporates such as Siemens piled into the market as well. Siemens is an industrial company that focuses on engineering and manufacturing with particular areas of interest in power, transportation, and automation. The company has over 70 billion euros in revenues per year, boasts a market capitalization of about the same, and has over 300,000 employees. In 2014, the company spent over 4 billion euros on research and development.

Siemens made a series of acquisitions to get a foothold in the burgeoning solar market. In March 2009, it invested in Archimedes for an undisclosed amount. In October 2009, it spent over $400 million to acquire Solel. Then, June of 2011, it invested in Semprius.

Then, just a little over a year later in October 2012, it announced it was leaving the solar business after having suffered losses over $1 billion. How did this happen, especially when investments were made just a few quarters ago? The main reason given was that the cost of a competing technology, solar photovoltaics, declined so much that their technologies (solar thermal and HCPV) could not compete well. This is a true statement describing what happened, but not that helpful in understanding why it happened or was not anticipated better.

It was unlikely that information or knowledge gaps were the problem. Siemens knows power markets extremely well given its long history with utilities and power customers. It undoubtedly had access to considerable numbers of consultants and industry experts to assess where various technologies were trending.

There was potentially a challenge in correctly ascertaining the system dynamic of costs for the competing technology of photovoltaics. First, the system dynamic it assumed was in place changed due to the entrance of the Chinese. Second, the reinforcing loop of cost declines was likely misunderstood in terms of just how fast costs could come down. The result was that its solar thermal and HCPV technology fell further behind than anticipated. **Anchoring bias** is a particular challenge when competing technologies are undergoing exponential cost declines (such as PV was experiencing); one can simply continue to anchor to the current costs and not fully appreciate where future costs end up.

Siemens likely was subject to problems with **overconfidence, the endowment effect, and commitment/consistency. Overconfidence** can creep in to groups that have significant experience in an area. The Siemens engineers likely had extreme confidence in their non-PV solar technologies given their significant manufacturing expertise and knowledge of power markets. They likely had too much confidence in their ability to hit cost declines relative to PV's cost declines, potentially not fully appreciating that PV was in the sweet spot of a powerful reinforcing loop driving costs down lower.

The **endowment effect** and **commitment/consistently bias** were likely impactful as well. As the last investment was made just 12 months before pulling out of the entire segment, this was possibly due to executives trying to make something work that was far gone. They valued their strategy as they were "endowed" with it; they wanted to be consistent with prior decisions but the market shifted and they moved too slow. The result was hundreds of millions in late investments that likely could have been avoided.

Figure 69: Significant Money was Wasted at Siemens in Solar

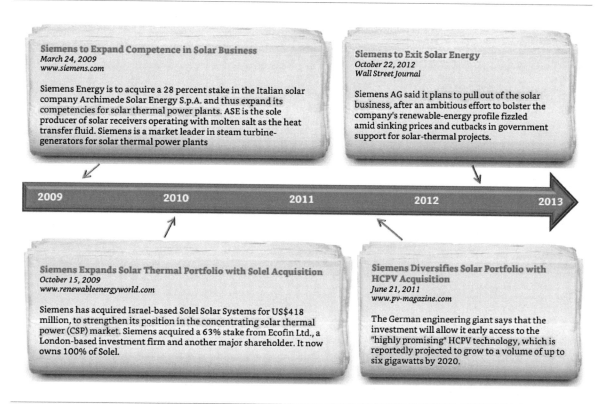

Siemens to Expand Competence in Solar Business
March 24, 2009
www.siemens.com

Siemens Energy is to acquire a 28 percent stake in the Italian solar company Archimede Solar Energy S.p.A. and thus expand its competencies for solar thermal power plants. ASE is the sole producer of solar receivers operating with molten salt as the heat transfer fluid. Siemens is a market leader in steam turbine-generators for solar thermal power plants

Siemens to Exit Solar Energy
October 22, 2012
Wall Street Journal

Siemens AG said it plans to pull out of the solar business, after an ambitious effort to bolster the company's renewable-energy profile fizzled amid sinking prices and cutbacks in government support for solar-thermal projects.

2009   2010   2011   2012   2013

Siemens Expands Solar Thermal Portfolio with Solel Acquisition
October 15, 2009
www.renewableenergyworld.com

Siemens has acquired Israel-based Solel Solar Systems for US$418 million, to strengthen its position in the concentrating solar thermal power (CSP) market. Siemens acquired a 63% stake from Ecofin Ltd., a London-based investment firm and another major shareholder. It now owns 100% of Solel.

Siemens Diversifies Solar Portfolio with HCPV Acquisition
June 21, 2011
www.pv-magazine.com

The German engineering giant says that the investment will allow it early access to the "highly promising" HCPV technology, which is reportedly projected to grow to a volume of up to six gigawatts by 2020.

Source: Sourced above

A Penny Saved is a Penny Earned

There are many areas better judgment could have helped. Less anchoring on relative valuation multiples would have potentially led some investors to pass on the investment or structure a better deal. Less confidence might have driven an investment process to be more focused on all the aspects of the power markets and competing technologies, which might have highlighted hidden risks. The point is *not* that money was lost. This happens all the time as business and investment is about taking risk. Anyone who takes risks for a living knows that many ideas will not work out well no matter how good one's judgment. That said, better decision-making may have helped to avoid losses in some cases and lessen losses in others. An ability to avoid large losses as much as possible is often the difference between a good and a great investor.

Fracking and the Changing Nature of Supply in Oil and Natural Gas

Fracking 101

Historically, much of oil and gas drilling was entirely vertical. Fracking (more properly said, horizontal drilling and hydraulic fracturing) is a new technique that has fundamentally changed oil and natural gas supply. After drilling down vertically, the drill is then turned and moves horizontally through shale rock that contains significant amounts of oil and natural gas trapped in the rocks. Then, the drillers employ hydraulic fracturing which is a method of pushing sand, water and chemicals to bust open countless small fissures in the shale. These openings release the natural gas and oil which then flows to the surface. The result is that a previously unimaginable supply of oil and natural gas is now accessible. Figure 70 highlights the process.

Figure 70: Horizontal Drilling and Hydraulic Fracturing

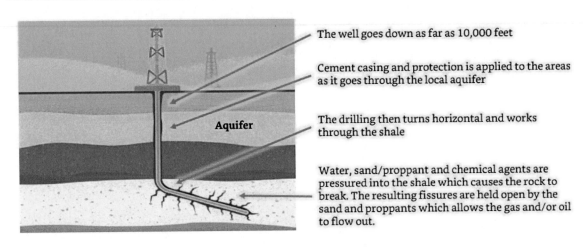

Source: Michael Molnar

The combination of these techniques (called "fracking" or "fraccing" for short), have led to a remarkable resurgence in U.S. oil and gas production. Oil production, on a downward trend since the early 1970s, has spiked to levels not seen in decades. Natural gas production, once flattened out, now has resumed a strong upward trajectory.

Figure 71: U.S. Natural Gas and Oil Production Has Increased a Lot in Recent Years

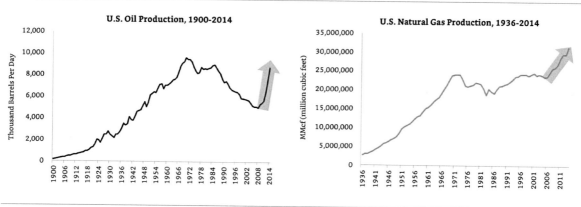

Source: Energy Information Administration (EIA)

There have been many reports indicating that the potential unearthed by this drilling technique is massive as much of the previously unattainable oil and gas in shale is now accessible. The map below shows various shale basins in the U.S. Some are mainly gas, some mainly oil, and many contain both. Maps for many other geographies show similar potential.

Figure 72: Shale Gas and Oil Locations in the U.S.

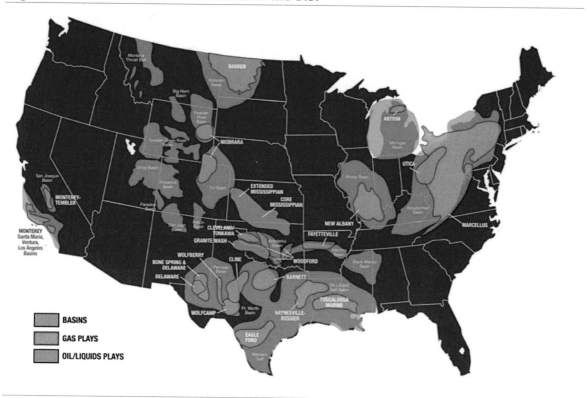

Source: PacWest Consulting Partners

While increased domestic production of oil and natural gas is a positive, there are risks; the most contentious of which relates to contamination of the water supply. Fracking requires drilling through a water aquifer and pumping down millions of gallons of chemicals to break and hold open the shale. While it is true that this occurs far below the aquifer, if the cement casing protecting the aquifer fails, these chemicals and the resulting sludge can leech into the water supply. Given that these drill sites are growing exponentially, there are more possibilities for this to occur each day. In my view, mitigating this risk is a clear area for government regulation to ensure safe drilling. If done well, America stands to benefit from more domestic production with less risk of water contamination.

The Impact of Fracking on the Gas and Oil Supply Dynamic

The potential for shale to help the U.S. become energy independent is discussed in the section following this one. This section discusses what shale technology has done to the dynamic of supply – something arguably just as impactful but much less discussed. It is a great example of a technology that has the potential to fundamentally change the dynamics of supply.

Historically, large amounts of supply could come to market via big discoveries and subsequent development. These were projects that could cost tens of billions of dollars and take years to come online. Once online, they can have producing lives of 20 to 50 years, with production typically peaking anywhere from 0 to 20 years after first output.

Shale is very different. Shale projects can cost $5 million to $20 million per well and can begin producing in 30 days. They have durations of three to six years, and often peak in year one with nearly all production coming out early. The figure below highlights the decline curve for a shale well. In this example, 75% of the total production is generated in year one. After five years, this well is basically done producing.

Figure 73: Mega Projects versus Shale Wells

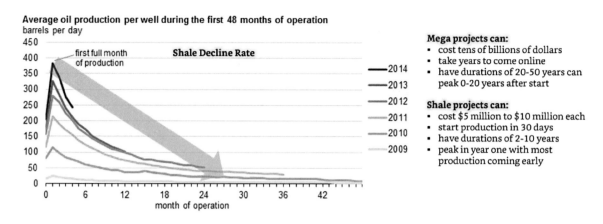

Source: Energy Information Administration

Figure 74, a standard system map of a commodity system, highlights why this matters. There are two time delays that cause price volatility. One is the demand substitution delay where, even if one wants to switch to another fuel or technology, there is often a considerable delay. For example, one has to wait for alternative technology vehicles to come to market if they are not already developed. This dynamic makes the demand response to increasing prices fairly inelastic in the short-term (i.e., not that powerful).

The second delay concerns supply. Finding, commissioning and developing mega-projects takes time. Once projects are developed, they often produce for many years and thus adjustment to changing market conditions was slow. The end result of these supply-and-demand response delays are periods where this is more supply than demand (oversupply) and vice versa (undersupply). These periods happen quite often and result in volatile pricing. As Figure 75 shows, this is exactly what oil and natural gas markets have experienced.

Shale technology has changed the dynamics of supply responses, mainly decreasing time delays to be much shorter. If there is a large amount of oversupply in the market, shale production is *already* coming down naturally as decline rates happen immediately versus trending up for years and *then* down in many mega-projects. During periods of undersupply, shale can bring supply online much quicker, taking 30 days versus many years for mega-projects. The result of these new dynamics of supply should result, all else equal, in lower price volatility as supply will adjust more quickly to market conditions.

Figure 74: Shale Technology Has Fundamentally Changed the Nature of Time Delays

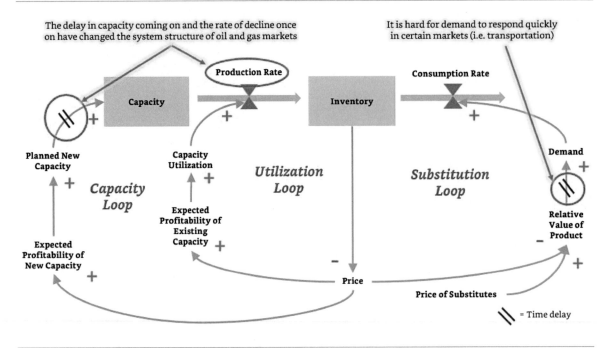

Source: Michael Molnar

Figure 75: Price of Oil and Natural Gas 1990-2015

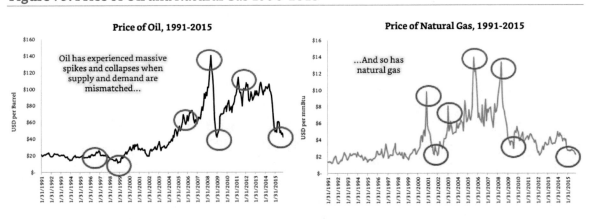

Source: Energy Information Administration

Shale fracking also provides an inherent check on human psychology. Historically, when prices spiked historically, oil and gas executives would **anchor** their views of future economics to the present prices. This would often lead to considerable investment in finding new reserves which, after some delay in developing those reserves, resulted in tremendous supply coming online. Because other macroeconomic factors are changing independent of this activity, this often resulted in supply coming online at just the wrong time. Oversupply and a big decline in prices were the result.

Shale's high decline rates in year one with shorter producing lives mean that a conscious decision to drill a new well has to be made to increase supply. This helps to reduce the risk of both the **endowment effect** and **commitment/consistency bias** where one is biased to over-value something that he or she already owns or previously committed to in the past. Mitigating behavioral biases requires a process of some sort as simple awareness is not enough to counteract the pull. Shale technology's high decline rates have inadvertently built in such a process for executives' decisions on adding or reducing supply.

U.S. Energy Independence – The Challenge and Fracking's Potential

Understanding the Dominance of Internal Combustion Engines (ICE)

As the automobile was gaining initial popularity in the late 1890s and early 1900s, there were gasoline, steam and electric-powered vehicles available. In fact, only 25% of the 4,200 cars produced in 1900 were gasoline-powered because electric and steam had advantages in terms of ease of use, noise and emissions. Gasoline had the advantage of lasting longer distances, but was dirty and unreliable at the time.

In 1901, the discovery of the huge oil field in Spindletop, Texas, was the beginning of a big increase in oil production in the United States. Just a few years later, in 1908, the Model T came to market providing a low-cost gasoline-fueled car available for the masses. These factors, combined with improving roadways (which thus allowed for longer driving distances), led to the start of three reinforcing loops that together created a massive tailwind for ICE engines to dominate for the next 100 years.

- **Fuel Loop:** The market for gasoline in the early 1900s led to additional oil exploration and development as companies recognized the market opportunity. More exploration was done, supply increased, and fuel costs stayed low.

- **Technology Loop:** As more cars were purchased, companies continued to invest in internal combustion engine technology which lead to a continued stream of improvements in efficiency, power and comfort. Therefore, by the time other technologies tried to break into the market, the internal combustion engine already had nearly 100 years of learning and development as a huge head start.

- **Infrastructure Loop:** Similarly, as cars were purchased, the supporting infrastructure was built out. This included the fueling stations across the country as well as the various parts of the supply chain that supplied parts and service.

As both ICE-driven engines and oil demand grew massively, the combination of all of these factors was that the internal combustion engine continued to grow in value (see Figure 76). Electric vehicles would not be a material risk to ICE dominance for the next 100 years.

Figure 76: Critical Reinforcing Loops Support the Internal Combustion Engine Dominance

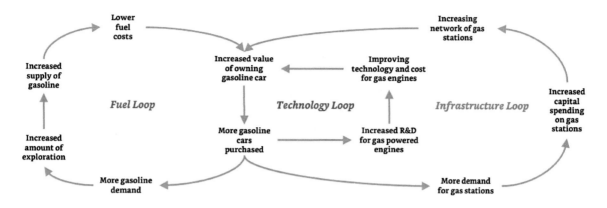

Three loops were all reinforcing one another – fuel infrastructure, technology and fuel cost. They all hinged on increasing the value of owning a gasoline car, which led to more gasoline-powered cars being purchased, which drove the feedback.

Source: Michael Molnar

This system dynamic was helpful for much of the 20th century as ICE engines allowed for relatively inexpensive transportation for more and more Americans. However, beginning in the late 1960s, U.S. oil production could not meet demand. Imports filled the gap and continued to grow in line with U.S. demand.

Figure 77: Americans Got Hooked on Oil, But Then Could Not Produce Enough Domestically

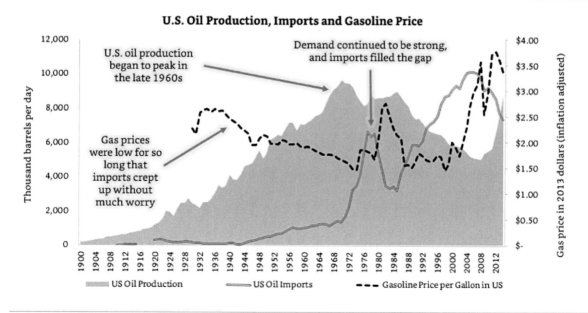

Source: Energy Information Administration

The Arab Oil Embargo of 1973 was a clear wake-up call to the risk of dependence on imports (see page 13). Since that oil crisis in the early 1970s, every U.S. President has made "energy independence" a key goal. Yet, all have failed.

Figure 78: Energy Independence Has Been a Goal of Each President Since Nixon

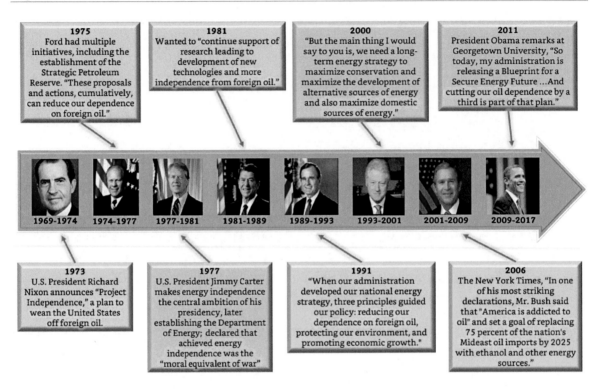

Source: Grist.org; Foreign Policy magazine; CanaryUSA; Reason.com; The New York Times; The Daily Show with Jon Stewart; Google Images

The challenge for new technologies or competing fuels to compete with such dynamics is intense. In system dynamics terms, the system is "path dependent" given the value of the internal combustion engine and the barriers to change (see page 37). There are also a set of large, powerful and economically sensitive interests that have no desire in seeing the system change, another barrier.

Fracking's Potential to Make the U.S. Energy Independent

One obvious strategy to become less dependent on foreign oil is to produce more domestically. Until recently, this has not been a viable option as oil production peaked decades ago. However, shale-drilling techniques have changed the potential for U.S. production of oil and natural gas in material ways. The increased production has driven down the amount of oil imported to levels not seen in decades.

Figure 79: Increased Production Has Made the U.S. Less Dependent on Foreign Oil

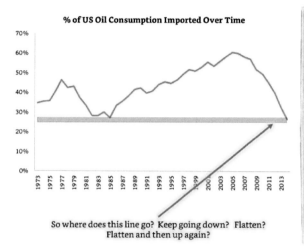

% of US Oil Consumption Imported Over Time

So where does this line go? Keep going down? Flatten?
Flatten and then up again?

How much petroleum does the United States import and from where? (per the EIA Website)

The United States imported approximately 9 million barrels per day (MMb/d) of petroleum in 2014 from about 75 countries. Petroleum includes crude oil, natural gas plant liquids, liquefied refinery gases, refined petroleum products such as gasoline and diesel fuel, and biofuels including ethanol and biodiesel. In 2014, about 80% of gross petroleum imports were crude oil, and about 46% of the crude oil that was processed in U.S. refineries was imported.

The United States exported about 4 MMb/d of crude oil and petroleum products in 2014, resulting in net imports (imports minus exports) of about 5 MMb/d in 2014. Net imports accounted for 27% of the petroleum consumed in the United States, the lowest annual average since 1985.

The top five source countries of U.S. petroleum imports in 2014 were Canada, Saudi Arabia, Mexico, Venezuela, and Iraq. The country rankings vary based on gross petroleum imports or net petroleum imports (gross imports minus exports).

Source: Energy Information Administration

To evaluate the potential for U.S. energy independence from producing more oil, it is imperative to understand some of the key data and definitions first. The charts below contain the latest EIA data for natural gas and oil for the following:

- U.S. production and reserves

- Worldwide reserves

- Worldwide consumption by country along with growth rates

- Calculations of years of proved reserves and total technically recoverable reserves

The definition of reserves is important to understand as it is critical data to understanding the future potential. It is subjective as one needs to estimate the amount of the resource that is physically there and what can be economically extracted. For $25/barrel, there is a lot less oil that can be extracted economically than if oil was $150/barrel, for example. So reserves are a moving target based on these estimates and technological improvements. The EIA definition of "proved reserves" is as follows:

> *Proved reserves are estimated volumes of hydrocarbon resources that analysis of geologic and engineering data demonstrates with reasonable certainty are recoverable under existing economic and operating conditions. Reserves estimates*

change from year to year as new discoveries are made, as existing fields are more thoroughly appraised, as existing reserves are produced, and as prices and technologies change.

Revisions primarily occur when operators change their estimates of what they will be able to produce from the properties they operate in response to changing prices or improvements in technology. Higher fuel prices typically increase estimates (positive revisions) as operators consider a broader portion of the resource base economically producible, or proved. Lower prices, on the other hand, generally reduce estimates (negative revisions) as the economically producible base diminishes.

Beyond this, there are "technically recoverable resources" (TRR), which are resources that could be extracted but with considerable more uncertainty as to "if" and at "what" cost. Basically, we think it is there, but really do not know the cost to get to them.

There are several takeaways from looking at the oil data in Figure 80:

- **U.S. Oil Production Trending Sharply Upwards:** U.S oil production had been steadily declining since the early 1970s. However, the increase due to shale drilling techniques has been remarkable. Production has gone from 5 million barrels per day in 2008 to 8.7 million by 2014.

- **U.S. Reserve Estimates Trending Up:** Seeing data on reserves shows just how volatile these estimates are as well. As one would expect, the trend has been up sharply as shale drilling has made these areas of the country economical to drill.

- **U.S. Consumption and Reserves:** The U.S. consumes 21% of total world oil demand, but only has 2% of the reserves. One can merely look at the list of where resources are – Venezuela, Saudi Arabia, Iran, Russia – to see why energy security is very important. China's oil demand growth has been impressive, with a 6.5% CAGR compound over the past 10 years, which is in line with GDP growth as one would expect. U.S. demand has actually declined.

- **Years of Reserves Highlights the Uncertainty of TTRR:** Comparing U.S consumption (2013 levels) to proven reserve estimates and total technically recoverable resources (TTRR) yields a shorthand measure of reserves called "years of reserves." This helps to understand, at current consumption, how many years of reserves are available. The U.S. has five years of proved reserves and 38 years of TTRR.

Figure 80: Key Data on World Oil Markets

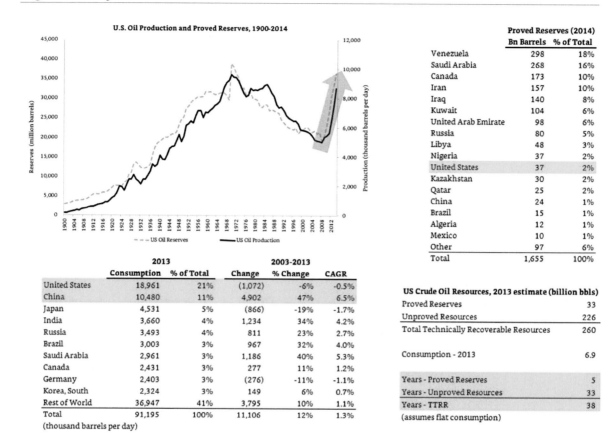

	2013		2003-2013		
	Consumption	% of Total	Change	% Change	CAGR
United States	18,961	21%	(1,072)	-6%	-0.5%
China	10,480	11%	4,902	47%	6.5%
Japan	4,531	5%	(866)	-19%	-1.7%
India	3,660	4%	1,234	34%	4.2%
Russia	3,493	4%	811	23%	2.7%
Brazil	3,003	3%	967	32%	4.0%
Saudi Arabia	2,961	3%	1,186	40%	5.3%
Canada	2,431	3%	277	11%	1.2%
Germany	2,403	3%	(276)	-11%	-1.1%
Korea, South	2,324	3%	149	6%	0.7%
Rest of World	36,947	41%	3,795	10%	1.1%
Total	91,195	100%	11,106	12%	1.3%

(thousand barrels per day)

Proved Reserves (2014)

	Bn Barrels	% of Total
Venezuela	298	18%
Saudi Arabia	268	16%
Canada	173	10%
Iran	157	10%
Iraq	140	8%
Kuwait	104	6%
United Arab Emirate	98	6%
Russia	80	5%
Libya	48	3%
Nigeria	37	2%
United States	37	2%
Kazakhstan	30	2%
Qatar	25	2%
China	24	1%
Brazil	15	1%
Algeria	12	1%
Mexico	10	1%
Other	97	6%
Total	1,655	100%

US Crude Oil Resources, 2013 estimate (billion bbls)

Proved Reserves	33
Unproved Resources	226
Total Technically Recoverable Resources	260
Consumption - 2013	6.9
Years - Proved Reserves	5
Years - Unproved Resources	33
Years - TTRR	38

(assumes flat consumption)

Source: Energy Information Administration

Doing the same analysis on natural gas yields different insights:

- **U.S. Natural Gas Production Trending Sharply Upwards:** U.S natural gas production never declined in such a way as oil had, but it was flat for some time. Shale drilling, however, has driven up production of gas sharply to new highs.

- **U.S. Reserve Estimates Trending Up:** Estimating natural gas reserves are no easier than oil and the takeaways are similar. There has been considerable volatility in the estimate and it has trended up sharply with the potential for shale drilling to uncover more previously inaccessible natural gas.

- **U.S. Consumption and Reserve Data:** The U.S. consumes 22% of total world oil demand with about 5% of world reserves. While those higher in the list are not necessarily friendly to the U.S. (Russia, Iran), the U.S. does not face a security risk in this area given it is self-sufficient in meeting its demand. As opposed to oil demand, natural gas demand has been growing in the U.S. For China, growth is very strong off an admittedly smaller base.

- **Years of reserves highlights the uncertainty of TTRR:** The U.S. has considerably more potential based on current estimates for natural gas versus oil. It has 12 years of proved reserves and 87 years of total technically recoverable resources (TTRR).

Figure 81: Key Data on World Natural Gas Markets

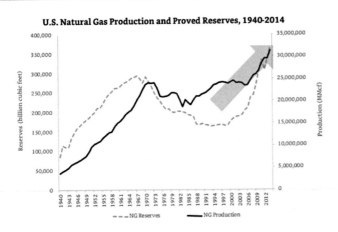

U.S. Natural Gas Production and Proved Reserves, 1940-2014

--- NG Reserves   — NG Production

	2013		**2003-2013**		
	Consumption	% of Total	Change	% Change	CAGR
United States	26,168	22%	3,891	15%	1.6%
Russia	15,599	13%	1,395	9%	0.9%
China	5,760	5%	4,617	80%	17.5%
Iran	5,556	5%	2,646	48%	6.7%
Japan	4,492	4%	1,393	31%	3.8%
Canada	3,655	3%	282	8%	0.8%
Saudi Arabia	3,533	3%	1,412	40%	5.2%
Germany	3,123	3%	(37)	-1%	-0.1%
United Kingdom	2,735	2%	(624)	-23%	-2.0%
Italy	2,474	2%	(269)	-11%	-1.0%
Rest of World	48,262	40%	15,458	32%	3.9%
Total	121,357	100%	30,162	25%	2.9%
(billion cubic feet)					

	Proved Reserves (2014)	
	Tcf	% of total
Russia	1,688	24%
Iran	1,193	17%
Qatar	885	13%
United States	338	5%
Saudi Arabia	291	4%
Turkmenistan	265	4%
United Arab Emirates	215	3%
Venezuela	196	3%
Nigeria	181	3%
Algeria	159	2%
China	155	2%
Europe	136	2%
Iraq	112	2%
Indonesia	105	2%
Rest of World	1,053	15%
World	6,973	100%
(tcf = trillion cubic feet)		

US Natural Gas Resources, 2013 estimate (trillion cubic feet)	
Proved Reserves	308
Unproved Resources	1,968
Total Technically Recoverable Resources	2,277
Consumption - 2013	26.1
Years - Proved Reserves	12
Years - Unproved Resources	75
Years - TTRR	87
(assumes flat consumption)	

Source: Energy Information Administration

Reasons to be Hopeful but Also Cautious

On the positive side, there is clearly much more potential for oil and natural gas in the U.S. than there was five or 10 years ago. Given is still relatively early, there are likely further improvements in shale-drilling techniques and thus potential for lower cost extraction of more-than-expected resources. These cycles of learnings (self-reinforcing loops) early on in a technology's development can lead to positive surprises.

Yet, there are some reasons to be cautious. The rate declines previously discussed means lots of wells have to be drilled to continue to grow supply. This, in and of itself, is not disastrous as it is the total amount of resource that can be found that is important, not the number of wells that have to be drilled. However, exponential growth in drilling is subject to constraints as we discussed. Just how many wells can be drilled in the U.S. and, more specifically, what might the side effects be? It is daunting to think of that number 30, 40 or 50 years out in order to continue to grow supply. Risks to aquifers would increase as the number of wells drilled increase.

Psychologically, there is also a risk that bad decisions are made as we **anchor** to a single, very uncertain number. For example, in February 2013, President Obama commented, "We have a supply of natural gas that can last America nearly 100 years. And my administration will take every possible action to safely develop this energy." This is not illogical, but one needs to appropriately understand the uncertainty associated with that number. As shown in the articles below, the revisions of estimated reserves declined by as much as 50% in certain regions, highlighting the uncertainty involved.

Figure 82: Reasons to be Cautious About Unproven Resources

Energy Information Administration
Estimates of technically recoverable resources are highly uncertain, particularly in emerging plays where few wells have been drilled. Early estimates tend to vary and shift significantly over time as new geological information is gained through additional drilling, as long-term productivity is clarified for existing wells, and as the productivity of new wells increases with technology improvements and better management practices.

Natural Geographic – February 2012
The 2011 estimate figured "unproved reserves" in the Marcellus were 410 tcf, but the new estimate plummeted by two-thirds, to 141 tcf. In the "core area" of the Marcellus—where most of drilling activity has taken place so far—the EIA had assumed before that each well would, in time, produce 3.5 billion cubic feet of gas. But with new data on how much gas wells have produced to date, the EIA's calculation came out lower, with each well expected to produce about 2 billion cubic feet, a drop of about 40 percent.

Excerpts from: "There's no way to tell" how much gas the US can produce – E&E, February 2013
"We think the resource is vast," said John Staub, who heads the oil and gas estimates team for the Energy Information Administration. But estimates of shale gas resources and reserves are still based on a small sample of actual wells. A year ago, EIA dropped its estimate of "unproved technically recoverable resource" for shale gas to 482 tcf, from the year-before estimate of 827 tcf.

...the size and shape of the shale formations is among the longest-studied and best-defined variables, said Coleman's colleague, Charpentier. "You can tell where the shale is, and isn't," he said. There is much less certainty on other issues, such as estimating how much of the Marcellus gas or oil is concentrated in prime exploration zones called "sweet spots," versus less potentially productive areas. The low estimate for the hydrocarbons in sweet spots is 10 percent, the high 75 percent.

Source: Cited above

For those extremely confident in the potential for U.S. shale, the United Kingdom's experience with the discovery of oil in the North Sea in the 1970s is a lesson worth remembering. The North Sea discoveries were deemed "game-changing" by many at the time. The discoveries led to huge capital investments which took U.K. oil production from zero to three million barrels per day in just a few years. The U.K. shifted from being an oil importer to an exporter. However, as often happens, situations change. As the chart below shows, oil production flattened out and then started to decline. Just several years, later, the U.K shifted back to an importer.

Figure 83: The U.K. Example: From Importer to Exporter, Back to Importer

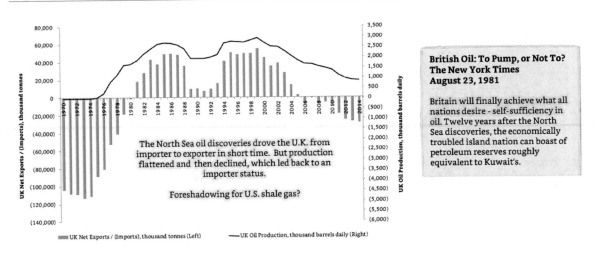

Source: DECC; EIA; The New York Times

The point of mentioning this story is not to say that the U.S. shale revolution cannot continue to trend up as there is a good probability that it does. Shale has provided the U.S. with its best shot at energy security in decades. However, the reality is that correctly assessing the amount of resource extractable at specific costs relative to other resources around the world is very difficult. Side effects, especially around water contamination, from drilling so many wells are equally challenging to predict.

It is very easy to envision a situation where supply flattens for whatever reason and the U.S. import trend reverses. Equally easy to imagine are scenarios where side effects of the exponential growth in wells end up being more problematic than some expect. If either of these happen, the shale revolution will simply have created another time delay in the necessary revolution in transportation that the U.S. needs.

Electric Vehicles and Windows of Opportunity

The Saudi Strategy to Keep the U.S. Addicted to Oil

There are two ways to mitigate the risk of oil imports.

1. **Produce More Oil:** Producing more oil was deemed an obvious but irrational strategy until shale-drilling techniques opened up new sources of oil in the U.S. See the prior section for this discussion.

2. **Use a Fuel Source Other Than Oil:** There are other ways to power vehicles such as fuel cells, electricity or natural gas. If these fuels are produced domestically, the risk is mitigated.

The Saudis, as the largest and marginal supplier of oil in the world, have had a clear strategy to keep the U.S. path-dependent on using oil as the main fuel for transportation: Keep the price of oil consistent and low. Their strategy is smart in preventing the system from changing based on the dynamics and judgments involved:

- **Prevent Substitution Loop from Scaling:** The strategy is intentionally attempting to prevent the substitution loop from taking hold. While the Saudis would make more money in the near term if the price of oil was higher, they recognize the potential negative dynamics it could create for them long-term. A higher oil price would increase the relative value of other fuels and technologies, which would begin to entice investment and research in order to exploit the market opportunity. If this continued, the potential for competing technologies and fuels to decline in cost was higher and the self-reinforcing loop could continue.

- **Anchoring, Availability and Hyperbolic Discounting Biases:** The Saudi strategy also recognizes several biases of people. First, people anchor their view to the current price so if the price is low, most people view the price as likely to stay low and vice versa. Second, high prices stimulate the availability bias as older people remember the oil crisis of the 1970s and the media begins to report on the risks to high prices on the economy and our security. Finally, hyperbolic discounting – over-valuing today versus tomorrow – is at work as well. When prices are low, people overvalue any change that could cause prices today to increase, even if long-term it makes much more sense.

The net effect of the strategy of low and consistent prices set by Saudi Arabia has been very effective so far in preventing other technologies from ramping.

Figure 84: Saudi Strategy to Maintain Oil Dominance for Transportation

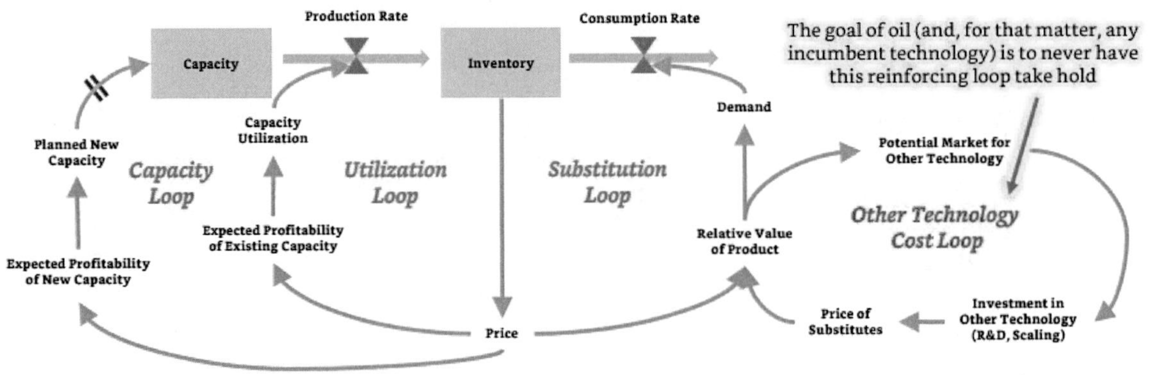

The goal of oil (and, for that matter, any incumbent technology) is to never have this reinforcing loop take hold

Source: Michael Molnar

Fuel Cells Provide a Case Study with a Tough Ending

Fuel-cell vehicles in the early 2000s and electric vehicles today provide interesting case studies to understand the challenge and opportunity in breaking oil's grip on transportation. Both fuel cells and electric vehicles garnered significant interest during their initial push. Ballard Power Systems, one of the companies with technology critical to the fuel-cell market in the late 1990s, saw its market capitalization rise from just a couple hundred million to $10 billion in a short amount of time (over $15 billion in 2015 dollars). Tesla, Elon Musk's electric vehicle company, has seen an even more dramatic ramp in valuation, to $30 billion.

While these companies operated during different time periods, there were several similarities in the environment. The price of oil, and thus gasoline, had either increased or stayed high. For Ballard, the price of oil doubled from $15/barrel to $30/barrel. For Tesla, the price of oil stayed at $100/barrel during much of its initial ramp. Additionally, both companies experienced the positive tailwind of a government focus on energy security as U.S. oil imports were perceived as a risk to national security. Finally, the stock market was very strong in the U.S. during these times, which is critical as the auto industry is a capital-intensive business and having access to the markets to fund plans is important.

Figure 85: Tesla and Ballard Power Systems Market Capitalization

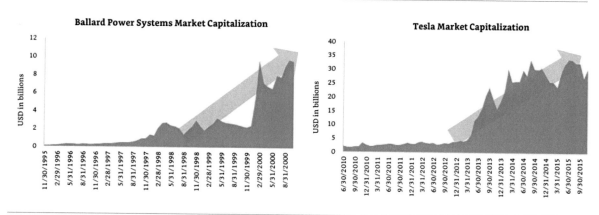

Source: Bloomberg

Figure 86: The Up Cycle - Oil Prices, Stock Prices and Market Valuation

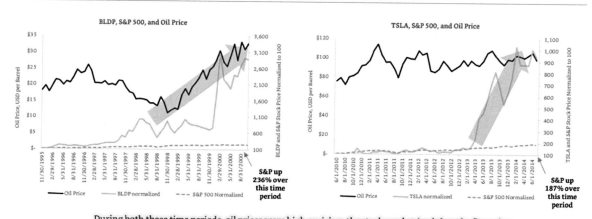

During both these time periods, oil prices were high or rising, the stock market (and thus the financing potential for capital-intensive businesses) was strong and the share prices traded higher

Source: Bloomberg

Fuel-cell companies' goal to disrupt the auto market came to an abrupt end for several reasons. First, stock market valuations crashed as the tech bubble burst from 2001 to 2002. The economic correction reduced demand, driving oil prices lower. Ballard and other fuel-cell companies never were able to scale to bring costs materially down, and were thus left in a position where oil was cheap and their costs were still high. They needed capital to scale operations but the capital markets were now closed, or at least only open at a very high cost.

Their business never ramped and the equity value sold off tremendously, from $10 billion to less than $500 million in a short amount of time.

Figure 87: The Down Cycle - Oil Prices, Stock Prices and Market Valuation

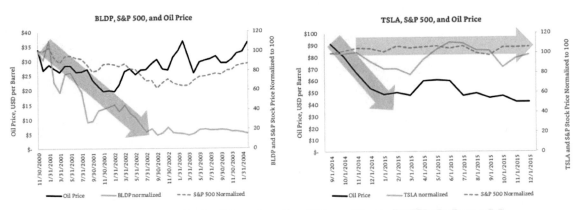

For Ballard, oil prices declined and the market collapsed; they could not scale within the time needed.
Tesla has just encountered a massive decline in oil, but the market is still strong. The next chapter here is yet to be written.

Source: Bloomberg

Electric Vehicles: Key for Success, Risks, and Positives Trends

Will Tesla and other electric vehicle manufacturers meet a similar fate as Ballard? The next chapter in the Tesla story is still to be finalized, but the fuel-cell case study has two important learnings.

- **Key is to Get Reinforcing Loops Moving Your Way:** Breaking the stronghold that internal combustion engines have on transportation requires getting the reinforcing loops of fuel, technology and infrastructure ramping. This is a "chicken-and-egg" problem as the loops begin to ramp as demand forms, but until they ramp, demand can be hard to find.

- **Exogenous Factors Can Prevent This, So Speed is Important:** To get these loops ramping, one needs certain exogenous factors to be in your favor. Specifically, it is helpful to have high oil prices, fears related to energy security robust, and a strong stock market providing access to inexpensive capital. These factors are out of any one company's control and thus speed is critical, as these tailwinds can turn into headwinds as the business cycle changes.

This is exactly what happened to fuel cells, which unfortunately never had the chance to ramp these feedback loops in their favor. The entire system turned the other way and fuel cells fell by the wayside. What makes these factors particularly risky are that they can shift in a highly correlated manner. An economic shock will hurt oil demand, lower oil prices and thus improve the economics of ICE technology. Also, it is likely that energy security fears lessen and capital markets are weak. All of these are problematic for new companies trying to unseat an incumbent.

Each situation is different, but Tesla currently faces two clear risks. The first risk is related to a large decline in the price of oil. This has made ICE engines very economic relative to when oil was higher. Second, the shale boom in the U.S. has many believing energy security is possible in a few years via producing more oil versus changing how we power automobiles. This presents a headwind for some consumer demand and government support. These situations can change but people and policymakers often have skewed judgment related to the present given the anchoring and availability biases which should never be underestimated.

That being said, Tesla has done a good job of stimulating its reinforcing loops and has achieved a level of scale that fuel cells never did. There are several positives in place for them currently:

- **Raised a Lot of Inexpensive Capital During a Boom Stock Market:** Tesla has raised a huge amount of capital during the booming stock market from 2010 to 2015. Upcycles do not last forever, but the company has taken advantage of the opportunity the capital markets have presented.

- **Tapped Emotions with First Car (Roadster):** Tesla had a smart strategy to initially scale with more than just an economic case of their car's cost versus a gasoline engine. The roadster was "cool" and people were buying into a brand as much as an economic case. This allowed for revenue to ramp which presented the opportunity to scale operations and invest more in research.

- **Infrastructure Buildout Has Begun:** Tesla built out an initial framework of the fueling infrastructure as it recognized that it had to solve this "chicken-and-egg" problem to some degree first. It built on sales momentum by subsequently launching its own "fueling" factory – the gigafactory – and recruited some key corporate partners. It is common knowledge that companies should focus on their areas of competence only. This is usually true but there are times when companies have to get these dynamics moving first and *then* find partners.

- **Environmental Benefits Likely Valued More Than in the Past:** The environmental benefits are likely to be valued more today given the increasing consensus that climate change is a real problem. This can help mitigate the reduced risk of oil imports as U.S. shale supply increases.

- **The "Enemy of Your Enemy" is Your Friend – and a Potentially Powerful Ally:** The electric power industry is salivating over the opportunity for electricity demand if electric cars take off. Electricity demand is currently anemic, due the maturity of the market. Also, distributed solar power is driving individuals to generate their own power and efficiency regulations are allowing people to do more with less power – two more risks. The potential new demand from electric vehicles is perhaps the only upside demand boost for utilities. As the Acid Rain Program success showed, when trying to create change, there are times the "enemy of your enemy" is your friend. Electric vehicles pose a clear threat to oil companies and the related products. Having an industry that is nearly as powerful – the U.S. utility industry – backing this disruption can go a long way. The fuel-cell industry had no such ally. See Figure 89.

In short, Tesla has effectively stimulated the technology, infrastructure and fueling reinforcing loops. However, as shown below, the potential for exogenous factors to crimp this dynamic is a considerable risk. While they are executing well given the window of opportunity presented to them, uncontrollable market conditions can change fast and materially impact the dynamics for the worse.

Figure 88: There are Many Vital Parts of the System that are Not in Management's Control

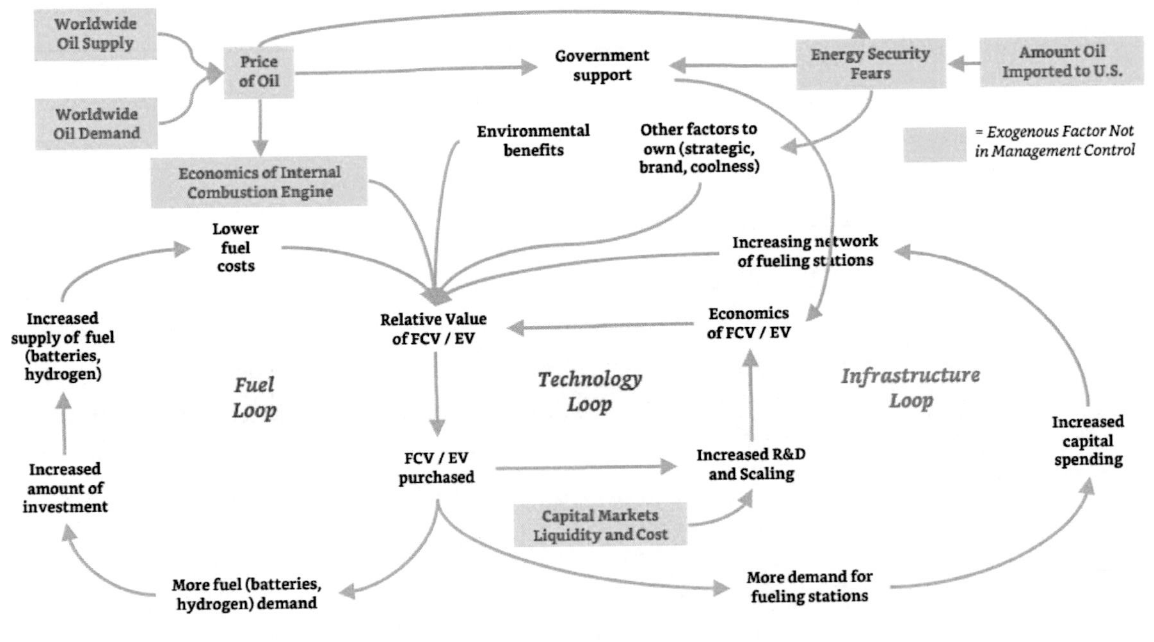

Source: Michael Molnar

Figure 89: Utilities See Electric Vehicles as a Major Source of Growth

Utility Industry: We Need to Promote Electric Vehicles in Order to 'Remain Viable'
Facing flat or declining electricity sales, electric vehicles are a path to growth for power companies.
July 30, 2014
Greentech Media

The Edison Electric Institute, the power industry's main trade group, is calling on utilities to better promote electric cars in order to stimulate demand for electricity and help reverse trends that threaten the long-term viability of some in the industry.

11. Conclusion

The bottom line is that the electric utility industry needs the electrification of the transportation sector to remain viable and sustainable in the long term. While the market has started moving in this direction and the technology has been proven, there is still more to be done. Without active engagement, we may not realize the many benefits that could be derived from widespread electric-based transportation. We must continue to innovate, invest and work closely with regulators, automakers, and other partners to develop policies and best practices that will allow electric transportation to flourish. Electrifying our own fleets is an important first step in moving the industry forward. The Edison Electric Institute in partnership with and on behalf of its member companies is requesting each member utility to dedicate 5% of its annual fleet purchase plan to plug-in vehicles. In many applications, this choice already makes economic sense. The 5% ask is a starting point. It is an investment in the future of our business. We must lead by example—showing our customers the benefits and possibilities of making the switch.

Source: Edison Electric Institute, Transportation Electrification – Utility Fleets Leading the Charge, June 2014

Source: Cited Above

Wait a Minute, Doesn't the Best Technology Always Win?

The discussion here has focused on the system dynamics necessary for success and the risks that changing non-controllable market conditions present. Intentionally excluded is a debate as to whether fuel cells and/or electric vehicles face some sort of technological limit or fault. That is clearly part of the analysis one would need to undertake if investing capital or running such a business. Understanding both the technology and system dynamics are needed, yet in my experience, much too little attention has been given to the latter.

One way to look at this issue is the following. Flawed technology will fail if it gets to the point of scaling and reinforcing loops take hold. By definition, there is a technical problem and eventually that will doom its success. However, while superior technology can succeed if those loops are working in its favor, it will likely fail if they are not. *In short, good technology has a better chance of winning, but by no means is it guaranteed – especially if the dynamics of the system are working against it.* Managements and investors need to recognize this dynamic and ensure their business plans are sufficient to get the system working for them before outside factors potentially work against them.

Decoding Business Cycles and Business Models

The success or failure of a company is dependent on many factors. Two factors that have, at times, caused massive success and horrific failures are discussed: the boom-bust cycle and risks to specific business models.

All business is cyclical, waxing and waning as general macroeconomic conditions change. **Boom-bust cycles** are different, however. Characterized by huge positive momentum followed by a sharp crash, they are industry-specific and driven by unique dynamics and psychological factors. While hard to anticipate, they consistently occur. Power generation is one example highlighted here, but the learnings are applicable to countless other industries.

Business models, essentially how a company makes money, are different. While there are countless business models in energy, this section focuses on two timely ones. **The utility death spiral** describes a situation where a long-existing and stable business model faces pressure given self-reinforcing feedback occurring *outside* the core business. Next, the dynamics of **the yieldco model**, where the model *itself* is self-reinforcing in nature, is evaluated. This reinforcing dynamic can be either a headwind or a tailwind and presents a unique challenge.

Time Delays, Skewed Judgment and Boom-Bust Cycles

Utilities 101

All business is cyclical, meaning that it fluctuates up and down with the general business cycle. However, in many areas of the energy world, there is severe cyclicality given time delays, capital expenditures fueled by debt, and judgment of market participants that is often very myopic and anchored to the current operating environment. The result: Great booms followed by terrific busts.

The electric utility industry is a complicated web of local markets and regulatory structures whose goal is fairly simple: provide low-cost and reliable electricity to homes and businesses. While each market is structured a bit differently, there are certain core concepts that are important to understand. On the supply side of power, each market has some mix of generating capacity such as natural gas, coal, nuclear, hydropower, wind and solar. Some of these are sources are baseload power, which means they are always operating, such as nuclear power. Others are intermittent in nature, such as wind and solar, that only produce power when the wind blows or the sun shines.

There are two types of generators involved – regulated utilities and independent power producers (IPPs). Regulated utilities are granted a regulated rate of return by the local regulator on the capital they spend. This then allows them to charge a certain rate to their customers per unit of electricity used. IPPs build capacity that is subject to market rates. So when market rates are increasing, then IPPs can make significant profits (all else equal). However, when rates go down their business is worse off.

On the demand side, the key drivers are population growth, wealth per capita, efficiency, and economic growth. As populations grow either in absolute numbers or in wealth per capita, the demand for electricity typically grows. As GDP and the economy grows, power demand tends to grow with it. On the flip side, efficiency reduces demand as technologies such as LED lighting use significantly less power to do the same amount of work.

Figure 90: High Level Mental Map of the U.S. Power Market

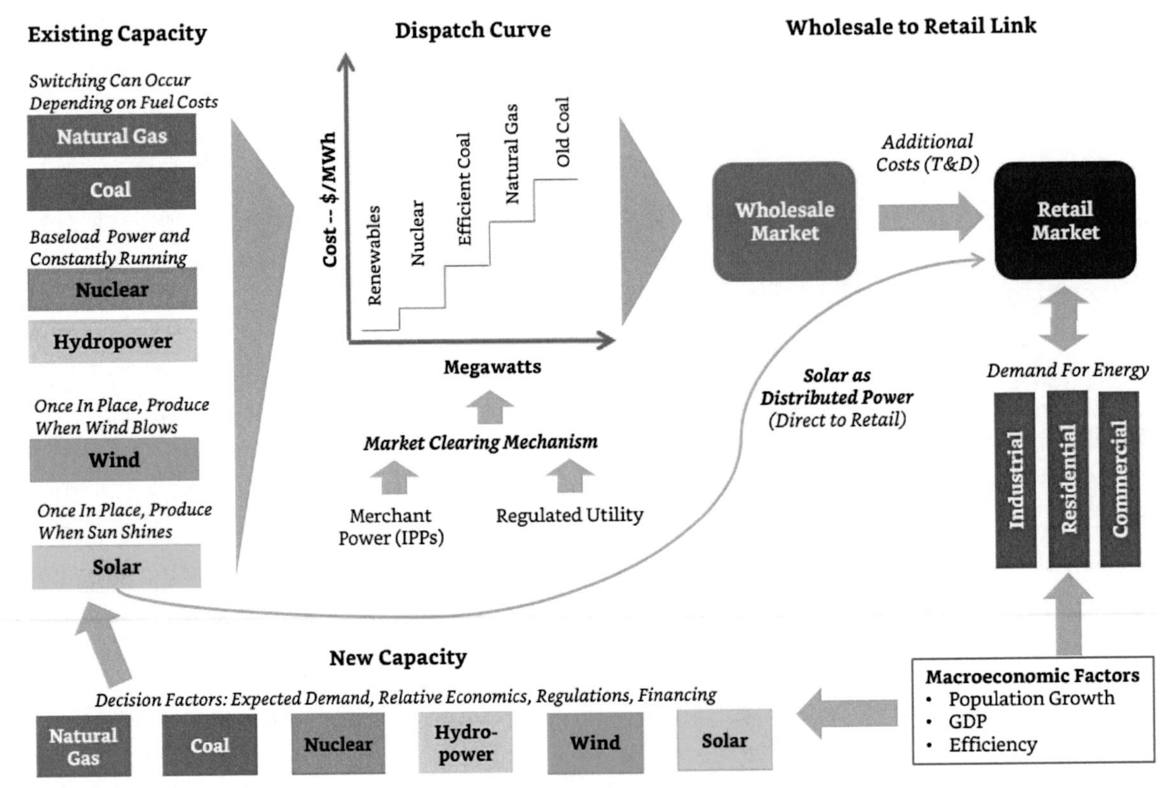

Existing Capacity

Switching Can Occur Depending on Fuel Costs
- Natural Gas
- Coal

Baseload Power and Constantly Running
- Nuclear
- Hydropower

Once In Place, Produce When Wind Blows
- Wind

Once In Place, Produce When Sun Shines
- Solar

Dispatch Curve

Cost -- $/MWh

Renewables | Nuclear | Efficient Coal | Natural Gas | Old Coal

Megawatts

Market Clearing Mechanism

Merchant Power (IPPs) | Regulated Utility

Wholesale to Retail Link

Additional Costs (T&D)

Wholesale Market → Retail Market

Solar as Distributed Power (Direct to Retail)

Demand For Energy

Industrial | Residential | Commercial

New Capacity

Decision Factors: Expected Demand, Relative Economics, Regulations, Financing

Natural Gas | Coal | Nuclear | Hydro-power | Wind | Solar

Macroeconomic Factors
- Population Growth
- GDP
- Efficiency

Source: Michael Molnar

Boom-Bust Dynamics

The IPPs are subject to boom-bust cycles. As they make money on the spread between the market price of electricity and their cost to generate it, their model is subject to variables not all under their control. It is a classic situation where not understanding the system dynamics and having judgment skewed by various biases can lead to massive business failures.

Typically, the cycle starts with new generation being built out. This is a judgment call by the companies involved based on the estimated demand for electricity and their view on the profit of building that capacity. If that looks promising, capital is spent and power generation facilities are built. Importantly, this takes time. This time delay – which can be several months to multiple years – is a risky situation as that asset is often coming online to an unanticipated future. New capacity can cost billions of dollars and take years to come online before it begins to generate cash flows for the utility.

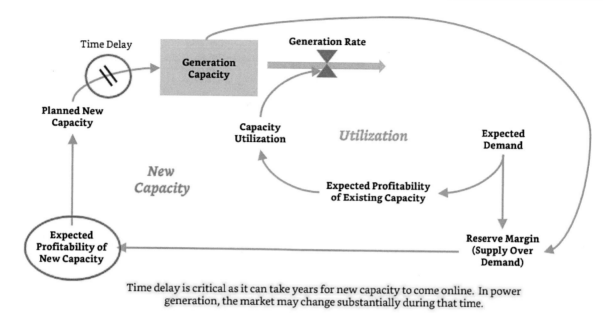

Time delay is critical as it can take years for new capacity to come online. In power generation, the market may change substantially during that time.

Source: Michael Molnar

The result of this dynamic is a boom cycle. When times are good, companies build capacity given the anticipated profits to be achieved. As market conditions are always subject to change, various assumptions inevitably prove incorrect. When the increases in capacity are fueled with excessive debt, companies can face dire situations as the cycle turns.

The Calpine Example

An example can help to bring the boom-bust cycle concept to life. Calpine was an IPP that was doing incredibly well during 1999 to 2000 as power demand was strong, deregulation was taking place, Calpine's expansion plan seemed to be working and its financials were improving. The market took notice with Calpine's stock price rising from less than $10/share to over $50/share. As shown below in their 10K filings at the time, business was strong and it was on track for more growth. The company did highlight the risk of its increasing debt load, but most investors saw that as a distant risk given the current state of the business.

Figure 92: Select Excerpts from Calpine's 1999 10K Annual Filing

THE MARKET

There is a significant need for additional power generating capacity throughout the United States, both to satisfy increasing demand, as well as to replace old and inefficient generating facilities. Due to environmental and economic considerations, we believe this new capacity will be provided predominantly by gas-fired facilities. We believe that these market trends will create substantial opportunities for efficient, low-cost power producers that can produce and sell energy to customers at competitive rates.

OUR STRATEGY

Our strategy is to continue our rapid growth by capitalizing on the significant opportunities in the power industry, primarily through our active development and acquisition programs.

RISK FACTOR

We have substantial indebtedness that we may be unable to service and that restricts our activities. We have substantial debt that we incurred to finance the acquisition and development of power generation facilities. As of December 31, 1999, our total consolidated indebtedness was $2.1 billion, our total consolidated assets were $4.0 billion and our stockholders' equity was $964.6 million. Whether we will be able to meet our debt service obligations and to repay our outstanding indebtedness will be dependent primarily upon the performance of our power generation facilities. This high level of indebtedness has important consequences, including:

- limiting our ability to borrow additional amounts for working capital, capital expenditures, debt service requirements, execution of our growth strategy, or other purposes
- limiting our ability to use operating cash flow in other areas of our business because we must dedicate a substantial portion of these funds to service the debt
- increasing our vulnerability to general adverse economic and industry conditions
- limiting our ability to capitalize on business opportunities and to react to competitive pressures and adverse changes in government regulation.

Source: SEC filings

Unfortunately for Calpine, competitors noticed similar market opportunities and developed similar expansion plans. As shown in Figure 93, capacity additions were 30 to 60 gigawatts per year from 2000 to 2003 but had been averaging only five to 10 gigawatts in the years preceding these additions.

Figure 93: A Huge Amount of Capacity Was Added in the U.S. from 2000-2003

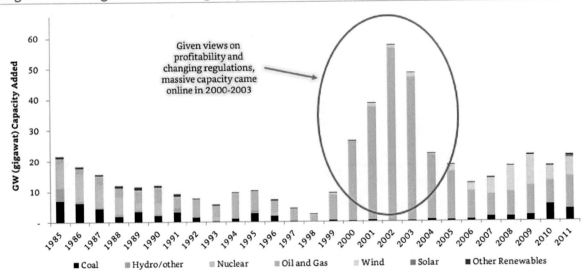

Source: Energy Information Administration

The world changed as the U.S. tech bubble burst in the early 2000s. The U.S. economy was weak and entering a recession which drove power demand lower. For a period of time, natural gas prices were rising just as demand got weak. This exacerbated the pain as costs increased just as demand was weakening. Worse yet, the looming supply that had been built out in prior years was starting to come online as well.

All these factors resulted in Calpine having higher costs and lower revenues. That meant less cash flow as interest payments were becoming due on its debt. Calpine declared bankruptcy in 2005 and billions of dollars of capital was destroyed. Unfortunately, Calpine was not a one-off situation. Mirant Corporation, NRG Energy, and National Energy and Gas Transmission were others that faced similar situations and filed for bankruptcy as well.

Figure 94: Calpine Went on a Debt-Fueled Capacity Binge at Exactly the Wrong Time

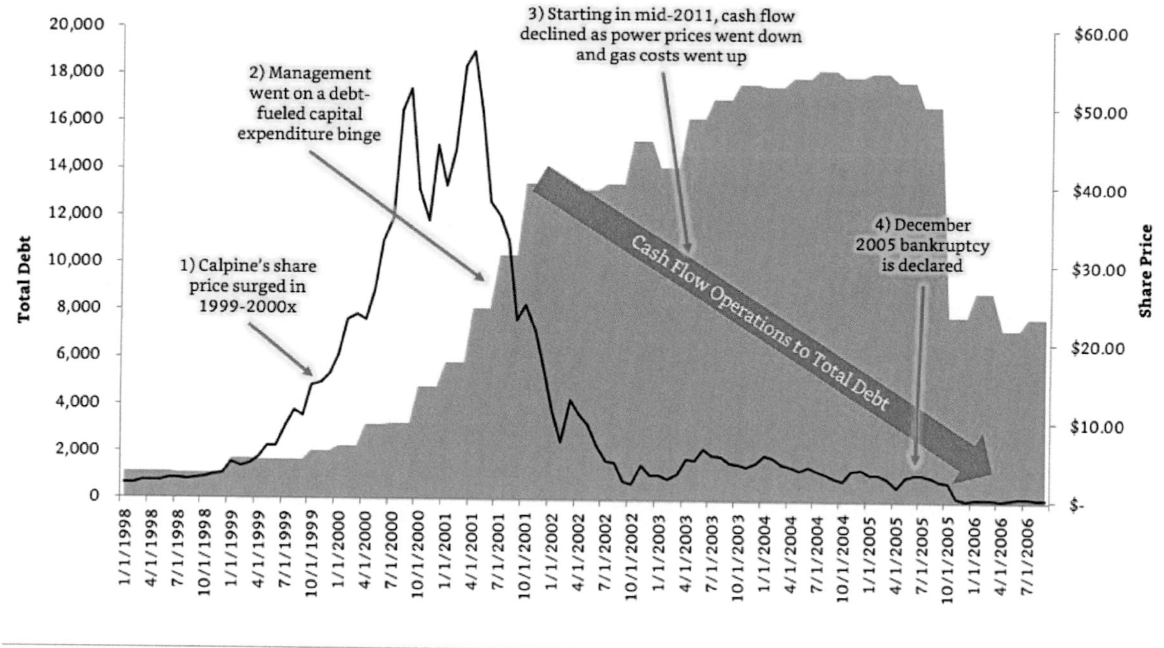

Source: Bloomberg; Michael Molnar

Figure 95: Additional Bankruptcies at the Time

Mirant Files for Bankruptcy Protection
The New York Times
July 15, 2003

Mirant, an energy producer that operates power plants in 14 states, filed for bankruptcy protection yesterday after slumping power prices and higher costs left it unable to refinance a $4.9 billion debt.

Mirant is the third major energy producer to file for bankruptcy in the past two months, joining the NRG Energy unit of Xcel Energy and the National Energy Group unit of PG&E. With $19.4 billion in assets listed in an April 30 annual report to the Securities and Exchange Commission, Mirant's bankruptcy is the largest since WorldCom filed in July 2002.

NRG Energy Files for Bankruptcy Protection
The New York Times
May 15, 2003

NRG Energy Inc. filed for Chapter 11 bankruptcy reorganization yesterday, a long-expected action that includes a $752 million commitment by its parent, Xcel Energy Inc., to help settle debts. In its filing in United States Bankruptcy Court in the Southern District of New York, NRG said it expected operations to continue as normal during restructuring. The filing does not include Xcel or any other Xcel subsidiaries. NRG is the debt-laden wholesale power generating unit of Xcel, which is based in Minneapolis. It operates power plants in Queens and on Staten Island.

Source: The New York Times

Psychology of the Boom-Bust

The time delay inherent in the system, from planning capacity to physical production is a big driver in the boom-bust cycle. However, managements know there is a time delay and yet this patterns happens often. Why? Typical explanations are focused on the tough timing of the recession, or the gas price move, or the power price move – all of which were unknowable. This is true, but the question remains: Why do companies have such poor judgment about the risk of these factors, especially if they agree that they are challenging to predict?

The answer lies in the biases that skew management judgment. Typically, there is a view that capacity is needed as reserve margins (which is simply supply relative to demand) will get tight and thus new capacity will be valuable. The **herd instinct** is often endemic where many management teams come to the same view, often quite quickly. Once that herd view is developed, managements are often myopically focus on how best to bring that capacity online, sometimes losing sense of changing market conditions and the risks it poses.

Next, managements often will **anchor** their view to current fuel prices in evaluating future cost structures. No doubt predicting future fuel prices is hard, but anchoring poses the real risk that they are skewed towards the status quo and not giving enough credit to possible future changes or ranges of scenarios that may happen.

Finally, **commitment and consistency** is likely a culprit in slow reactions. Having communicated their strategy and begun to execute, it is very hard to quickly change direction. Unfortunately, when markets turn, speed is critical to being able to survive as cash flows get tight very fast, especially for highly indebted companies.

Boom-Bust Dynamic Inherent Throughout the Economy

The boom-bust cycle is endemic throughout all parts of the energy and industrial world. While the sectors may look quite different (e.g., offshore drillers, salmon farmers, agriculture equipment manufacturers), the drivers are typically the same. Time delays and skewed judgment drive the boom, and the bust.

Reinforcing Feedback Impacting the Business Model; the Utility Death Spiral

Understanding the Utility Death Spiral

Academically speaking, reinforcing feedback loops result in exponential system behavior as discussed (see page 48). Practically speaking, for those who have invested in companies that have undergone this type of feedback, the word "violent" is more likely to come to mind. What if a sleepy industry that is used to consistent profits and limited competition suddenly encounters reinforcing feedback loops that are hurting its business model? That is the risk of the so-called utility death spiral.

Utilities are natural monopolies as it does not make sense to have each geography replicate the same infrastructure for numerous companies to compete. Therefore, it is regulated to ensure that the monopolist does not derive extraordinary economics from the customers in the region. The utility is tasked with ensuring safe, reliable power to the customers in the region and that requires some level of investment in infrastructure such as the plants to generate electricity and the lines to carry it to homes and businesses. The regulated utility will get its spending approved by the local regulator. A return is added to this spending and, depending on the number of customers and usage, a charge to be levied is calculated.

If there is a reason for customers to leave the utility, or use it less, the utility has to either charge a higher rate to the remaining customers or face earning a lower return on its investment. However, increasing rates will stimulate more customers to leave. This feedback then drives the rate up again if the utility wants to get to its prior expected rate of return, incenting more customers to leave and the feedback continues.

The example below is shown with solar as the "other" option for customers. Solar can be put on roofs by customers to generate their own power (or sell that power back to the utility per local regulations), which threatens the centralized power model of the utility. Also, as discussed earlier (see page 116), solar has a self-reinforcing loop related to its cost structure coming down. The interaction of the utility customer rate loop with solar's cost reduction loop presents a very unique system dynamic as shown in Figure 96.

Figure 96: Mapping the Utility Death Spiral

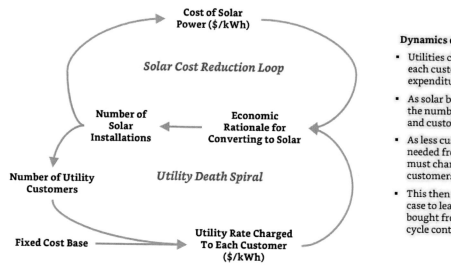

Dynamics of the Utility Death Spiral

- Utilities charge a rate per kWh to each customer to cover their capital expenditures

- As solar becomes more economic, the number of installations increase and customers need the utility less

- As less customers (or less kWh needed from the grid) the utility must charge more to the remaining customers

- This then strengthens the economic case to leave or reduce what is bought from the utility...and the cycle continues

Source: Michael Molnar

Utility Death Spiral, European-style

Germany's case study highlights a slight variation of the utility death spiral. Solar has been heavily promoted by the German government as a means to have more secure power, wean itself from nuclear power and reduce emissions. A "feed-in-tariff" was implemented, allowing farmers, residences and others to put solar panels on their property and receive a guaranteed rate per kWh generated paid for by the utility. As the economic returns were high, a lot of solar was installed. As more solar was installed, the system price fell as companies became more efficient at installing it.

Figure 97: German Installed Solar System Costs and Generation Statistics

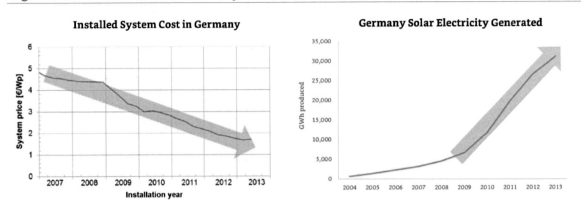

Source: Solar Energy Support in Germany – SEIA Report (left); Bloomberg (right)

The costs of the feed-in-tariff (FIT) are distributed to citizens via the so-called "EEG payment" on their utility bill. Typical costs of delivered electricity are generation, transmission/distribution, various taxes/fees, and – for Germany – the EEG payment. As one would expect given the increase in solar, the EEG payment has been increasing in Germany.

Figure 98: Residential and Industrial Retail Electricity Rates in Germany

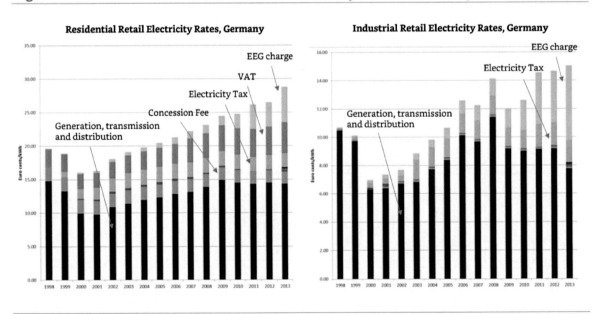

Source: SEIA Report on Germany FIT

However, wholesale rates (wholesale rates are paid when selling to the grid; retail rates are paid when selling to the end user) have headed in the opposite direction. Solar as well as other renewable sources of generation like wind have a higher installed cost initially, but then the fuel is free when the sun shines or the wind blows. So these sources of generation will get dispatched first to the market at a very low marginal cost. What has happened – in addition to carbon pricing and other fuel-cost issues – is that such a large amount of solar and wind were installed that they drove the wholesale market price down massively. There have even been times during the day that the price of power has been negative due to the mismatch of supply and demand.

Figure 99: Wholesale Power Prices in Germany Have Been on a Massive Downtrend

Germany Wholesale Power Prices

Renewables Take Top Share of German Power Supply in First
Bloomberg
October 1, 2014

Germany for the first time got more electricity from renewables than any other source of energy, evidence Chancellor Angela Merkel is making progress in weaning the nation off nuclear power. Clean-energy sources met 27.7 percent of Germany's demand in the nine months through September, for the first time exceeding the 26.3 percent share held by lignite coal, according to calculations by Agora, an influential researcher owned by the Mercator Foundation and European Climate Foundation.

Wind and solar power, unlike atomic reactors, don't produce around the clock. Renewables provided 44 gigawatts of electricity, or three quarters of the nation's demand, on May 11. With conventional plants producing a further 24 gigawatts, it created an oversupply that led to negative power prices, Agora said.

Source: Bloomberg

Low wholesale prices mean that utilities with power-generating assets supplying into the wholesale market will garner lower prices and thus earn less revenue. This was one of the key drivers that pressured RWE and EON, two of the largest utilities in the area. As an example, EON had a valuation of 100 billion euro at its peak and by late 2015 it was down to 20 billion. RWE was once valued at 54 billion euro, but fell to 7 billion euro.

While Germany's situation is not the exact death spiral described, it does highlight the impact that exponential growth can have on a market. Customers were not leaving per se, but were heavily incented to put up solar generation and sell to the grid. The exponential growth in solar changed the wholesale market dramatically.

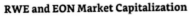

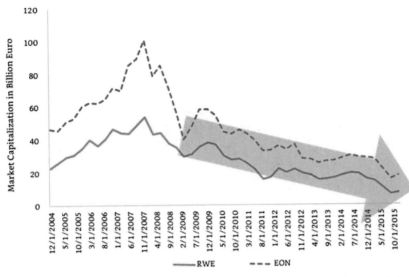

- EON and RWE market capitalization peaked at 100 billion and 54 billion euro.

- The stocks have been on a constant run downward as shown at left with market capitalizations at 20 billion and 7 billion at the end of 2015.

Source: Bloomberg

Early Signs of the Death Spiral in the U.S.? The Hawaiian Example

Hawaii provides a good case study for the potential of the utility death spiral in the United States. Hawaii is landlocked and imports oil for electricity generation. This results in very high-cost electricity rates of $0.35 per kWh relative to the rest of the country at around $0.10 per kWh. Also, as any anyone who has traveled there knows, Hawaii gets a lot of sun.

These factors – high costs from the utility plus low-cost solar potential – combined with a supportive government policy resulted in a massive surge in solar installations. By 2015, nearly 12% of Hawaiian Electric's customers had installed rooftop solar, a multiple of the level of penetration that has been achieved elsewhere. As described the article in Figure 102, the utility was threatened with the death spiral as customers continued to leave, as the economics of leaving only got better as more left.

Figure 101: Hawaii Retail Rates and Solar Resource

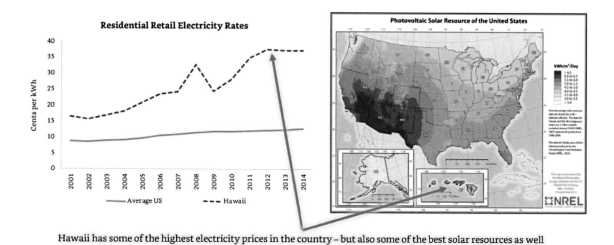

Hawaii has some of the highest electricity prices in the country – but also some of the best solar resources as well

Source: Energy Information Administration (EIA); National Renewable Energy Laboratory (NREL)

Figure 102: Hawaii is a Case Study for the Risk of the Utility Death Spiral

In Hawaii, rooftop solar panels threaten 'utility death spiral'
Energy experts worry that the rise of solar power will raise prices for utility customers left to subsidize the grid
August 26, 2015 - Aljazeera America

Hawaii's electricity prices are higher than anywhere else in the nation. The burdensome cost of power, paired with the island state's plentiful sunshine, has led to an unparalleled adoption of residential rooftop solar energy. On the island of Oahu, where 80 percent of the state's population lives, more than 12 percent of Hawaiian Electric Co. (HECO) customers have rooftop solar systems — about 20 times the solar penetration rate of any mainland utility. As homes increasingly morph into mini power plants, some residents are winding down their HECO bills to net zero.

The problem is this: When solar customers provide their own power, they don't pay for the fixed costs the utility has outside of electricity generation. As more and more people switch to solar, an ever-shrinking pool of utility customers still connected to the grid are left to cover these operating and maintenance expenses. This causes bills to spike for traditional customers, which incentivizes even more people to switch to solar, raising bills for nonsolar customers even more. Every new rooftop solar installation added to the grid contributes to this cost shift.

As less energy is sold in Hawaii because of rooftop solar installations and energy efficiency gains, fixed costs are rising. And utility customers reliant on the grid, like Kong, are paying the price. Roberts estimated that the average nonsolar HECO customer on Oahu is subsidizing solar customers by 1 or 2 cents per kilowatt hour, or about $5 to $10 per month.

"What's causing a lot of tension right now is oil prices have come down quite a lot and the utility is generating less electricity but bills are not going down," he said. "About two-thirds of a resident's bill is fixed costs. People are pointing at the solar customers and saying that they are not paying their fair share."

Source: Cited above

There are many reasonable arguments as to why this is unfair to the utility and its remaining customers. Utilities make investments to ensure safe and reliable power. Solar customers are able to use that infrastructure to sell their power back, often at very high rates (retail versus wholesale), as well as use it for power when needed (i.e., when the sun is not shining). The rates that the utility is charging likely did not anticipate such dynamics. Non-solar customers face the risk that their rates will go up to compensate for solar customers.

The debate centers around the economics. What rate should solar customers be allowed to sell to the grid? When they buy power, is there a different rate? Should there simply be a surcharge for solar customers to account for this? It is a very contentious issue as the current regulatory framework did not anticipate the growth of distributed power. As shown in the articles below, even utility executives have very different thoughts about how this might play out.

Figure 103: Opposing Views on the So-Called Utility Death Spiral Risk

Utility 'Death Spiral' Will Accelerate Quickly Over Next 5 Years, NRG Chief Says November 2015 SNL – via eei.org While the use of the utility "death spiral" argument has slowed in recent months, NRG Energy President and CEO David Crane on Nov. 13 said that although U.S. utilities are fighting to keep a monopoly status, grid defection is inevitable, SNL reports. "They just finished their big conference … and the message I heard that came out of the conference is that everyone wants to do regulated, everyone wants to hide behind fortress monopoly walls," Crane said during a talk at Columbia University in New York City, referring to the recently concluded EEI Financial Conference in Florida. "The thing is, if you actually empower people to provide their own electricity, that's beyond the scope not only of the utility, because it's on the other side of the meter, but it's actually out of the scope of the state regulator as well."	**Southern Co. CEO Says 'Heck No' to Notion of 'Industry Death Spiral'** July 2015 Environment and Energy Publishing – via eei.org Southern Co. CEO Tom Fanning on Tuesday was asked during an appearance at the National Association of Regulatory Utility Commissioners' summer meetings in New York what he thought about a prominent New York official's assessment that utilities could become a "zombie business" if they don't change to adapt to a more distributed reality. "In a back-and-forth interview segment before hundreds of attendees, the president of NARUC, Florida Public Service Commissioner Lisa Edgar, wondered what Fanning thought of the notion that utilities are headed for an 'industry death spiral.' Fanning bluntly replied, 'With all due respect, heck no,'" Environment & Energy Publishing reports.

Source: Cited above

The Psychology of Slow Reactions

My favorite utility joke is as follows (in reality, I only have one utility joke):

- Question: How did the utility executive commit suicide?
- Answer: By stepping in front of a glacier.

While this joke is perhaps overly harsh, it does beg the question: Why have so few utility executives and analysts been at the forefront of recognizing some of the changes in the industry?

The utility business model has been incredibly stable – and effective – for the past 100 years. The most-needed skills are project management, cost cutting and regulatory expertise. In such an environment, one would expect slower reaction times compared to, say, the technology sector where dramatic industry change is constant. With this as context, several psychological biases most likely were at work in executives' minds:

- **Semmelweis Reflex, Confirmation Bias and Herd Instinct:** The Semmelweis Reflex, rejecting information contrary to one's view, is likely at work as this is a radical paradigm shift for utility executives to ponder. The other side of the coin, confirmation bias (where one seeks information to confirm a pre-existing view) is likely at work as well for a similar reason. In an industry which has not seen a change like this, these biases can be tough to overcome. In the technology world, business executives are used to more disruptive change and often have a different mindset.

  There was, and likely still is, a herd mentality among utility executives and analysts on solar that goes something like this: "We need the grid and while solar has gotten cheaper, it can only go so far." This may be an accurate assumption, but how many of these companies have truly brought contrarian views into their boardrooms? Herds can, and often do, get slaughtered when change happens as opposing viewpoints are cast aside without proper reflection.

- **Anchoring Bias:** Anchoring bias, having one's judgment skewed towards recent data, is a clear roadblock for many involved in the incumbent industry. For example, I had a conversation with a utility analyst about 10 years ago. His comment was, "Solar is so expensive, do people really think this will ramp?" I have had countless similar conversations over the past decade where people are simply anchoring their views to current data versus where that data will be in the future.

- **Bayesian Bias:** This bias, where one is too conservative in assessing change, is similar to the anchoring bias in some ways. When I would explain that costs could come down substantially in solar, some would disagree with a response such as, "Okay, let's assume costs go down 20%, it is *still* extremely expensive." Exponential growth – or, in this case, cost declines – are incredibly hard to accurately predict. For industries ramping in a self-reinforcing manner like solar, forecasts are often much too conservative.

To utility executives still pushing back on the potential for disruptive change, I would offer two thoughts. First, if the dynamic was understood earlier, would they have pushed back harder on allowing solar to be sold to the grid at retail rates, or lobbied to have surcharges put in once certain levels of installation were hit? Now that has become harder as the solar industry has become more powerful. Second, while the utility industry will not "go away" as we need the grid and economic battery storage is likely many years off, why be so complacent? Utilities do not have to die for massive value to be destroyed. There also might be a hidden opportunity for those willing to look for it.

Reinforcing Feedback Inherent to the Business Model; the Yieldco Example

Yieldco 101

The utility death spiral is driven by a reinforcing feedback loop that initially starts outside its own business but eventually impacts its core operations. However, there are businesses where the model *itself* is based on reinforcing feedback. Their goal is to drive that feedback to work for them and, when that happens, the benefits can be enormous. But the model sometimes turns the other way and the risks can be catastrophic. The so-called "yieldco" business models that pervaded Wall Street in 2014 and 2015 are good examples.

A "yieldco," short for yield company, is a publicly traded company that holds long-term contracted assets that provide annual cash flow to the company (e.g., a solar field that generates power and sells it to a company for 20 years). The company has a policy where these cash flows are distributed to shareholders at some very high rate, say 80% or more of the cash received, to investors searching for yield. For example, if the stock price is $10/share and investors get $1 in a dividend annually, yield investors will see a 10% return for, say, 20 years if that is the length of time that contracted assets are held.

The rationale for their creation was twofold. First, companies like SunEdison, the solar developer, felt they were not garnering the true economic benefit by selling projects to others for a one-time fee. So it wanted to hold onto the assets longer to realize the better economics over time. However, given the other varied business lines of the parent company, the risk was that the market would not be able to properly parse out the yieldco and poor valuation was possible. Putting all these projects that were generating cash flows into an entity would solve this problem and also have a clear investor group – those searching for yield.

Second, infrastructure-development businesses need low-cost capital to be successful. While there are many sources of capital available, a related yieldco could help be another source that not only provided low-cost capital, but also helped to speed the turnover of capital versus having to run unique funding processes for each asset (as the capital-raising criteria was pre-determined). Lower capital and higher turnover of capital had the potential to create significant value.

While yield vehicles have been around in various forms for some time, the success of NRG Yield's IPO (the entity formed by NRG, the utility) gave confidence to others in the renewable space to analyze these structures. Abengoa, NextEra, and SunEdison soon followed in developing their own yieldcos and had good success as the business model was applauded by investors and the share prices rose.

Figure 104: Yieldco Stocks Were Very Much of Interest in Early 2014 to Mid-2015

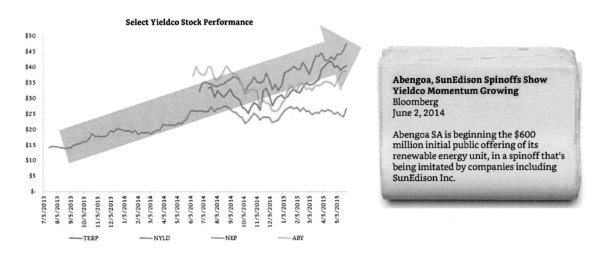

Source: *Bloomberg*

Reinforcing Loops Can Be Good or Bad

Unfortunately, events took a turn for the worse in mid-to-late 2015. The stocks turned down massively, a big surprise to many investors who thought they were investing in stable dividend-paying stocks. To understand what could drive this, one has to understand the inherent reinforcing loop to the business model.

SunEdison (SUNE) and Terraform (TERP) provide a good example. The very essence of the business model of SunEdison and Terraform is based on a self-reinforcing feedback loop with the following dynamics when it is working in the company's favor:

1. SunEdison, the development company, would continue to generate the pipeline of projects.

2. This pipeline of growth would translate into low yield at Terraform (the yieldco), meaning that investors would only require a low current yield given the potential for growth in the future.

3. Terraform would pay dividends, a good amount would go to SunEdison as the majority owner.

4. This, in turn, would allow it to grow and create more pipeline. As long as its cost of capital was lower than the project returns, capturing value was possible. This cycle of events then continued (i.e., more pipeline, lower yield).

Figure 105: Yieldco Stocks Sold Off Harshly after Their Big Run Up

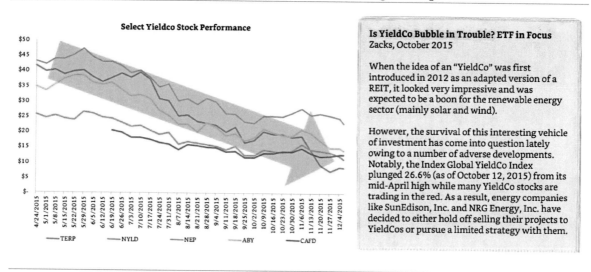

Is YieldCo Bubble in Trouble? ETF in Focus
Zacks, October 2015

When the idea of an "YieldCo" was first introduced in 2012 as an adapted version of a REIT, it looked very impressive and was expected to be a boon for the renewable energy sector (mainly solar and wind).

However, the survival of this interesting vehicle of investment has come into question lately owing to a number of adverse developments. Notably, the Index Global YieldCo Index plunged 26.6% (as of October 12, 2015) from its mid-April high while many YieldCo stocks are trading in the red. As a result, energy companies like SunEdison, Inc. and NRG Energy, Inc. have decided to either hold off selling their projects to YieldCos or pursue a limited strategy with them.

Source: Bloomberg; Zacks

Unfortunately, feedback works both ways as shown in Figure 106. It can turn against a company when the following happens:

1. If for some reason, TERP experienced a drop in share price, then issuing equity would come at a higher cost.

2. This translates into a higher cost of capital, which means that it would be less competitive in bidding or building assets.

3. This translates into lower growth potential which, in turn, impacts the stock price...and the cycle continues.

While it should be obvious, the loop's impact is just as impactful when working against a company as when it is working for a company.

Positive Reinforcing Loop

The positive reinforcing loop as indicated during the SunEdison Capital Markets Day (February 24, 2015)

Negative Reinforcing Loop

The negative reinforcing loop. Bears would point to a possible balance sheet, business model and/or valuation issue

Source: SunEdison; Michael Molnar

The Trigger That Changed Feedback from Positive to Negative

The challenge with business models that are inherently based on reinforcing feedback is in assessing the risk of feedback shifting from a tailwind to a headwind. Sometimes it is a single event that shifts the model, others times there are multiple where each in isolation would not be a problem but combined were a risk. The latter is what happened to the yieldcos late in 2015.

Higher interest rates were the key risk many investors were monitoring. If this happened, yield-oriented investors would have other options which could lower demand, and the share price, for the yieldco shares. During this time, however, interest rates did not move much as shown in Figure 107.

The driver of the initial decreases in share price were not any one factor, but a confluence of factors that came together at the same time. What made this even trickier to assess was that many of these factors were technical and not fundamental in nature. Most analysts recognize that technical factors can drive share prices over shorter periods of time. For many businesses, this is a mere annoyance, but not particularly impactful. For example, if a large industrial company faces technical pressure on its share price for a few weeks, it will not typically damage its ability to sell products and service customers. Yet, if one's business model is fundamentally based upon a self-reinforcing loop in which the level of its share price is critical, technical factors can lead to fundamental pain.

Several factors moved at the same time and contributed to the initial decline in share price that, in turn, changed the self-reinforcing nature of the business model from positive to negative:

- **Market Valuation Declined:** While not the biggest factor, the stock market sold off during this time and that will impact all valuations.

- **Oil Price Fell:** The price of oil also declined. While oil does not impact the opportunity for many of these predominately solar builders directly, it can lead to a negative sentiment on energy-related investments. For confidence-based business models such as yieldcos, *perception is reality* so the price of oil does matter as long as people think it does, whether it does in reality or not.

- **MLP Buyers Felt Pain:** Master Limited Partnership (MLP) investors are yield-searching investors that often invest in oil- and gas-related investments. The decline in oil prices significantly hurt this group of investors; the pain they encountered forced them to sell their portfolios. Because they previously had become the marginal buyer of yieldco equity, this created selling pressures on yieldco shares.

- **Equity Issuances Create Supply/Demand Mismatch:** Leading up to these events, the yieldcos had issued a lot of equity to the market. Given the loss of the MLP buyer, the equity issuances created a supply/demand mismatch and lower share prices resulted.

- **Company-Specific News Flow Decidedly Negative:** During this time, Abengoa warned investors of bad results, which the market interpreted as a negative for other yieldcos. Also, SunEdison bought residential solar company Vivint at a high valuation by using debt, thereby increasing perceived risk.

Once the reinforcing loop shifted negatively, there was nearly nothing management could do to stop it.

Figure 107: Yieldco Reinforcing Loop

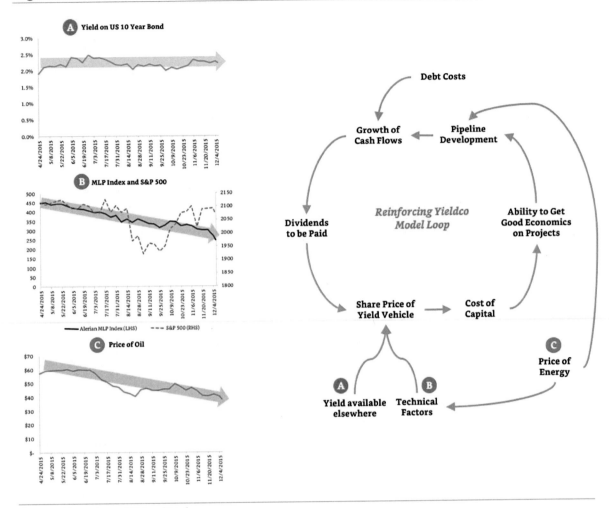

Source: Bloomberg; Michael Molnar

Figure 108: Select Yieldco Capital Raises

Date	Company	Type of Offering	Gross proceeds	Shares (M)	Price / share	Cumulative
7/31/2015	TerraForm Global	IPO	$ 675	45.0	$ 15.00	$ 9,129
7/21/2015	Pattern Energy Grou	Follow-on/Converts	$ 350		$ 23.00	$ 8,454
6/22/2015	NRG Yield	Follow-on/Converts	$ 850		$ 22.00	$ 8,104
6/18/2015	8point3 Energy Part	IPO	$ 420	20.0	$ 21.00	$ 7,254
6/18/2015	TerraForm Power	Follow-on	$ 599	15.8	$ 38.00	$ 6,834
5/12/2015	NextEra Energy Part	PIPE	$ 109	2.2		$ 6,236
5/11/2015	Abengoa Yield	PIPE	$ 670			$ 6,127
2/3/2015	Pattern Energy Grou	Follow-on	$ 351	12.0	$ 29.25	$ 5,457
1/15/2015	Abengoa Yield	Follow-on	$ 328	10.6	$ 31.00	$ 5,106
1/15/2015	Terraform Power	Follow-on	$ 352	12.0	$ 29.30	$ 4,778
11/21/2014	Terraform Power	PIPE	$ 350			$ 4,426
7/23/2014	NRG Yield	Follow-on	$ 652	12.1	$ 54.00	$ 4,076
7/17/2014	Terraform Power	IPO	$ 577	23.1	$ 24.97	$ 3,424
7/3/2014	Terraform Power	PIPE	$ 65			$ 2,847
6/26/2014	NextEra Energy Part	IPO	$ 467	18.7	$ 25.00	$ 2,782
1/12/2014	Abengoa Yield	IPO	$ 829	28.6	$ 29.00	$ 2,315
5/8/2014	Pattern Energy Grou	Follow-on	$ 586	21.1	$ 27.75	$ 1,486
9/26/2013	Pattern Energy Grou	IPO	$ 405	18.4	$ 22.00	$ 900
7/16/2013	NRG Yield	IPO	$ 495	22.5	$ 22.00	$ 495

$ in millions, except for per share data

A significant amount of capital was raised in a short amount of time. Then with the crash of the MLP index, the marginal buyer of this capital became a seller.

Source: Multiple sources; Company filings

Psychology Played a Role as Well

The yieldco case study represents how reinforcing feedback loops can be an inherent part of a business model and the unique risk that poses. This is true in many confidence-based businesses. The challenge in running a company where sentiment, perception and confidence can materially damage the business was not fully appreciated by most executives or investors. This, combined with several of the psychological biases below, led to some very tough results:

- **Anchoring and Bayesian Bias:** As conditions changed, anchoring bias skewed judgment. For example, many analysts would assume that the cost of equity would increase by, say, 50 basis points and conclude that the business was still strong. Unfortunately, reinforcing loops need a reason to stop and, until that happens, they keep moving. So 50 basis points became 100 basis points and then multiples of that in subsequent weeks.

- **Herd Instinct and Confirmation Bias:** Investors plowed into these stocks as a herd with several well-known investors touting their potential. No doubt confirmation bias played a role for those who stayed too long as like-minded investors sought comfort in each other versus actively seeking out and truly listening to the contrarian view.

- **Fundamental Attribution Error:** Several managements likely over-ascribed the early share price rises to their strategic choices versus situational factors (i.e., fundamental attribution error). Not enough credit was given to the macroeconomic factors that helped the business model historically, which potentially drove a level of overconfidence and decisions that pushed the model too far. By failing to ascribe some credit to these outside factors on the way up, one faces the risk of not seeing their potential to change things dramatically and force things down.

This case study is not meant to describe a model that has no future as yield companies have a place in the market. However, the risks of managing and investing in such businesses are unique. Failing to respect – and manage – these differences can lead to negative surprises when market conditions change.

Decoding the Politics of Energy

Energy and politics are inextricably intertwined. There are countless issues surrounding regulation, foreign policy and economic growth – each of which could be a book in and of itself. This section evaluates three situations where politics and energy mix, each located in a different part of the world.

Policy sets the rules from which behavior follows in many energy systems. **U.S. energy policy** is an interesting amalgamation of disparate policies. While each policy in isolation might makes sense, the culmination of all of them form an ineffective system dynamic. A more coherent policy strategy is put forth.

China faces a challenge similar to that of the U.S. and Europe during their industrial booms: how to most reap the benefits of economic growth with the least damage to the environment and citizens' health. While this has been a clear opportunity to show its prowess as a government, the results have so far been uninspiring as evidenced by the horrid air and water pollution.

Finally, **oil-dependent economies** face extreme risks if energy prices stay low for extended periods of time. The economic impact of low oil prices combined with large youth populations and politically volatile climates are a recipe for civil unrest, war and increased forms of terrorism.

The Structure of U.S. Energy Policy and the Ineffective Dynamics it Causes

The United States government intervenes in energy markets in countless ways on both the supply and demand side. The government makes direct expenditures to producers or consumers, creates countless tax incentives, funds certain research and development, grants loans and guarantees, and mandates efficiency programs. Often the focus of debate centers around an individual subsidy or the total amount of subsidies. Less discussed are the unintended consequences that all these subsidies create.

Demand Interventions: Government-Driven Efficiency

On the demand side, the United States government has created a series of efficiency regulations. For example, there are government mandates for efficient lighting, appliances and automobiles. This sounds logical, but the effectiveness is often muted due to the **rebound effect** (see page 111).

There is also a pushback by the consumer against such policies when energy is cheap. For example, SUV purchases rise when gasoline prices are low, resulting in complaints by automakers that they are being mandated to produce cars that people do not want. U.S. energy policy intervention on the demand side is what I call a **"Government-Driven Efficiency"** policy. It is not awful, just not particularly effective.

Supply Interventions: Government-Driven Supply

On the supply side, there are countless subsidies doled out to nearly all energy industries. This puts the government in the role of choosing which technologies or companies to support. While nearly everyone would agree this is not the best role for government, all energy companies play the game since that is how the system is structured. Lobbyists are hired to make their companies' cases to government officials. I call this the **"Government-Driven Supply."**

Once enacted, subsidies can be difficult to stop. Combined with a massive government budget, the fungibility of money, and the influence of lobbyists, the end result is that the U.S. ends up over-subsidizing supply in an inflexible manner.

When people talk about energy's impact on the economy, it typically goes as follows: *"Cheap energy is needed to have a healthy economy. If energy prices are low, the economy will grow and that is beneficial to U.S. citizens."* This is linear thinking with a start (cheap energy) and an end (healthy economy). Unfortunately, this is not how systems work. Systems are interconnected and contain feedback.

Figure 109 details the feedback loops at work due to current U.S. energy policy. I convert the linear thinking above into a what I call the **"Energy Cost Economic Impact"** loop. The relationship is fairly simple: Economic growth drives energy demand which – when matched to supply – drives energy pricing. The feedback is completed as energy pricing feeds back into impacting economic growth (Note: To simplify, we include all "energy" as one, when in reality there are different markets for electricity or auto fuel, for example).

There are two other sources of feedback that people intuitively know exist, but seem to forget when discussing U.S. energy policy:

1. **Health, Security and Environmental Economic Impact:** The first is the impact that health, security, and the environment have on the economy. I call this the "Health, Security and Environmental Economic Impact" loop. In this feedback loop, economic growth impacts energy demand which, depending on the energy mix (clean versus dirty, secure versus less secure), impacts our health, security and environment. This, in turn, impacts economic growth.

   This is why the framing of "either/or" for economic growth versus the environment and citizens' health is an incomplete analysis. Unhealthy citizens are less productive and incur higher healthcare costs. If sea levels rise due to global warming, the negative economic impact will be massive (See *The Stern Review: The Economics of Climate Change*). The costs of less-secure forms of energy are nearly impossible to calculate, but very meaningful (e.g., terrorism, U.S. Middle Eastern military presence).

2. **Subsidy Funding Economic Impact:** Subsidies need to be funded through some combination of higher taxes, larger government debt or lower spending on other areas. Each of these three items negatively impacts economic growth. I call this feedback the "Subsidy Funding Economic Impact" loop.

Figure 109: System Dynamics Created by Current U.S. Energy Policy

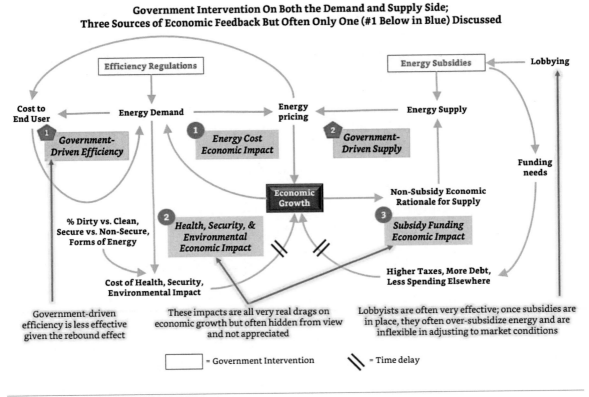

Government Intervention On Both the Demand and Supply Side;
Three Sources of Economic Feedback But Often Only One (#1 Below in Blue) Discussed

Source: Michael Molnar

The Results Are Not Particularly Impressive

U.S. energy policies have not generated particularly impressive results:

- **Health and Environment:** Pollution still impacts Americans too much. For example, coal combustion contributes to four of the top five leading causes of death in the United States: heart disease, cancer, stroke, and chronic lower respiratory diseases (Source: *Coal's Assault on Human Health*, Physicians for Social Responsibility). The risk of global warming includes higher sea levels impacting coastlines, and severe weather events damaging lives and infrastructure (Source: IPCC).

- **National Security:** For the past 40 years, the U.S. has depended on foreign oil from often outright hostile regions of the world. While the situation has improved somewhat as domestic sources have increased due to fracking, the U.S. still imported 27% of its petroleum in 2014 – still too much for something so critical.

- **Economic Impact:** By intervening in supply directly, the government plays the role of venture capitalist and private equity funder. Because this is not a core competency of government officials, there is little doubt that capital is wasted. Likewise, while there are human costs to health, security and environmental impacts as described above, there are also economic ones. Sick citizens are less productive and incur costs to get better. Rising sea levels and extreme weather damage infrastructure (See *The Stern Review: The Economics of Climate Change*).

  The cost of energy security should not be considered lightly either. To put the matter in perspective, the U.S War in Iraq has cost $1.7 trillion, with an additional $490 billion owed to veterans for benefits. Given this was funded with debt, it has been estimated to grow to more than $6 trillion over the next 40 years including interest (Source: *Costs of War Project* by the Watson Institute for International Studies at Brown University). This is not to say the U.S. will never be involved in the Middle East or that the Iraq War was entirely about energy security. Rather it highlights that even small reductions in these costs could mean a massive saving in money as well as lives of U.S. military.

Better Policy Can Drive More Effective System Dynamics

Existing U.S. energy policy, driven by subsidies to specific industries and companies, creates a dynamic where lobbyists are often the critical factor between success and failure. A better dynamic creates an environment where talent and capital flow to exploit a market opportunity that is the same for all participants regardless of their lobbying skill or partners.

What could that look like? Government has a clear place in intervention, but it should not be directly involved in supply or demand. Rather policy should focus on pricing what the market cannot (e.g., pollution, carbon, energy security) and regulating safety. The concept is simple: you levy a fee (dare I say a "tax") on the activity or product that is less desired (e.g., fossil fuels). Then the government should simply step aside and let entrepreneurs, business owners, and investors drive towards exploiting the market opportunity that this pricing (i.e., fee) has created. It is by far the most limited form of government intervention and will get to the outcomes desired, faster as it creates much more effective set of dynamics. In terms of supply and demand, there are two impacts:

- **Consumer-Driven Energy Efficiency**: As prices increase due to the pricing of pollution and energy security, consumers – not government – will demand more efficient appliances and vehicles. Entrepreneurs and investors will form companies and products that will drive efficiency in ways that the government could never imagine.

- **Market-Driven Supply:** Once clear rules are in place that increase the cost of polluting and less secure forms of energy, talented entrepreneurs and capital providers will form companies and develop technologies to exploit this opportunity. Cleaner and more secure forms of energy will scale exponentially faster in a world where talent and capital strive for solutions than in a world of competing lobbyists.

In terms of the economic impact dynamics, the "**Energy Cost Economic Impact**" loop is basically the same. Economic growth drives energy demand which, when matched to supply, drives energy pricing. As pricing will be higher, the isolated impact of this feedback will be negative. That said, these other two often hidden economic sources of feedback will be markedly better.

- **Health, Security and Environmental Economic Impact:** As long as the price of these three issues are set at a sufficient level, the energy mix will become cleaner and more secure.

- **Fee Revenue Economic Impact:** Subsidy payments are eliminated and replaced with fee revenue. The resulting fees obtained by the government can be used to cut taxes, reduce debt or increase productive spending in areas such as infrastructure or education, for example. These all are net benefits to the economy if the money is used wisely.

Figure 110: Changing How the Government Intervenes Can Lead to Much Better Dynamics

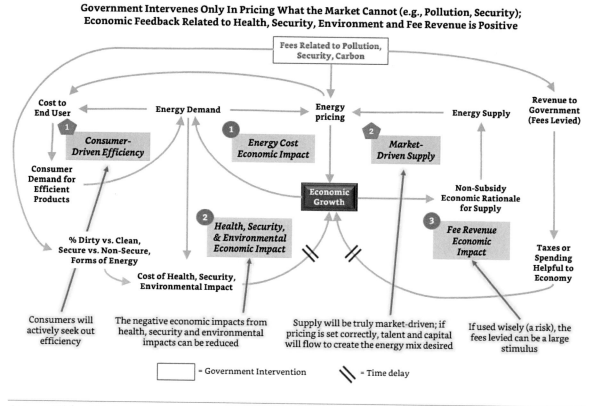

Source: Michael Molnar

My focus here is not on the specific processes by which to levy these fees but, rather, in explaining how doing so fundamentally changes the dynamics of the system for the better. For those with interest in the possible mechanics of implementation, the IMF published a book *Getting Energy Prices Right – from Principle to Practice* in 2014 which is a good reference.

What About "Cap-and-Trade" Versus Levying Fees (e.g., Taxes) Directly

Both policies (cap-and-trade and a tax) have the same objective, increasing the cost of forms of energy that are less desired thereby driving the market to shift to a better outcome. While both can work if implemented well, a tax is far more efficient yet politically more tenuous.

Cap-and-trade systems are more complex and often can result in volatility of the cost of pollution. For example, in Europe, the price of carbon fluctuated massively – from 5 euro per ton to 30 euro per ton (see page 101). These fluctuations are a risk to the existence of the very market opportunity the regulation was designed to create. Conversely, a consistently applied fee (e.g., tax) provides a clear line-of-sight into the opportunity for entrepreneurs and capital providers.

Why is "cap-and-trade" popular then? As this policy provides the opportunity for each company to either buy a permit to pollute or invest in abatement, this can allow the market to find the lowest cost solution. However, there are two other drivers: Politicians like it because they can market it without saying the word "tax" and Wall Street likes it because it provides another product to trade.

Addressing Two Critiques

There are two critiques of such a change in energy policy. **First, some will immediately argue that if we price carbon and other countries like China do not, then certain industries will be hurt and the U.S. risks losing its manufacturing base even further.** This is a logical concern but I would offer two thoughts. First, Germany – a country far more economically tied to exports than the U.S. – has seen an increase in electricity prices due to energy policy yet has not encountered an economic meltdown. Second, there are other actions the U.S. can take against countries who do not comply with certain pollution guideless and unfairly compete. Given the growing risk, proactively moving on effective regulation is a much better alternative versus doing nothing and continuing the stalemate.

Second, **others will argue that a tax simply will not work politically.** Beyond getting public support – addressed in the following section – there are three reasons that there is a window of opportunity that this can get done:

- **First, the proposed revamping of energy policy has features that are attractive both Democrats and Republicans.** Democrats would like the transition to cleaner forms of power, which pricing pollution and carbon dioxide would stimulate. Republicans would find decreased government intervention appealing.

- **Second, the "enemy of your enemy is your friend" principle is a possible tailwind.** Any bold change in policy such as this will drive some incumbents to lose (e.g., fossil fuels if carbon is priced) while others win. The winners can be very influential in mitigating the noise that the losers will be intent on creating. For example, the electric utility industry (given electric vehicles), the solar industry (given it is clean power), and U.S. shale drilling companies (given it is secure power) all potentially stand to benefit from increased demand for their products.

- **Third, while these factors constantly change, a decent economy and low energy prices present a window of opportunity in early 2016.** Implementing a policy change that drives the direct costs of energy higher even though it can lead to better economic outcomes over time, is politically tenuous. Doing so when energy prices are high and the economy is weak will likely lead to substantial pushback. Figures 111 and 112 show recent economic and energy data as of the end of 2015. Gross domestic product (GDP) has grown about 2% to 3% the last several years, unemployment has declined, inflation is at record lows and the stock market has been strong. Combined with low energy prices, this presents a window of opportunity to change U.S. energy policy.

Figure 111: Key U.S. Economic and Market Statistics

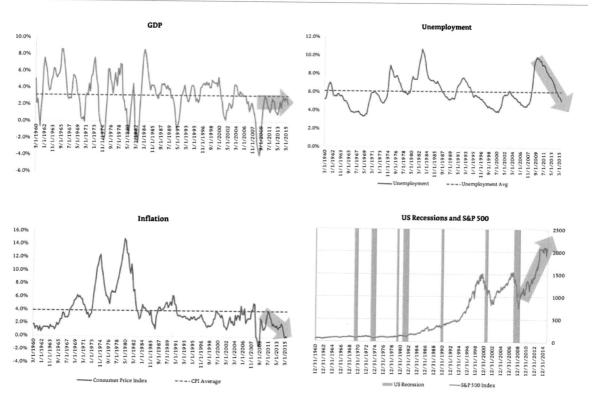

Source: Bloomberg

Figure 112: Oil and Natural Gas Prices

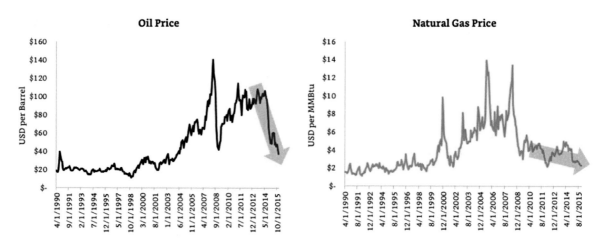

Source: Energy Information Administration

The X Factor: Garnering Public Support

The science behind climate change, the desire for less pollution, and the need for energy security is sound and logical. Yet, while necessary, they are not sufficient on their own to rally substantial public support. Companies that stand to lose from this policy change will hire lobbyists and public relations firms that are well-versed in how to sway opinion. Anyone that wants to change policy needs to have an equally effective communication plan with a focus on emotions and psychology, not merely facts.

While a detailed communication plan is beyond the scope of this section, several thoughts are detailed below to help begin to think about effectively communicating this topic:

1. **Create a Policy Name That Taps into Emotions:** Do not underestimate the name of the policy itself. Words matter as the "estate tax" versus "death tax" debate showed; estate taxes seem reasonable while death taxes seem outrageous to most. The name should contain what all people undeniably want. Keywords could include safety (cleaner air and water), opportunity (better economic impact), and security (less foreign risks).

2. **Frame the Change as a both a Savings and a Stimulus:** Behavioral economics has shown that the same economic outcome merely framed in a different way can lead people to choose different paths. Too often, proposed changes in energy policy are framed as delivering costs to the public now, for uncertain gains in the future. The

policy should be framed as a savings (less government waste, lower costs of security and health impacts) and a stimulus from the impact of the fee revenue.

3. **Tell Personal Stories of the Consequences of Current Policy:** Rather than spewing statistics, personal stories of the costs of current policy hold more sway. Stories about the personal health costs of pollution, the monetary and human costs of our involvement in foreign affairs, and the risks to specific geographies due to global warming all need to be told in a personal way.

4. **Counter Fake Authorities and Phony Reports:** The opposition will fund phony authority figures and bogus research reports from biased think tanks. As people listen to authority figures – even when they are a sham – these need to be proactively countered.

Better Outcomes Are Possible, for both the U.S. and the World

Individual subsidies – such as subsidizing a high-potential technology or granting a company a loan for a high-return project – can feel right in isolation. Cumulatively, these policies create poor system dynamics which lead to suboptimal outcomes. Better policy can drive to better overall outcomes, faster.

While this section has focused on U.S. environmental policy, there are implications for governments around the world. The International Monetary Fund (IMF) issued a Working Paper called *How Large are Global Energy Subsidies* which researched the costs and potential impacts for the world as a whole. A key takeaway was the following:

> *The fiscal, environmental, and welfare impacts of energy subsidy reform are potentially enormous. Eliminating post-tax subsidies in 2015 could raise government revenue by $2.9 trillion (3.6 percent of global GDP), cut global CO2 emissions by more than 20 percent, and cut pre-mature air pollution deaths by more than half. After allowing for the higher energy costs faced by consumers, this action would raise global economic welfare by $1.8 trillion (2.2 percent of global GDP).*

In short, the world could actually gain – not lose – by managing this situation better.

China's Quest for Growth and Its Related Consequences

Understanding China's Growth and the Pollution Side Effect

From 1990 to 2014, China's economy has grown at a compound annual growth rate of three times the U.S., at 15% versus 4.6% in nominal terms. In 1990, China's economy was 10% the size of the U.S. economy, growing to 60% by 2014. Millions of people have emerged from poverty as evidenced from per capita income increasing from $465 to $3,866 from 1990 to 2014 (in 2005 USD per person, adjusted for inflation). Such per capita GDP growth is impressive for a population of 1.3 billion people (compared to 320 million in the U.S.).

Figure 113: China's Economic Growth Has Been Impressive

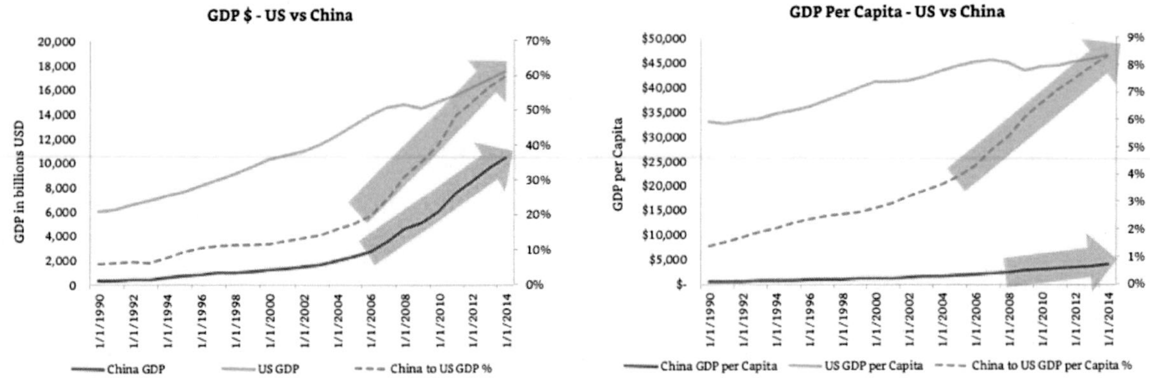

Source: Bloomberg

In terms of energy mix, the U.S. mirrors the world with similar usage of oil, natural gas and coal followed by much smaller share of nuclear, hydroelectric and renewables. In contrast, 66% of China's primary energy usage is produced by burning coal. From 2000 to 2014, China's annual coal usage increased from 1.5 billion tons to about 4 billion tons. By comparison, U.S. coal usage has stayed flat at 900 million tons from 1990 to 2014.

Figure 114: Coal Comprises a Greater Percentage of China's Energy Mix

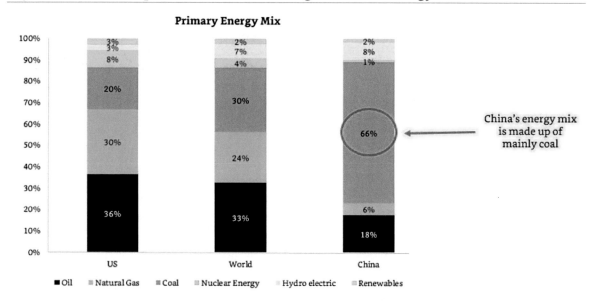

Primary Energy Mix

Source: BP Energy Statistics – 2014 Data

Given coal is such a dirty fuel, this growth in coal consumption has created pollution problems for China. PM2.5 levels, a measure of air pollution, show just how dire the situation in China has become. PM 2.5 stands for particulate matter that is less than 2.5 micrometers in diameter (as a reference, that is 25% the width of a human hair).

Particulate matter is often a byproduct of combustion, for example burning coal. The particles are so small that they can end up in people's lungs when they breathe or, if small enough, pass through lung tissue and enter into the bloodstream. Health impacts can include premature death for those that have heart or lung disease, irregular heartbeats, asthma, issues with lung function, and respiratory problems.

Environmentally, the particulates can settle in the ground or water, altering their compositions and damaging the ecosystem. The most visible outcome is haze. The picture below is one I took in June 2014, in a city called Shijiazhuang, which is about four hours outside of Beijing in the Hebei province. This picture shows, believe it or not, a sunny day. The haze was the result of a massive amount of particulate matter in the sky which prevented the sun from shining through.

Figure 115: Particulate Matter is a Major Issue in China

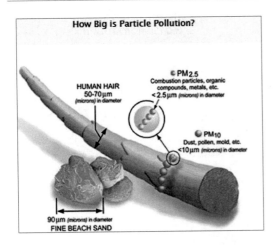

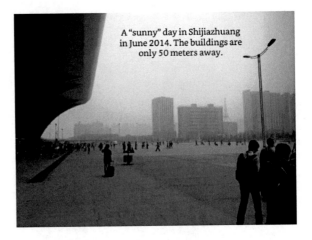

Source: Environmental Protection Agency (left); Michael Molnar (right)

The picture below shows the levels of PM 2.5 levels around the world. One can see the level of pollution in China and India, which is due largely to the volumes of coal burned there. The scale for PM 2.5 goes from 0 to 500 as shown below right. Some cities in China have registered values over 500 – literally beyond the measurement scale.

Figure 116: China and India Have the Worst Air Pollution in the World

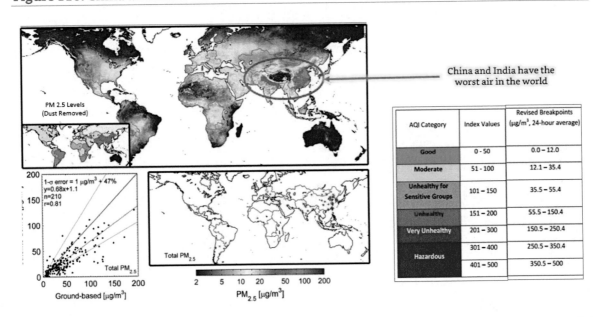

Source: "Use of Satellite Observations for Long-Term Exposure Assessment of Global Concentrations of Fine Particulate Matter," Aaron van Donkelaar, Randall V. Martin, Michael Brauer, and Brian L. Boyses

China faces a system dynamic that many countries have experienced during their industrial booms. Strong growth has had many positives, but also the unfortunate side effect of significant pollution. Eventually, increasing levels of pollution drive the public to pressure the government to act. There are two important time delays as shown in Figure 118.

1. First, the **pollution and growth impact loop** contains feedback and a time delay that is obvious but not always appreciated. Simply put, pollution – especially at the levels China is currently experiencing – impacts people's lives. There will be increased cancers, premature deaths, and respiratory problems, all which lead to a less healthy and productive population over time.

   The challenge is often **framed** as "growth" versus the "environment and citizen's health." As growth improves lives on average and makes China more powerful overall, it is easy to come to a simple conclusion that – at least for now – growth takes precedence. However, this short-term growth has the potential to massively impact medium- to long-term growth of the country in ways that are not in China's own best interests. China's pollution problem illustrates how bad framing can skew good judgment.

   Numerous studies have researched the cost to human health. One showed the average person's life expectancy was cut short by five years for people that lived in highly polluted areas in the 1990s. Another estimated 670,000 deaths were tied to this pollution in 2012. This study highlighted that 70% of the population were exposed to PM 2.5 levels higher than deemed "healthy." Even more shocking, 157 million people were found to be living in areas where the PM 2.5 levels were 10 times what the World Health Organization recommends. See Figure 117.

China's coal burning cutting lives short by years
Historical study links higher levels of pollution to higher mortality.
Nature – July 2013

High levels of particulates from coal burning in China's highly polluted north may have cut more than five years from life expectancy for the 500 million people who lived there in the 1990s, scientists report today in Proceedings of the National Academy of Sciences1. The study can help to forecast the health effects of pollution in present-day China — where air quality has only gotten worse — as well as in other countries.

Chinese air pollution made global headlines during the 2008 Beijing Olympics and again this winter, when particulate levels in Beijing exceeded 700 micrograms per cubic metre — more than 50 times higher than those allowed by US air-quality standards.

The cost of China's dependence on coal - 670,000 deaths a year
Study urges Beijing to raise taxes on coal-burning by up to 10 times.
Fortune – November 2014

A new study has revealed the staggering cost of China's dependence on coal to power its economy: 670,000 deaths in one year alone.

The study, by Tsinghua University associate professor Teng Fei, lays bare the extent of the country's pollution problem that is the darkest side effect of the country's rapid growth over the last 20 years: over 70% of China's 1.4 billion population are exposed to pollution levels above national regulatory norms, and over 10% are exposed to concentrations of harmful particles 10 times the level considered safe by the U.N.'s World Health Organization.

Source: Cited above

2. Second, the **regulatory response loop** has a delay at each step: from actual pollution, to perceived pollution, to putting pressure on the government, to action and – finally – to results. This has been exacerbated in China due to an **information gap.** Given restrictions on people's movements to other potentially cleaner cities and restrictions on the dissemination of data, it is not easy for local citizens to understand the gravity of the situation they may face.

This information gap began to narrow slightly in 2012, when the U.S. embassy installed a PM 2.5 monitor on top of its roof and started to tweet the results. The resulting public pressure drove citizens to demand more information. China subsequently installed and disclosed more information about air quality and citizens have continued to demand it. For example, during my last visit to China in 2014, several friends showed me apps on their iPhones that detailed air quality data. Good information widely disseminated can help get the regulatory response loop moving.

Figure 118: China Delay in Managing Pollution is Similar to Other Countries

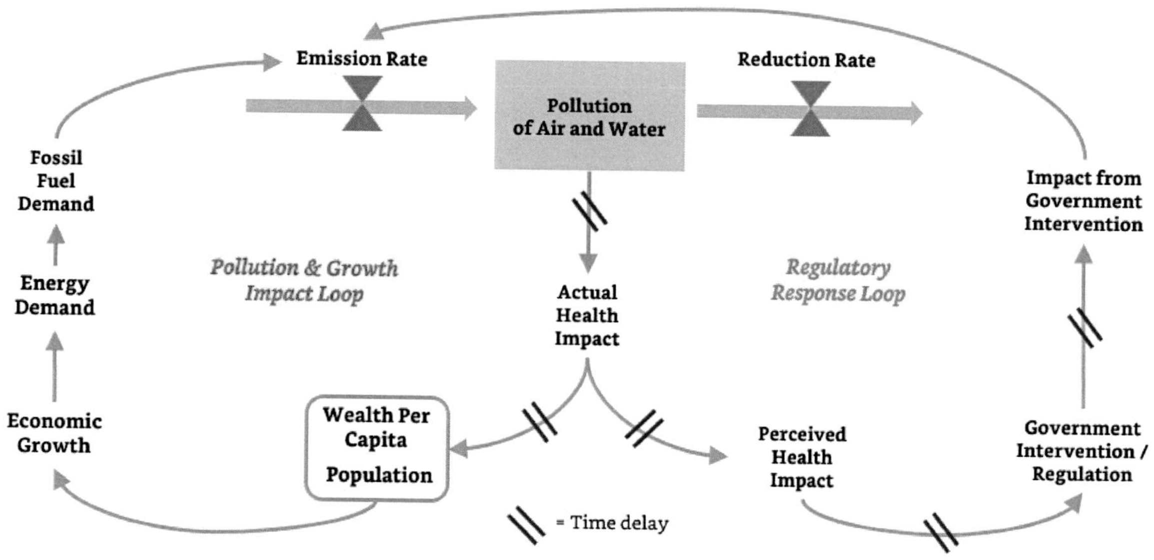

Source: Michael Molnar

China is No Worse, But No Better in Managing the Issue – So Far

Western governments such as the U.S. have, at times, proven to be inept in dealing with intra-generational issues such as pollution or climate change. Election cycles make it challenging for most politicians to think long term. The result is short-term thinking and large time delays in responding effectively.

China's growth has helped millions people out of poverty to better lives. This is a great accomplishment and should be recognized. The horrid pollution is arguably no worse than what occurred in the U.S. and in Europe during their industrial booms. Yet, the world today is more advanced in terms of understanding the costs involved and having technologies and methods to reduce pollution. As Figure 119 shows, while China might not be faring any worse than the U.S. or the E.U. did during their industrial booms, it is clearly not doing any better either.

Figure 119: The Costs of Increased Use of Fossil Fuels Continues to Mount in China

The World This Week
The Economist, December 2015

The authorities in Beijing issued the city's first ever "red alert" for smog. This involved closing schools, shutting down building sites and banning the use of half of the city's cars. The government's failure to act previously when pollution had reached worse levels had caused public anger.

Shenzhen, Embodying China's Growth, Falls Risk to It
New York Times, December 2015

SHENZHEN, China — Rescuers searched for survivors in a sea of red mud on Monday, a day after dirt and construction debris engulfed dozens of buildings in this city in southern China, the latest of several man-made disasters in recent years to lay bare the perils of the nation's rapid growth.

...

"They started piling up the dirt and waste roughly two years ago," Li Xigui, a 52-year-old metal craftsman who has lived in the area for 15 years, said in an interview. "I knew something would go wrong in the future."

...

Chinese news media have suggested that officials have allowed risks to fester, through corruption or laxity. The official response to such accidents, while often impressive in scale and speed, has done little to mute that criticism — in this case, by ignoring the danger from a growing pile of construction tailings and debris near factories and homes.

Source: Cited above

Fluctuating Energy Prices, Civil Unrest and Shifting World Powers

The Arab Spring Case Study

Energy and politics are intertwined, perhaps more than any other sector in the economy. Regulations are an inherent part of the industry whether due to pollution issues or to natural monopolies like the local utility company. International politics is entangled with energy as much as domestic politics are given energy has been used as a weapon and a driver for war. For example, Russian President Putin threatened to stop natural gas flows to the Ukraine in early 2015, a massive threat given heating needs in the middle of winter.

The Arab Spring is an interesting example. The Arab Spring seemed to come out of nowhere when a street vendor in Tunisia set himself on fire in December 2010. More civil unrest occurred elsewhere and, for a time, it seemed like the entire area of the world would fall into chaos. Just two years later, the rulers of Tunisia, Egypt, Libya and Yemen were forced out. There were major and minor protests throughout the region (as highlighted below) and the impacts are felt to this day.

Figure 120: Timeline of the Arab Spring

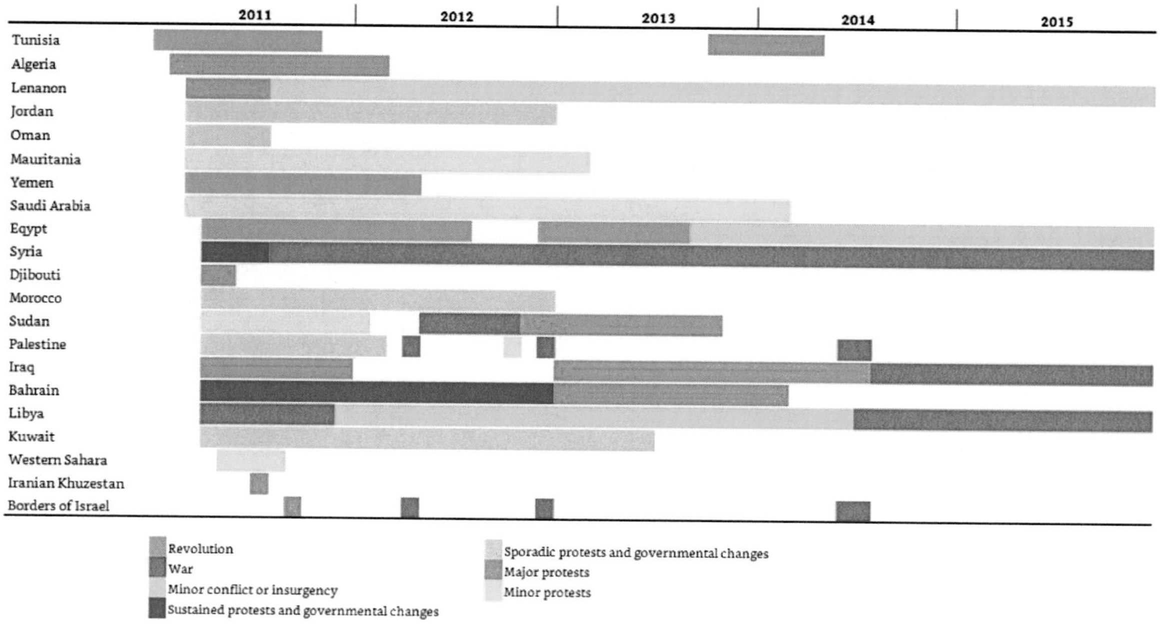

Source: Wikipedia contributors. "Arab Spring." Wikipedia, The Free Encyclopedia

What triggered the Arab Spring? The Center for American Progress published a report that describes a series of events that, at first, seem irrelevant but make sense.

A key source of discontent among the population was food inflation, as 10% to 40% of income is spent on food. Many of these countries are net importers of food, specifically wheat. In the months leading up to the outbreaks of civil unrest, major wheat producers around the world experienced severe weather that hurt production. China experienced a bad drought and the Ukraine, Russia, Canada and Australia encountered major heat waves and floods. Global wheat pricing surged, increasing from $157 per ton to $326 per ton from June 2010 to February 2011. This is not to say that the Arab Spring was *entirely* driven by the increase in food prices, but rather that food inflation was quite possibly an igniting factor in an area ripe for unrest.

Figure 121: System Map of Civil Unrest During the Arab Spring

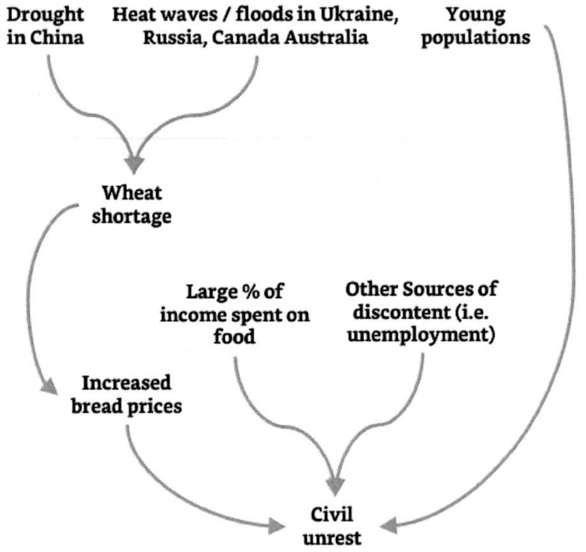

Percent of income spent on food and average age per-capita of the top wheat-importing countries

2010 Wheat imports per capita			Per capita		Age
Rank	Country	Metric tons (in '000s)	Income (in U.S. dollars)	Food - percent of income	Percent under 25 years
1	UAE	370.659	47,400	8.7	31.1
2	Libya	242.803	12,062	37.2	47.4
3	Israel	238.968	27,085	17.6	43
4	Jordan	173.611	4,435	40.7	54.4
5	Algeria	101.439	4,477	43.7	47.5
6	Tunisia	89.330	4,160	35.6	43.2
7	Yemen	86.843	1,230	45	65.5
8	Egypt	81.284	2,771	38.8	52.4
9	Iraq	76.701	2,625	35	60.6
10	Cuba	70.503	5,000	n/a	34.6

Source: Michael Molnar (left); Arab Spring and Climate Change Report, Center for American Progress (right)

Oil-Dependent Economies Are Facing Significant Risks

The selloff of commodities, specifically oil, will drive similar pressures for many oil-revenue-dependent countries. While lower oil prices for consumer-oriented countries like the U.S. is a positive as the reduced costs act like a tax cut, this is not the case for economics that are less diverse. Many of these economies are not diverse due to the so-called "resource curse" and could soon face major challenges.

The "resource curse" is a term used for the paradoxical situation in which many countries that have great mineral wealth experience slower and serious economic issues down the road due to the following chain of events:

1. Resources are discovered (e.g., minerals, oil).
2. Demand for these resources drives increased demand for that country's currency.
3. This drives up wages, inflation and the value of the currency.
4. These increases make it harder for other sectors, such as manufacturing, to compete.
5. Talent clusters around that one resource because it is often the best way to make money.
6. Government has a windfall and spends massively.

The end result is a non-diversified economy that spends too much. Severe economic and social challenges follow when the price for that resource declines.

Some countries, like Saudi Arabia, have prepared for downturns by saving a massive amount of money. At the end of 2015, the Saudis had accumulated about $700 billion. However, the current budget is running a large deficit given its oil-dependent economy and the collapse in the oil prices. The International Monetary Fund stated that if the deficit continues that Saudi savings would be depleted by approximately 2020.

Saudi Arabia has never developed a diversified economy outside of the oil industry. The majority of the population are in government jobs, many of which are dubious in nature and simply a means of paying people to keep them happy. So while some may do back-of-the-envelope math and suggest that the Saudis simply have to cut subsidies and reduce government waste to survive, they not are taking into account the implicit social contract. This contract allows the royals to make billions if they give the public a comfortable life. If that dissolves, a balanced budget might be followed by severe civil unrest.

A quick way to understand other countries at risk is to look at the World Bank's calculation of oil rents as a percentage of GDP (defined by the World Bank as the difference between the value of crude oil production at world prices and total costs of production over GDP). Figure 123 shows 26 countries that have more than 10% of GDP tied to oil. In 2013, the United States oil rent was 0.9% of the economy compared with 43.6% for Saudi Arabia.

Figure 122: Saudi Arabia Has Reserves but They Are Falling Fast

Excerpts from: "How Much Longer Can Saudi Arabia's Economy Hold Out Against Cheap Oil?"
Bloomberg News - August 2015

The difference is the sheer cost of maintaining the state as an employment machine and guarantor of the riches that Saudis have become accustomed to since the last squeeze. Subsidized gasoline costs 16 cents per liter and while there's the religious levy called zakat, there is no personal income tax in the nation of 30 million people.

"The Saudi government can't continue to be the employer of first resort, it can't continue to drive economic growth through the big infrastructure projects and it can't keep lavishing on subsidies and social spending," said Farouk Soussa, chief Middle East economist for Citigroup Inc. in London.

"These are things that are absolutely politically explosive," he said. "You've gotten accustomed to a certain lifestyle and that lifestyle is far in excess in terms of luxury that was prevailing in 1998.

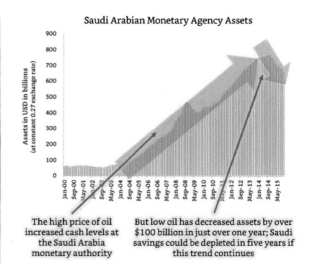

The high price of oil increased cash levels at the Saudi Arabia monetary authority

But low oil has decreased assets by over $100 billion in just over one year; Saudi savings could be depleted in five years if this trend continues

Source: Bloomberg (left); Saudi Arabian Monetary Authority Data

Figure 123: Numerous Countries' Entire Economy is Dependent on the Price of Oil

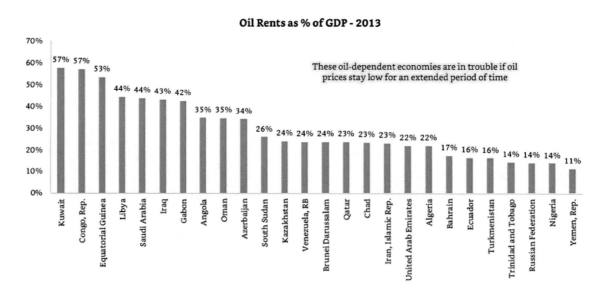

Source: World Bank

Even more concerning is the average age of the population in many of these oil-dependent areas. A so-called "youth bulge," a large population of typically young males, has been a key determining factor in social unrest in many studies. If oil rents decline, many young men will be unemployed and resentful. This is a major risk for the governments of these countries and should be a major concern to terrorist analysts around the world. Figure 124 shows two maps, the median age by region and oil rent as a percentage of GDP by region. The overlaps of these two factors is a clear risk to civil unrest if oil prices stay low for extended periods of time.

Figure 124: Oil Dependent Economies Are Mostly Very Young as Well

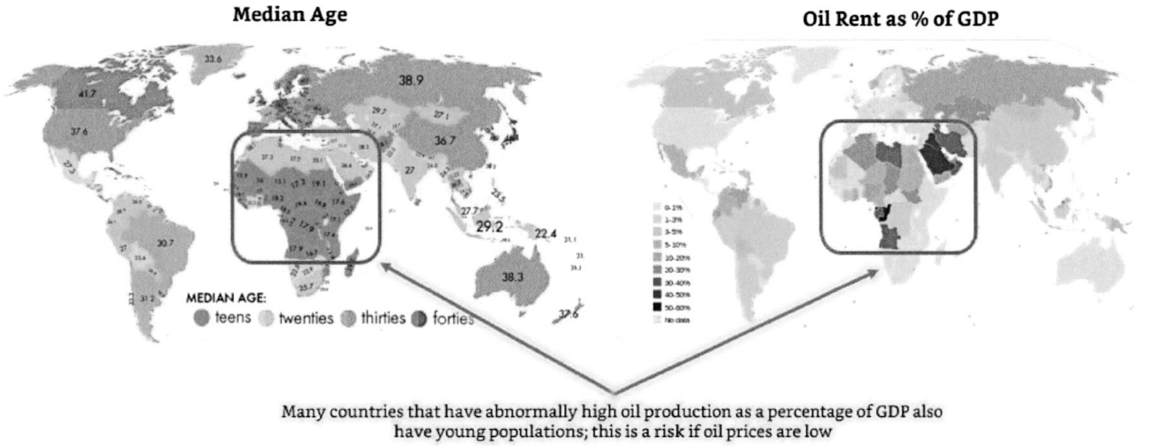

Many countries that have abnormally high oil production as a percentage of GDP also have young populations; this is a risk if oil prices are low

Source: Global Post; CIA Factbook

If oil prices rebound sharply after declines this might not be such a concern. That would take a medium-term risk and make it a short-term blip. The concerns for an extended low oil price centered around the following two factors:

1. **On the Supply Side, U.S. Shale Has Changed the Supply Curves for Oil (see Figure 126).** The supply curve for shale currently cost more than some traditional sources, but is very flat (which means a lot can be supplied at that price). If these techniques continue to improve and costs decline further, certain countries' supply might be pushed farther out on the cost curve resulting in lower profits.

2. **On the Demand Side, China Holds the Key.** China's GDP growth has driven a huge amount of oil demand, making them the marginal demand source. If China's economy hits a soft spot, world oil demand may be much less than expected.

The end result could be more supply and lower demand, resulting in an extended period of low oil prices. Oil-dependent countries that have no real non-oil economy will face the risk of civil unrest. See Figure 125.

Figure 125: System Dynamic of Civil Unrest in Oil Dependent Countries

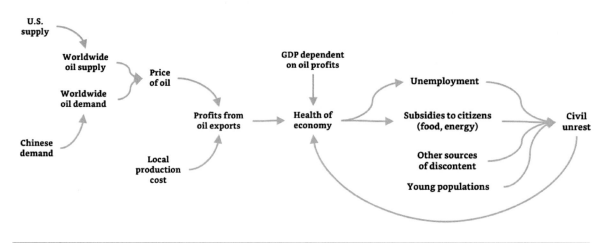

Source: Michael Molnar

Figure 126: U.S. Oil Supply and China Demand

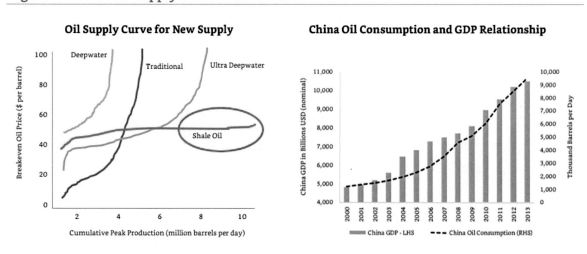

Source: Michael Molnar (left); Bloomberg (right)

Venezuela provides an unsettling case study for other oil-dependent economies. During the oil boom in the mid-2000s, the country experienced large inflows of cash given its oil reserves. President Hugo Chavez was a power in world politics, often mocking the U.S. and nationalizing foreign assets in his country.

Just a few years later, the country is now in dire circumstances. With 24% of Venezuela's GDP tied to oil, the collapse in oil price has devastated the economy. As *The Economist* reported in October 2015:

> *"Venezuela's economy will be one of the worst performers this year, according to the IMF. The fall in oil prices and macroeconomic imbalances will cause GDP to shrink by 10% in 2015. Inflation will be well above 100%. Price controls and a lack of foreign exchange have led to shortages of goods."*

This is very unfortunate for the Venezuelan people and likely a blueprint for what may happen in many other areas of the world if oil stays low. The foreign policy implications – shifting power dynamics and increased terrorism, to name just two – are tremendous.

Figure 127: More Situations Like Venezuela are Likely if the Price of Oil Stays Low

As Economy Lags, Hugo Chávez's Movement Fades in Venezuela
New York Times, December 2015

...but boom has turned to bust, the economy is in shambles and the love affair is over...

High prices for oil, natural gas, coal, copper, gold, silver, bauxite, soy beans and other products led to steady growth, a sharp drop in poverty and an expansion of the middle class throughout the region. That growth, in turn, brought political stability, with leaders and parties being repeatedly re-elected. Many of those were on the left, having come to office on a wave of public discontent following a lengthy period of economic stagnation.

"Chávez covered up problems with money," said Miguel Aguín, a Barinas policeman who became disillusioned with Chavismo years ago. "He didn't think about the future. He just gave out handouts to get through today."

Long lines to buy hard-to-find products like diapers and detergent in Sabaneta, Mr. Chávez's hometown. Government price controls of some basic goods have led to shortages. *Credit Miguel Gutierrez for The New York Times*

Source: Cited above

Section IV

Final Thoughts

The Future of Growth

This book discussed many issues in energy: the challenges of pollution, the potential for certain game-changing technologies, the structure of business cycles and models, and the impact of energy on world politics and power. While each situation is unique, there is a common thread: *the interplay between human judgment and complex systems.*

As discussed, this interplay manifests itself in two ways. Human judgment can drive behavior from within existing systems (e.g., the business executive who decides to expand operations and add to industry supply). It can also motivate the creation of new system structures (e.g., the policymaker who decides to regulate pollution).

Unfortunately, human judgment can be skewed by countless biases. In particular, it often misinterprets and underappreciates the path that growth will take and the constraints that it will inevitably encounter. These deficiencies spur several of the enigmas discussed: industry oversupply and undersupply, mispriced shares in the stock market, ineffective government policy and failing business strategies, just to name a few.

Consider the following: If you folded a standard piece of paper over and over again, how many folds would it take to be 1 centimeter thick? After one fold of a 0.001 centimeter-thick piece of paper, the resulting stack would be 0.002 of a centimeter thick. After two folds, 0.004 of a centimeter thick. Then 0.008, 0.016 and so on, doubling with each fold.

After 10 folds, you would have a stack 1 centimeter thick. Another 10 folds (20 total) and the stack would be 34 feet tall. Just five more folds (25 in total) and it would be about as tall as the Empire State Building (1,100 feet). Folding the paper just 45 times in total would reach the moon *over 200,000 miles away.* You can check the math; I did when I first heard this myself.

This is an incredible illustration of how challenged human judgment can be in grasping the extraordinary speed of exponential growth. Each fold represents exponential growth of 100%, but the takeaways are the same for any compound growth rate over time. *Growing anything by a percentage on an ever-increasing base yields massive numbers, very fast.*

This book analyzed exponential growth in many contexts, including solar installations, oil production, internal combustion engines and pollution. Underlying nearly all of the issues discussed was the influence of a critical factor – the goal of economic growth.

Economic growth should be applauded for affording beneficiaries a better quality of life. We should never forget how lucky we are to live in current times as opposed to hundreds of years ago when life was short, hard and lacking many of today's comforts. The result of this success is that that *goal* of most economies is exponential growth, specifically economic growth as measured by GDP.

Given the historical success of economic growth in improving the welfare of people – *which is the ultimate objective* – it can be easy to forget that economic growth is a *means* to an end, not an end in itself. That leads us to a logical question: *If nothing can grow exponentially forever, at what point do our growth-seeking economic models become ineffective?*

An economist would agree that there are constraints, such as the physical limits of the Earth in producing and consuming energy (which happens to be growing exponentially along with GDP and population). Yet, many would argue that technology and innovation will drive more GDP and sustain larger populations with less energy consumption. In short, it can be managed.

Figure 128: Exponential Growth in GDP, Population and Energy Usage

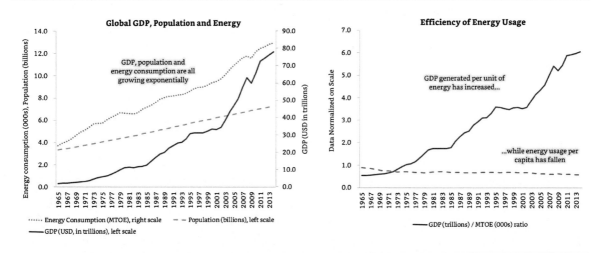

Source: BP World Energy Statistics (energy consumption); World Bank (GDP, population)

I tend to agree over the near term, but with some unease. To be clear, I do believe that energy consumption per unit of GDP and population will continue its positive trends, likely far beyond my life. Human ingenuity probably will continue to surprise us with future technologies and innovations that we cannot envision today. This should mean the goal of economic growth can continue to yield the outcomes we desire – improving welfare for the world's citizens.

That said, economies are complex systems filled with humans. If there is one lesson from the research highlighted in this book, it is that we should never be overconfident in predicting the behavior from such a system. Case in point: Barely any economists predicted the financial crisis of 2008, even though many would argue the signs were there.

What if technology and innovation's growth (which is exponential, by the way) stops earlier than expected? What if the constraints of finite physical resources are met faster than anticipated? More fundamentally, what if the goal of economic growth itself simply loses effectiveness beyond a certain level of wealth (signs of which are evident in many countries as feelings of satisfaction stagnate even as wealth increases)?

Human ingenuity is remarkable, creating countless companies, products and devices that have driven economic growth and a better quality of life. Yet, I wonder if the truly ingenious innovation will be to rethink the goal of economic growth itself. An enigma to be pondered another day.

About the Author

Michael Molnar has been involved in the energy sector as a hedge fund investor, investment banker and sell-side equity analyst. Most recently, Michael was a Founding Partner of Lorem Ipsum Partners LLC, a long/short equity hedge fund focused on the energy, industrial and agriculture sectors.

He was also a Founding Partner of Greentech Capital Advisors where he advised clients on M&A transactions, strategic joint ventures and private capital raises. He served on the Board of Directors and the Commitments Committee, helping the firm to grow nearly 10 times, raise two rounds of capital and expand to three offices around the world.

Prior to Greentech Capital Advisors, Michael was the lead equity analyst for the U.S. alternative energy and coal sectors at Goldman Sachs. At Goldman, he also helped to start the Small and Mid-Cap Research Team and was a member of the Special Situations Research Team.

Prior to Goldman Sachs, Michael was a Visiting Research Fellow at Accenture's Institute for High Performance Business, a company-sponsored think tank. His research focused on management techniques to most effectively maximize shareholder value and was published in both internal and external business journals. He was also a manager in Accenture's strategy consulting practice.

Michael received an MSc with Merit from the London School of Economics, an MBA from the University of Chicago, and a B.S. with Honors from Rutgers University. He is a CFA (Chartered Financial Analyst) charterholder and is a former CPA (Certified Public Accountant - inactive), CMA (Certified Management Accountant – inactive) and CFM (Certified in Financial Management - inactive).

Notes

Notes

Notes

Notes

Notes

Notes

Notes

Notes

32196745R00124

Made in the USA
Middletown, DE
26 May 2016